Unnamed Country
The Struggle for a Canadian Prairie Fiction

Dick Harrison

The Struggle for a C

1977

Unnamed Country
adian Prairie Fiction

The University of Alberta Press

First published by The University of Alberta Press
Edmonton, Alberta, Canada.

This book has been published with the help of a grant
from the Humanities Research Council of Canada, using
funds provided by the Canada Council.

Canadian Cataloguing in Publication Data

Harrison, Dick, 1937-
        Unnamed country

        Bibliography: p.
        ISBN 0-88864-019-6

        1. Canadian fiction (English) - Prairie
Provinces - History and criticism.* 2. Prairies in
Literature. I. Title.
PS8191   C813'.009'32   C77-002132-8
PR9192.6.P7

Cover design: P. Bartl/ M. Chan
Printed by Printing Services of
The University of Alberta

For Pearl and Elmer Harrison
who pioneered this West

Contents

Plates

Canadian prairie fiction is about a basically European
society spreading itself across a very un-European
landscape. It is rooted in that first settlement process in
which the pioneer faced two main obstacles: the new
land and the old culture. The land was a challenge not
only physically but psychologically; like all unsettled
territory it had no human associations, no ghosts, none
of the significance imagination gives to the expressionless
face of the earth after men have lived and died there.
The prairie, in effect, lacked the fictions which make a
place entirely real.

Howard O'Hagan, in his *Tay John*,
describes vividly the sensation of facing totally unknown
country. Though he writes specifically about the
mountains, his insight is equally valid for the plains:

> . . . a country where no man has stepped before
> is new in the real sense of the word, as though it
> had just been made, and when you turn your back
> upon it you feel that it may drop back again into
> the dusk that gave it being. It is only your vision
> that holds it in the known and created world. It
> is physically exhausting to look on unknown
> country. A name is the magic to keep it within
> the horizons. Put a name to it, put it on a map,
> and you've got it. The unnamed—it is the
> darkness unveiled.[1]

O'Hagan points up the magical quality of naming, our
way of ritually controlling the unknown so that we will
not lose it or be lost in it. He also balances the promise
and the threat held out by radically new land. On the
one hand it is a glimpse of the first creation—O'Hagan
earlier mentions a feeling of almost surprising the
Creator at his work. On the other hand, it is "the
darkness unveiled," a threat of chaos. The two images
draw out the ambivalence of this impulse to name which
O'Hagan states so flatly: "Put a name to it, put it on a
map, and you've got it." With the nice balance of threat ix

and promise, either "you've got it" before it gets away or "you've got it" before it gets you, before the chaos overwhelms you. This was the challenge to the pioneer imagination, and one to be met not just verbally and ritually but by surveying, fencing, building—anything to capture the new space within a known order.

The known order was naturally the old culture. It constituted the only names the pioneer knew, the only maps he had brought with him. When he attempted to take inventory of the unnamed country, his choices were limited by the vocabulary of another place and another life.[2] This was inevitable, of course, and not necessarily a handicap, but the English-speaking settlers, most of them bred in the sheltered towns and farms of Britain and Ontario, were drawing upon a culture that was ill adapted to the life and the landscape of the prairie. Their efforts to capture it in their known world, in everything from land survey to literature, tended to distort, to obscure, and to isolate them from the plains. The long struggle to adjust physically and psychologically to the environment goes on, but successive generations of prairie people have lived with the lingering effects of those initial incongruities between the old culture and the new land.

Writers encountering the prairie even after settlement had begun found it "unnamed" in the sense that it lacked the verbal traditions upon which a literature builds. To varying degrees they have been subject to the same cultural limitations in their "naming" as the settlers, but they have also been among the first to recognize the incongruities between the culture and the land. It may be because of this awareness that they have so often emphasized the prairie's implied threat to civilized order. The fiction, at least, which has won critical acclaim has been dominated by the hostile face of the plains. The settlers themselves who faced the unnamed country must have felt the promise as well as the threat, and both are reflected in the mass of popular fiction, but we generally accept the development of prairie realism with its preference for the stark and threatening aspect of the plains as the culmination of prairie fiction. At the head of this tradition we place Sinclair Ross's *As For Me and My House* as the central expression of the prairie experience, because Ross's narrator, Mrs. Bentley, expresses so well the reactive, defensive function of the imagination confronting the prairie. In one frequently-quoted passage from her diary, she isolates the purest threat of the unknown country, which is intangible and indefinable. It is simply the empty spaces intimating chaos and unmeaning:

> The stillness and solitude—we think a force or presence into it—even a hostile presence, deliberate, aligned against us—for we dare not admit an indifferent wilderness, where we may have no meaning at all.[3]

At this extreme, Mrs. Bentley is engaged in a particularly negative kind of naming. She must give a definite form to what O'Hagan calls "the darkness unveiled," even a menacing form, because the alternative is a kind of spiritual annihilation

Over against Ross's novel we should place W. O. Mitchell's *Who Has Seen the Wind*. The book has been difficult to fit into fashionable generalizations about prairie fiction, despite the fact that it has enjoyed much wider popularity than *As For Me and My House*. It is obviously somewhere in the "realist" tradition, yet it emphasizes the positive response to the unknown country. Mitchell's Brian O'Connal can see the prairie as a glimpse of the first creation, and the boy's imagination reaches out to hold the experience and make it more real. There is one characteristic moment when young Brian is eager for the elusive feeling the prairie and its creatures inspire in him; he wants to know what has only been intimated to him:

. . . for breathless moments he had been alive as

he had never been before, passionate for the thing that slipped through the grasp of his understanding and eluded him. If only he could throw his cap over it; if it were something that a person could trap. If he could lie outstretched on the prairie while he lifted one edge of his cap and peeked under to see. That was all he wanted— one look.[4]

In one way the two novels represent the poles of prairie fiction, withdrawal and approach, and are the best examples in the realistic tradition of what might be called the tragic and comic views of man facing an unnamed country. Not surprisingly the promising view of the prairie and its mysteries is through the eyes of a child who hardly feels the constriction of adult society; Mrs. Bentley, on the other hand, knows she has been too long in the artificial enclosure of the towns to face the prairie without fear. Her problem of seeing the prairie darkly through the glass of an alien culture is one of Ross's conscious themes, but we can tell by the general tone of the novel that it is also something Ross himself struggles with, as do other prairie writers down to the present day. Contemporary novelists such as Margaret Laurence, Robert Kroetsch and Rudy Wiebe are engaging the same problem when they set out quite explicitly to draw the cultural and mythical world of prairie man into line with the physical and historical realities of the plains This book is in one sense about their struggle for an indigenous prairie fiction. It begins before the first prairie novel, with the encounter between the civilized imagination and an unnamed country. It then traces the growth of prairie fiction over the past century as part of our imperfect and often self-defeating efforts to humanize that country. Henry Kreisel, in his excellent essay, "The Prairie: A State of Mind," has said that "all discussion of the literature produced in the Canadian West must of necessity begin with the impact of the landscape upon the mind,"[5] but at the same time, the effects of that impact cannot be fruitfully discussed in isolation from the inherited culture which provides the other, unseen environment of that mind. I have therefore tried to go beyond the two major published studies of Canadian prairie fiction. The first, Edward McCourt's *The Canadian West in Fiction*, examines the novelist's need to capture the new land imaginatively in fiction. McCourt contends that his authors have failed to do this, or succeeded in only a limited way, but he stresses their limitations in literary genius and craftsmanship rather than any difficulties inherent in the subject itself. As a result, he does not concentrate directly on any unique challenge the plains environment presents to the writer's imagination. More recently, Laurence Ricou's *Vertical Man/Horizontal World* studies the power of the landscape as reflected in the fiction but does not concern itself directly with the influence of culture on man's reaction to the landscape. I have attempted to take into account this third basic element in the struggle for a prairie fiction.

The problem of new land and old culture is by no means peculiar to the prairie. It hampered Ontario pioneers in Susanna Moodie's day, as it must in some way affect the members of any migrating society. It is simply more acute on the prairie, where the topography as well as the climate is extreme. The landscape, with its vastness and its paucity of visual detail, lacks human dimensions. It remains particularly tough to humanize, particularly intractable to the imagination. It is also more different from what the English-speaking settlers were used to than the new lands of Central Canada had ever been. A study of the prairie as an extreme example may shed some light, obliquely, on the corresponding problem in other regional literature. The prairie, might, for another reason, be the ideal place to begin examining what can be seen as a typically Canadian problem. As Dave Godfrey once said in a C.B.C. interview with Alan Anderson, the prairie is the great source of our fiction; it is the archetypal region   xiii of Canada. Quebec and Ontario were settled by the French and the English, but the prairie was settled by us as a people.

Whether the prairie has been the source of our *greatest* fiction is a question I have not attempted to answer in this book. A wide-ranging study does not allow time for the carefully argued critical judgements which will be necessary before the central canon of this fiction can be confidently established and its value assessed. And the kind of study I hope to initiate here should properly come first. Critical judgments do not go on in a vacuum, and universal critical standards, even within one language and one century, are an abstraction convenient to the academic mind. All literature grows out of a time and a place, and cannot be understood or valued without an understanding of its cultural context. Where the cultural framework is overlooked, then the judgments are made within some other context. For prairie fiction the context tacitly assumed has usually been one appropriate to British, Western American, or Eastern Canadian literature.

I have concentrated entirely on fiction written in English, not only because of the practical need to limit the material examined and the evidence that the problem of cultural adaptation has been particularly acute for the English-speaking settlers, but because those settlers have controlled the development of prairie society. While never a majority on the prairie, they have always been the dominant minority, supported by the power that emanates from the institutions of Central Canada. The term "prairie" I apply to the settled areas of three prairie provinces. Though they include considerable variation, they share enough gross similarities of climate, topography, and mode of settlement to make them more like each other than like any other region of Canada. The variations within so large a region cannot, of course, be overlooked in any study of imaginative literature, especially where the chief feature to which the imagination must respond is the land itself. The climate and topography of the foothills of southwestern Alberta, for example, must have been both physically and imaginatively less inhospitable to a British or Eastern settler than the flatlands of the Regina plains. Geographers' descriptions are all too detailed and technical for present purposes, but some rough idea of the main prairie zones may be helpful.[6] The prairie consists, as Captain John Palliser noted in 1857, of three distinct levels or steppes, sloping gradually north-eastward from the Rockies in southern Alberta to the Hudson Bay basin. The high plains south of Calgary are at an altitude of over 3000 feet; and central portions of Manitoba, the dry bed of ancient, glacial Lake Aggazis, are less than 1000 feet above sea level. More significant for the traders and settlers has been the arrangement of typical vegetation, depending more on conditions of soil and precipitation than on altitude or latitude. Skirting the true bushland of the Laurentian Shield to the east, the taiga to the north and the Rockies to the west, there lies a crescent of lightly and irregularly wooded "park belt," averaging about two hundred miles in width and arching from southern Manitoba through central Saskatchewan and Alberta to the mountains. Enclosed by this park belt, and occupying a little of southern Manitoba, all of southern Saskatchewan and most of southern Alberta are the grasslands, the "true" prairie, what W. O. Mitchell's characters call the "bald-headed." Generalizations about the prairie can be assumed to refer especially to the high, flat, dry grasslands, as the extreme and for that reason most typical landscape, but distinctions among these areas as settings will be made where they seem important to the interpretation of the literary response to the land.

It will not surprise any westerner that I sometimes use the terms "prairie" and "West" interchangeably. As Edward McCourt says, "To the native of the prairies Alberta is the far West; British Columbia the near East."[7]

I would like to thank those who have

helped me at various stages in the preparation of this book, and especially these people: James Reaney, who, as director of my doctoral thesis, stimulated some of the first ideas for this study; the students in my graduate seminars at the University of Alberta, who helped to provide a climate of discussion in which those ideas could mature; Roy Holley of Austin, Texas, who typed the final manuscript patiently and intelligently; and my wife, Irene, who heard me out.

I am also indebted to the University of Alberta for the sabbatical leave during which I completed my research and writing, to the Canada Council for the grant which helped to sustain my work while on leave, and to the Humanities Research Council of Canada for a grant in aid of publication.

Portions of this book, in earlier forms, have appeared in "The Beginnings of Prairie Fiction," *Journal of Canadian Fiction*, No. 13 (1975), 159-177; "The Mounted Police in Fiction," in Hugh Dempsey, ed., *Men in Scarlet* (Calgary: McClelland and Stewart West, 1975), pp. 163-174; and "Cultural Insanity and Prairie Fiction," in D. E. Bessai and David Jackel, ed., *Figures in a Ground* (Saskatoon: Prairie Books [In Press]).

Dick Harrison
Department of English
University of Alberta
Edmonton, Alberta.

The Problem of
Seeing the Prairie

The first English-speaking people to come West, the
explorers, traders, settlers, artists, looked out on the
prairies with essentially "Eastern" eyes. Their perceptions
were so conditioned that in the most prosaic and literal
sense, they could not see clearly what was around them. [1]
This handicap may help to explain why they were so slow
in shaping their ways to the life of the plains. They did
not at first recognize how much they needed to adapt, and
they were reluctant to learn. As James M. Minifie says
of his family arriving from England as late as 1912, "we
thought the environment should adapt to us."[1] The
English-speaking pioneers were especially slow to realize
that making themselves psychically at home in their
surroundings was a vital part of any lasting adaptation
to the plains. For many the combination of physical and
psychic dislocation was too much. Nellie McClung
provides a classic description of settlers who had given
up and turned back in 1880. The people were from
Ontario, and it was the woman in particular who had
broken down:

> She wore a black silk dress and lace shawl and a
> pair of fancy shoes, all caked with mud. She
> would have been a pretty woman if she would
> only stop crying. She hated the country, she
> sobbed, it was only fit for Indians and squaws
> and should never have been taken from them.[2]

There is something poignant about this figure in silk and
lace on the plains of Manitoba, a kind of pathetic
gallantry in the face of defeat. She was, of course, an
extreme example, "a painted doll," as the practical Mrs.
McClung says, but her defences against the rigors of the
prairie were only slightly more incongruous than those of
many hardier pioneers who eventually succeeded
materially. In *Gully Farm*, Mary Hiemstra describes her
mother, one of the Barr Colonists, as a woman with "a
knack for home-making" who hung hand-made lace
antimacassars over the unglazed windows of their log

shack and swept the dirt floor every day. "The home-made broom wasn't very effective, and Mother often got down on her hands and knees and swept with the little handbrush she had brought from England . . . ."[3] The practical and even the aesthetic value of these activities is questionable, so evidently the antimacassars and the sweeping represented a type of human order this civilized woman depended on to protect her from the rude and chaotic world she had been confronted with. Her need for imaginative defences against the wilderness was capable of taking precedence over her need for physical comfort. The fiction written about the prairies every-where reveals this intimate and changing relationship between the need for imaginative order and the physical struggle for survival.

Mrs. McClung's woman in the silk dress and Mary Hiemstra's mother could, of course, have been confronting any wilderness. D. G. Jones, in his *Butterfly on Rock*, identifies the problem of an overpowering environment as the general lot of the Canadian imagination. It might be asked how these women's struggles differ from that of Margaret Atwood's farmer in "Progressive Insanities of a Pioneer," or of the trapper in Earle Birney's "Bushed," or of Susanna Moodie back in Upper Canada fifty years earlier. But as further accounts will show, the prairie with its openness and isolation does make its own peculiar assault on the civilized mind. Because of the strange topography, the experience of pioneering on the plains made unpredictable demands upon man's sense of order. As Robert Kroetsch says of even the more settled prairie of today, "The western landscape is one without boundaries quite often. So you have the experience within a kind of chaos, yet you have to order it somehow to survive."[4] Whether or not the "chaos" to which Kroetsch refers is like the environment of Atwood's pioneer, "not an absence of order / But an ordered absence," the desire to order it is both heightened and frustrated by the impact that the simple and gigantic forms of the prairie landscape have upon the imagination. In many respects the westerner's imaginative struggle is peculiar to the prairie environment, and its distinctiveness becomes more apparent as we look at the records of early travellers on the plains.

The prairie has long been thought of as prose (if not prosaic) country, inspiring much good fiction and little good poetry. It is ironic that the earliest written account of the first White man's encounter with the prairie should be in verse: Henry Kelsey's ninety rhymed lines about his lonely expedition inland from Hudson Bay in 1690. It is typical of our attention to western history, however, that Kelsey's journals were not discovered until 1926—in Castle Dobbs, Carrickfergus, Northern Ireland. Until then it had been assumed that La Verendrye, who reached the Red River in 1738, had been the first White man to travel the Great Central Plain of North America. Kelsey was a remarkable young man, but his awkward couplets must be regarded as a "sport"; most early responses to the prairie were non-literary and devoid of aesthetic intent. Kelsey's own poem says nothing much about the landscape, and his prose diary for the journey of 1691 is almost as laconic:

> August ye 20th   To day we pitcht to ye
> outtermost Edge of ye woods this plain affords
> Nothing but short Round sticky grass & Buffillo.[5]

Kelsey we know was a semi-literate youth of nineteen or twenty, keeping records under adverse conditions, but that does not entirely explain his response. It would be another century and a half before any traveller responded poetically to the sight of the prairie.

In the journals of the early explorers, traders and travellers, descriptions of the new landscape are not as common as one might expect.[6] These men had other things on their minds, of course, but since they took time to describe scenes of another sort, the very dearth of description is significant. This terrain was not

3

what they had come to know as picturesque; they had no
ready paradigms for describing it, and must have had
difficulty even observing it very carefully. In this respect
they had something in common with the earliest settlers
who, to judge from their diaries, kept their eyes firmly
fixed on the immediate menace of mudholes,
mosquitoes, and the occasional Indian. What impressions
we do find before the mid-Nineteenth Century are chiefly
remarkable for an absence of imaginative stirring. The
explorers and fur traders saw the plains in a severely
utilitarian way. Descriptions in their journals concern
mainly the means of survival and resources useful to the
fur trade. Anthony Henday, the first white man to cross
the Canadian prairie to within sight of the mountains,
records his emergence onto the true prairie in what is
now north-central Saskatchewan in the summer of 1754
with the following terse journal entry:

> [Aug] 30. Friday. Left the Asinepoet Indians, and
> travelled N.W. 10 miles. Level Barren land, not
> one stick of wood to be seen, & no water to
> drink.[7]

Henday's entry, like Kelsey's, could serve as a model for
one class of non-response to the landscape: the prairie as
unusable space. Alexander Mackenzie's journals of his
Voyages in 1789 and 1793 are much fuller and have more
pretensions to style, despite his modest disclaimers, yet
his description of the plains country shows the same
utilitarian concerns:

> The country between the [Assiniboine] and the
> Red River, is almost a continual plain to the
> Mississoury. The soil is sand and gravel, with a
> slight intermixture of earth, and produces short
> grass. Trees are very rare; nor are there on the
> banks of the river sufficient, except in particular
> spots, to build houses and supply fire-wood for
> the trading establishments . . . .[8]

Mackenzie at least recognizes the utility of the land: he understands the vital connection between the buffalo and the fur trade, but he offers an inventory rather than a description.

It is not until he reaches the park belt country of northern Manitoba that Mackenzie is stirred by the landscape. Here he describes a point on the Swan, Clearwater, or Pelican River:

> This precipice, which rises upwards of a thousand feet above the plain beneath it, commands a most extensive, romantic, and ravishing prospect . . . . a most beautiful intermixture of wood and lawn . . . . stately forests, relieved by promontories of the finest verdure.[9]

Mackenzie's two descriptions make an interesting comparison. The park belt scenery is obviously reminiscent of his native Scotland, but from the terms he uses, "romantic," "ravishing," "wood," "lawn," "stately forests," terms which might have come from an eighteenth-century topographical poem, it is clear that the scene lends itself to familiar conventions of landscape description. It is therefore easier to see, respond to, and record. For better or worse the White imagination had begun to find ways of applying the old culture to the new land.

Attempts at a more imaginative response to the true prairie began to appear in the last half of the Nineteenth Century. Sir William F. Butler was the first eloquent prairie traveller. His well known and often quoted *The Great Lone Land* is an account of his tour of the West in 1870-71, and the time may be significant. Butler was writing late enough to have read earlier accounts of the American West and quite possibly of the Canadian West, so his impressions may have depended to some extent upon romantic traditions, implicit in his descriptions. A thirst for adventure was his declared motive for coming to the West, though his

5

mission for this particular tour was ostensibly to report upon conditions prevailing among native tribes in the North West Territories. His mention of "the much-coveted passage to the long sought treasures of the old realms of Cathay" suggests that he must have picked up the first informing myth to possess the American people with regard to their own West, as described by Henry Nash Smith in his *Virgin Land*. Butler still regards the prairie as that passage, and this clearly adds to the glamour of his tour. In his attempts to explain the imaginative appeal of the plains, he returns consistently to the effects of space, the imposing aspect of the sky, the unexpected wild beauty of the land itself, and especially the silence, loneliness, and isolation he experienced:

> The great ocean itself does not present more infinite variety than does this prairie-ocean of which we speak. In winter, a dazzling surface of purest snow; in early summer, a vast expanse of grass and pale pink roses; in autumn too often a wild sea of raging fire. No ocean of water in the world can vie with its gorgeous sunsets; no solitude can equal the loneliness of a night-shadowed prairie: one feels the stillness, and hears the silence, the wail of the prowling wolf makes the voice of solitude audible, the stars look down through infinite silence upon a silence almost as intense.[10]

To give a form to the totally unfamiliar mixture of impressions, Butler has drawn from the old culture the familiar seascape which would have been part of the experience of most of his intended British readership. Not only the effectiveness of the comparison but the persistence of that culture is evident from the recurrence of the prairie-sea metaphor through the works of Stringer, Grove, Ross, McCourt, Kreisel, Kroetsch (the list could be extended indefinitely) as a way of drawing upon the literary experience, and often only the literary experience, of their Canadian readers. The imagination is always more at home with what has already been rendered imaginatively. For that reason the early writers must have suffered from the lack of any verbal tradition on the prairie which might have provided the humus out of which a well-rooted fiction could grow.

In phrases such as "feels the stillness" and "hears the silence," Butler's description testifies, like most later descriptions, to the elusiveness of the power this landscape exerts upon the imagination. Even the preoccupation of prairie novelists with "the impact of the landscape upon the mind," to use Kreisel's phrase, is less the indulgence of a satisfying theme than the sign of a continual and unfinished struggle. The power is elusive but in the more extensive descriptions certain elements recur, like the common impression that the vastness of the plains is at once enticing and threatening to the civilized imagination. In this respect the plains are the extreme form of O'Hagan's "Unnamed country." Butler emphasizes the beauty, but also the unpleasant or menacing elements such as the snow, grass fires, wolves, and loneliness. Surprisingly few of the descriptions dwell upon the routine discomforts of the climate, the bitter cold and blizzards in winter, the withering heat and persistent, dessicating wind in summer, to say nothing of periodic hazards of hail, cyclones, drought, and dust storms. Yet there is some ambivalence of feeling about even the most pacific features of the prairie. The openness of prospect which frees the spirit also threatens it with the loss of security, order, and ultimately all human meaning. Butler refers to a French writer who has said that "the sense of this utter negation of life, this complete absence of history, has struck him with a loneliness oppressive and sometimes terrible in its intensity" (p. 200). Butler denies any such feeling in himself, yet a few pages later he admits to feeling uncomfortably exposed to all those things inside as well as outside himself from which settled society normally protects an individual. "So, lying down that night for the first time with all this before me," he writes, "I felt as one who had to face not a few of those things from which is evolved that strange mystery called death, and looking out into the vague dark immensity around me, saw in it the gloomy shapes and shadowy outlines of the bygone which memory hides but to produce at such times" (p. 206). A menace undefined is potentially infinite, and it may be that the lack of clear definition in the prairie landscape is a part of its evocative power. For a robust adventurer like Butler the physical hardships can be accepted more readily than the uneasiness in the presence of mysterious and intangible shapes the immensity suggests to his imagination.

The prairie exposes him, above all, to disquieting levels of his own consciousness. The "darkness unveiled" that O'Hagan refers to is within the observer as well as without. This mirroring effect becomes almost as prominent in the later fiction of the prairie as it is in the sea stories of Conrad, which may help to explain the continuing popularity of the sea metaphor. D. G. Jones describes it well in *Butterfly on Rock*: he is considering Canadian literature as a whole, but his argument applies particularly well to prairie fiction from, say, 1920 to the present.

> The land is both condition and reflection, both mirror and fact. Particularly in literature it comes to symbolize elements of our inner life. As these elements are ignored or repressed, the land becomes a symbol of the unconscious, the irrational in the lives of the characters. And the more powerful those elements are, the more disturbing and demonic the land and the figures associated with it may become.[11]

One would only have to impose a severe Calvinist outlook on Butler's night reflections to produce the grim almost judgmental environment of Mrs. Bentley's diary in *As For Me and My House*, even without the drought, but unlike the prairie realists, Butler entertains both sunlit and night thoughts of the prairie, and he is equally eloquent about them.

Only a decade after Butler's tour of "The Great Lone Land" a traveller from Canada, George Monro Grant, edited a book called *Picturesque Canada* which includes a section on the North West Territories. The book was obviously meant to stimulate national pride if not immigration; its drawings are romantically embellished and its text sparkles with optimism about the West. Yet Grant records a reaction to the space and solitude of the open prairie very much like Butler's:

> Here, for day after day, the traveller moves like a speck on the surface of an unbroken and apparently interminable level expanse. Nothing intervenes between him and the horizon, and let him gallop as fast as he will the horizon appears ever the same and at the same distance from him. All the while, too, he sees no living thing on the earth or in the air. Silence as of the grave reigns supreme from morning to night. The spirits of the most buoyant traveller sink as he rides deeper and deeper into this terrible silence, unless he has learned to commune with the Eternal.[12]

It is clear that Grant's galloping horseman is not suffering from boredom. Nor is it mainly the emptiness which is bothering him (that, in any case, is partly a trick the prairie plays on Eastern eyes), but rather the sparseness of detail in the foreground which exposes him to an awareness of himself in a larger perspective of horizon and sky. He finds the silence "terrible" because the configurations of the land itself help to induce reflections upon death and eternity. As Wallace Stegner says in *Wolf Willow*, there is something suggestive of eternity in the "hugeness of simple forms" which makes up the prairie landscape.[13] They reduce man and

9

his temporal progress to a speck on an apparently interminable expanse.

This paradox of freedom and exposure has complicated the idea of the frontier West in North American consciousness as a whole. Jack Warwick, in *The Long Journey*, explains how in French Canadian literature that paradox is embodied as a dramatic tension in the figure of the voyageur, torn between the lure of anarchic freedom in the *pays d'en haut* and the commitments and attractions of ordered social existence in the settlements.[14] Henry Nash Smith had earlier identified the corresponding figure in American tradition as the backwoods hunter-settler typified by Daniel Boone, who was variously mythologized as a powerful civilizing agent carving the state of Kentucky out of the wilderness and as a man addicted to the savage way of life, who fled before the near approach of anything like civilization.[15] Cooper's Leatherstocking and the best of his literary descendents carried on the tradition. They balanced the two impulses excited by the virgin land, to preserve the wild freedom of it and to impose a better human order on it. Canadian prairie fiction in English may be weaker dramatically because it has developed no such character, but then it describes a very different western culture, one with very little time for anarchy. In this fiction the freedom of the plains is a freedom to cultivate the land nature has provided, and there is no doubt that this cultivation is part of a divine plan. The main internal tension embodied in typical pioneer heroes like Grove's Abe Spalding and Stead's John Harris is between the desire to work harmoniously with the land and the temptation to dominate and exploit it. Which impulse prevails will depend, in O'Hagan's terms, upon whether the unnamed country is seen as a glimpse of the first creation, where man would be a laborer in God's garden, or the darkness unveiled, a threatening chaos to be strictly subjected to man's will. In either instance, order and not wild freedom is the ideal, and man is an essentially orderly being. Consider even a romantic figure

10

like Butler, who writes that he cannot long endure "constraint within the boundaries of civilized life," while engaged in a survey to determine the best means of maintaining law and order among the native tribes.

The same elusive and ambivalent power felt by nineteenth-century writers seems to haunt later prairie travellers. Some of the features basic to the meeting of man and prairie become clearer and sharper when these accounts of early visitors are juxtaposed with a recent account by a writer who has lived on the prairie. Wallace Stegner's *Wolf Willow* (1955) describes his return to the area of southern Saskatchewan where he had spent part of his early childhood. Notice that his description includes the familiar sea metaphor as well as the feeling of an imagination powerfully moved but not entirely at ease with its own freedom.

The plain spreads southward below the Trans-Canada Highway, an ocean of wind-troubled grass and grain. It has its remembered textures: winter wheat heavily headed, scoured and shadowed as if schools of fish move in it; spring wheat with its young seed-rows as precise as combings in a boy's wet hair; gray-brown summer fallow with the weeds disked under; and grass, the marvellous curly prairie wool tight to the earth's skin, straining the wind as the wheat does, but in its own way, secretly.

. . . .

On that monotonous surface with its occasional ship-like farm, its atolls of shelter-belt trees, its level ring of horizon, there is little to interrupt the eye. Roads run straight between parallel lines of fence until they intersect the circle of the horizon. It is a landscape of circles, radii, perspective exercises—a country of geometry.

11

Across its empty miles pours the
pushing and shouldering wind, a thing you
tighten into as a trout tightens into fast water. It
is a grassy, clean, exciting wind, with the smell of
distance in it . . . .

It is a long way from characterless;
"overpowering" would be a better word. For over
the segmented circle of earth is domed the biggest
sky anywhere, which on days like this sheds down
on range and wheat and summer fallow a light to
set a painter wild, a light pure, glareless, and
transparent.[16]

In the intervening eighty-five years since Butler's journey
the prairie has been settled and to some extent pervaded
by human associations, enough that Stegner can attach to
it human metaphors of skin and hair. But the prairie
remains essentially unchanged by settlement; it is still
an "ocean" responsive only to the will of the elements;
and within the ocean metaphor the farms are not
even islands, but "ships," with all the fragility and
impermanence, the transient quality, implied by the
image. The entire panorama does not include a single
human being. The "over-powering" quality may be partly
a result of the observer being characteristically alone in
the landscape, as he is in so much of the fiction. The
prairie seems to deny the permanent signs of human
society which could reassure the observer that he is not
alone in the face of the huge, eternal forms of land and
sky. The best that man has managed, the lines of road
and fence, are as bloodless as geometry.
More than any of the earlier writers,
Stegner emphasizes how powerfully the imagination is
stirred yet how little it can seize upon in trying to
assimilate the strongly felt impression. Imagery is
difficult when the stimulus is reduced almost to the
abstraction of geometry. Travellers and settlers from
Britain and Ontario must have experienced difficulty

responding imaginatively to a landscape whose characteristic features evoked strong but ambivalent feelings. Their difficulty was aggravated by the fact that its elements hardly constitute a "landscape" in any sense familiar to them. Grant's impression that there is nothing between him and the horizon is a typical response to the paucity of visual detail a prairie offers. Consider, for example, the journals of early settlers, which contain almost no landscape description, or the responses of the average presentday traveller who has ridden the transcontinental train across the plains. Even fairly articulate travellers often proved uncommunicative about the true prairie. Dr. Cheadle and Viscount Milton, for example, in their *The North-West Passage By Land* of 1865 offer no description of the terrain until they reach the park belt on the North Saskatchewan, at which point, like Mackenzie, they begin to see landscapes, "not indeed grandly picturesque, but rich and beautiful."[17]

The fiction frequently bears witness to the same spare, incomplete visual quality of the plains. Sinclair Ross's narrator, Mrs. Bentley, remarks that "only a great artist could ever paint the prairie, the vacancy and stillness of it, the bare essentials of a landscape, sky and earth."[18] W. O. Mitchell echoes the latter phrase in the first two lines of *Who Has Seen the Wind*: "Here was the least common denominator of nature, the skeleton requirements simply, of land and sky—Saskatchewan prairie."[19] Further afield, Willa Cather has her narrator, Jim Burden, in *My Antonia* remark when he first sees the similar terrain of Nebraska, "There was nothing but land: not a country at all, but the material out of which countries are made."[20] Burden's remark emphasizes the incomplete or unfinished quality implied in the other descriptions while Mitchell's "lowest common denominator," like Stegner's "landscape of circles, radii, perspective exercises" shows how the mind is tempted by the open, inconclusive forms to impose some pattern of its own, even if it must go to the level of mathematical abstraction. Perspective too, as Marshall McLuhan

13

explains, is an artificial contrivance, but it provides an observer with at least a point of view and a rudimentary way of ordering what he sees. In just the topography, then, we can begin to see why the West has been particularly intractable to the civilized imagination, why the settlers, like the woman in the lace shawl, tended to cling to familiar patterns. And when, as Stegner's description suggests, the land resisted those patterns, the settlers and the writers felt something like hostility in the silence of the plains.

When we look from these first impressions of travellers to the early cultural response to the plains, we can see the strangeness did not end with the visible terrain. The first British and Canadian settlers must have found the dearth of familiar form and detail to the landscape equalled by the lack of cultural traditions developed to express man's response to these surroundings. They found no suitable conventions of landscape painting or description, very little in the way of architecture, song, story, or social custom, and what was there among the Indians and Metis they failed to recognize. Into this apparent absence they brought what was familiar to them. Alexander Mackenzie, in another passage from his *Voyages*, shows that his tendency to impose his own cultural patterns on what he found was not confined to the landscape. At one point he explains the failure of the missionaries to "civilize" the Indians, suggesting a program which looks very familiar today:

> They should have begun their work by teaching some of those useful arts which are the inlets of knowledge, and lead the mind by degrees to objects of higher comprehension. Agriculture, so formed to fix and combine society, and so preparatory to objects of superior consideration, should have been the first thing introduced among a savage people: it attaches the wandering tribe to that spot where it adds so much to their comforts; while it gives them a sense of property,

and of lasting possession, instead of the uncertain
hopes of the chase, and the fugitive produce of
uncultivated wilds.[21]

The passage is rich in unconscious irony, especially so
because it could be a description of our patent
misunderstanding of the native people to the present day.
The difference is in his absolute, unashamed faith that our
society based upon property and possession leads the
mind "by degrees to objects of higher comprehension."
He would not notice that the Indians could neither
comprehend the goals of such a society nor understand
how the rules of property could apply to the earth itself,
because he could not see that their habits constituted a
culture any more than he could see that the shapes of the
prairie constituted a "landscape." Mackenzie was an apt
representative of the culture which was to dominate the
settlement of the West.
          It was in a spirit not unlike Mackenzie's
that the pioneers set about, sometimes wisely but too
often unwisely, imposing a culture upon the land. As W.
L. Morton says about the accomplished cultivation of
southern Manitoba, "It was at once a material reshaping
of the land, and also a firm and confident expression of
a way of life, rarely defined, but well understood."[22]
Even in Manitoba, where the confidence was not
misplaced in a material sense, the broader cultural
adjustment was the difficult part to accomplish, partly
because of the incongruities that resulted from this
confident assertion of a way of life. Methodist
missionary Egerton Ryerson Young provides one striking
instance when he describes his first glimpse of Old Fort
Garry in 1863, reached after several days of travel over
uninhabited prairie:

We traveled on through the French half-breed
settlement, until we reached the quaint, old-
fashioned, medieval fortress of Fort Garry.

> Strangely out of place did it seem to us. As we
> first looked up at its massive walls and turrets
> and bastions it seemed as though some freak of
> nature or magic wand had suddenly transported
> it from some old historic European nation and
> dropped it down amid the luxuriant grasses and
> brilliant flowers of this wild prairie country.[23]

Significantly the Metis settlement does not seem out of
place to him, while the architecture and air of the
fortress testify to civilized man's response (or lack of
response) to the plains, a clinging to the familiar,
however incongruous in the new setting. Quite as
significantly Young never sees the shadow of an analogy
between the fortress and his missionary work among the
Indians. This sort of cultural conservatism is common in
the literature of the plains, first as a trait of the fiction
and later as a perennial theme. Grove develops the theme
extensively in *Our Daily Bread* and *Fruits of the Earth*,
and Fort Garry as the Rev. Young saw it could even be
taken as a distant ancestor of the grand house Abe
Spalding builds in *Fruits of the Earth* to dominate the
prairie, to proclaim his dominion. Houses, as Susan
Jackel demonstrates in her "The House on the Prairies,"
acquire a strong symbolic significance in prairie fiction.[24]
As the first creative assertion of the inhabitants and as
the most immediate defence against the environment,
they are also a useful index of the cultural adaptation of
various groups of settlers. The British and Canadian
settlers, whenever they could manage to, were inclined to
build imposing, slightly impractical houses, probably
because they embodied a style of life to which they
hoped to rise by coming to the free land of the West.
The prairie is everywhere dotted with tall, windswept
"upper Canada" looking houses, not only in the older
areas settled heavily by direct immigration from Ontario,
but also in the more westerly and later settled areas. The
contrast with the habits of the eastern European settlers
16 is still obvious today if one compares, for example, the

houses in the English-speaking farm communities south of Edmonton with the surviving pioneer homes of Ukrainian settlers north and east of that city.

There are some indications that, like their houses, the broad cultural patterns of the British and Canadian immigrants were unusually ill-adapted to prairie conditions. The same determination which brought them out in force seems to have made them insensitive to the disparity between what they brought with them and what they found there. Compared to the Metis or the smaller ethnic groups from eastern Europe, for example, the typical spatial arrangements they imposed on the landscape, and the social organization which accompanied them show a proneness to ignore and to work against the natural characteristics of the new environment. The Metis of Red River settled narrow strips of land extending two miles back from the river in the manner the French had adopted in Quebec two centuries earlier. All shared the river front as a source of water and as the natural means of communication, and the dwellings were kept conveniently, sociably near to each other. This survey also had the advantage that the Hudson's Bay Company allowed an additional two mile strip beyond the river lot as a hay meadow informally consigned to the use of the farmer.[25] It was in one of these hay meadows in 1869 that Louis Riel made his historic gesture of placing his moccasin on the chain of the surveyors sent to redivide the land.[26] The Metis were willing to be guided by the economics as well as by the geography of the land, dividing their time (not always too effectively) between the rude sort of farming possible there and hunting or freighting for the fur companies. Their buffalo hunting was essential to the provisioning of the fur "brigades," which could never have served the remote trading posts without a portable concentrated food supply like pemmican. The earliest of the "Selkirk" settlers were forced, whether they liked it or not, to depend on these same mixed activities for some years after they began breaking their land for cultivation.[27] The

Metis allowed this mixed mode of subsistence to shape
their social organization and to provide their ideals in
life. As Douglas Hill says in *The Opening of the
Canadian West*, "To the Metis, running the buffalo was
a sport and a way of life, symbolizing their freedom and
their mastery of the plains. The hunt also gave solidarity
and organization to the Metis communities. To this
social structure came laws to govern both the hunt and
the community life—and from it came their justifiable
sense of being the true children of the West, a separate
nation."[28] Rather than learn from this people, the settlers
despised their way of life, probably because it did not
tend toward either wealth or security. Milton and
Cheadle reveal a blindness to the value of the Metis
adaptation which was probably typical. They dismiss the
mixed-blood as a colorful but worthless sort of fellow,
without seeming to notice that throughout their long and
celebrated tour of the West their lives depended
continually on the special accomplishments of their Metis
guides and hunters.

My object here is not to tax the individual
pioneers with any personal lack of understanding or
flexibility; the local histories of western settlements are
abundant testimony to the resourcefulness of Anglophone
pioneers. It seems rather that the culture they brought
with them, including certain of their attitudes, ideals, and
institutions, was ill-designed to encourage adaptation. In
particular, the kind of individualism which pervaded this
culture was better adapted to a market economy than to
a subsistence economy, and to a settled land than to one
where the natural environment still poses a considerable
threat to the individual. From the Metis and from some
East-European groups such as the Mennonites they
might have gleaned strategies of adaptation which
encouraged community and cooperation. These in turn
could have eased some of the rigors of pioneering and
drawn the people into an earlier reconciliation with the
strange land. I say "gleaned" ideas from the smaller
ethnic groups because, of course, no other culture could

provide a complete model for adaptation. The Metis combination of hunting and agriculture, for example, would become obsolete with the end of the buffalo and the coming of a market economy, but it was ideally suited to its particular time and place. The river-lot survey, as the experience in Quebec reveals, has its limitations, but in the initial stages of settlement it has obvious advantages. The rectangular survey required for further settlement can, in fact, be fitted to it later, as it was along the North Saskatchewan in the 1880's. Similarly, the Mennonite system of farming their land communally in order to live in villages might not appeal to the independent Britisher, but the Mennonites themselves used the system only in the early period of development when the hazards and privations of isolation were greatest.

Many of the remedies for the painful incongruities in western settlement were beyond the control of the individual pioneers. Nor can individuals be blamed for an accultured resistance to change. Their natural reluctance to learn new ways would also have been reinforced by the circumstances of their immigration. The English-speaking pioneers were coming to an ordered West which they assumed to be already a part of their accustomed culture.

The Canadian government survey, in contrast to the Metis practice, seemed well designed to create hardship by ignoring the natural features of the land. It divided the West into townships six miles square containing thirty-six sections of 640 acres, each in turn divided into 160 acre quarter-sections, all without regard to fertility, access to water, or natural lines of communication. This was the American practice adopted apparently on the assumption that 160 acres would support a farm family. In the West, where modes of agriculture dictated larger farm units, it created even greater dispersal of the settlers. On the short grass range, for example, a hundred acres was often found to be sufficient to pasture only one steer. The isolation and

19

lack of community was further aggravated by the free
homestead policy framed in the Dominion Lands Act of
1872. "Free homesteads could be established only on
even-numbered sections. The odd numbers were
otherwise reserved. Two odd sections in each township
were to be sold, when needed, as an endowment for
schools. One and three-quarters sections of each
township (and an extra section in every fifth township)
went as H.B.C. reserve land. In some areas, Indian (and
Metis) reserves claimed a share. Much of the remainder
was set aside for the C.P.R. . . . ."[29] Obviously the
recipients of the "free" quarter sections were expected to
do the work which would make the C.P.R. and Hudson's
Bay sections valuable— then buy them.

One effect of this land policy was to
broadcast a scanty population along the routes of the
railways, frequently out of convenient range of
neighbours and thoroughly exposed to the intimidating
and often dangerous isolation of the empty prairie. And
this in a climate where the unremitting severity of the
weather could inhibit travel for long periods. A second
effect was to commit the settlers to a rectangular world,
and they went on to sustain the motif as they brought
the land under cultivation. W. L. Morton describes this
process in his "Seeing an Unliterary Landscape."

> Very quickly . . . in fact in less than three
> generations for the most part, the elegant undress
> of the wild landscape of poplar bluff and meadow
> had given way to the prim and level square fields
> made by the plough.
>
> The new landscape was that
> standard in North America, the homestead with
> shelter bluff, square white house and long red
> barn . . . . Around the homestead the fields and
> pastures spread out to the fenced limits of the
> farm, usually the road allowances. They were
> square or oblong, but always rectangular in
> response to the insistent demand of the plough

that it turn full, square furrows when at work.[30]

The utilitarian geometry of the fields was extended beyond any material need, to become "a cultural as well as a material landscape" as Morton says, and it had its larger scale in the townships, school districts, electoral districts and its smaller scale in the town lot, fenced and hedged on a rectangular grid of streets usually responsive to the railroad tracks rather than any of the natural topography.

Another characteristic Morton's description suggests is the enclosure and isolation inherent in the fencing and hedging. It was the most natural practice for the individualistic West Europeans but not necessarily the best way of living with the already isolating conditions of the pioneer West, as some of the less individualistic ethnic groups demonstrated. The Mennonites came to southern Manitoba in large groups, often entire villages, cooperating to arrange their removal and arrival and to help the villagers establish themselves on the land. They cultivated their farms cooperatively at first, living in villages rather than scattered across the prairie. The typically Canadian reaction to their settlements shown by J. B. McLaren in Grant's *Picturesque Canada* was to remark upon them without apparently seeing the advantages of their method:

> One street of steep-roofed, low-walled houses, with an old-country air of pervading quiet and a uniform old-country look about the architecture, describes them all. There are about eighty of these villages in the Reserve. The farms are innocent alike of fences and of buildings. Each village has its herdsman, who goes out daily with the cattle. The husbandmen live in the villages, submitting to the inconvenience of distance from their work, in order the better to

> preserve their language, religion and customs, and
> enjoy the pleasures of social intercourse. To a
> stranger these pleasures would appear not to be
> very great.[31]

In 1882 the Mennonites' desire to "preserve their
language, religion and customs" would not have been
thought entirely consistent with good citizenship.
The Mennonites resembled the Metis in their practice of
handling locally and communally all matters of property,
justice, religion, culture, and sociability. And though
McLaren sees that they have prospered partly because
they "at once accommodated themselves to the climate
and all the material conditions" of the new land, he can
never be more than good-naturedly condescending
toward their achievement. He is repelled by their living
habits, including their low houses of timber frame and
sun-dried bricks which must have proven serviceable in
the previous land of their adoption, the Russian steppes.
        Where the enclosures of the Mennonite
villages or the extended water-front community of the
Metis would tend to bind together, the typical North
American arrangements would tend to separate and confine, to shut out all society along with the threatening
environment. As the settlers fortified their separate
farms with fences and windbreaks they were shutting
themselves in, aggravating the loneliness and isolation
which were among the most threatening aspects of
the prairie landscape. Further, by working to cut themselves off, psychically, from nature, they were rejecting
some part of their own natures. Dorothy Livesay
recalls the effects of a similar kind of isolation surviving
into very different times and circumstances and describes
them vividly in a reminiscence of her Winnipeg childhood.
Her father, a reader of the classics, with a "passion"
for building fences, made his home and garden a model
of order and seclusion where the children were scarcely
allowed to play. Miss Livesay describes her first awakening
to the prairie beyond the fences:

1. Paul Kane, "Red River Settlement," Royal Ontario Museum, printed in *150 Years of Art in Manitoba* (Winnipeg Art Gallery, 1970), p. 29.

> For the first time I was really lifted from the
> earth to see the sky itself: a wide blue sky
> extending over the prairie like a winged bird,
> dropping soft feathers of light onto the horizon.
> And I saw the horizon! I saw its farther shores.
> From that day onward I had a different feeling
> about my father's house—the small white
> clapboard house, the brown fence railings, the
> boundaried street—these were no longer the
> hedge to keep me home. These had been like
> fetters holding me down.[32]

A stubborn cultural conservatism can be seen running
from the settler's rectangular world to Mr. Livesay's
passion for fences; both deny the natural environment,
and the cultural consequences are similar.

Direct aesthetic responses to the plains, in
painting and in fiction, reveal the same basic features we
have been looking at in early first encounters with the
prairie and in general cultural responses to it—an initial
difficulty in seeing the plains and a tendency to impose
familiar patterns on them. Writers like R. M. Ballantyne
and J. E. Collins gave the prairie a distinctly Walter
Scott or Fenimore Cooper cast, and they had their
counterparts among the painters who came out in
surprising numbers with various expeditions and on their
own. The work of W.G. R. Hind, William Armstrong, F.
A. Verner, Paul Kane, and Frederick B. Schell exhibits
this tendency in varying degrees. Paul Kane is probably
the most respected of the early painters to visit the
prairie, and his response to it is conveniently accessible
both in his paintings and verbally in *Wanderings of an
Artist*, the account of his tour of the west in 1847-48.
Laurence Burpee's introduction to a recent edition of
Wanderings describes Kane as having quite naturally
"seen through European eyes" despite his having grown
up in Ontario. Burpee quotes Charles W. Jeffreys'
assessment of Kane's western scenes:

"Trained abroad, he naturally adopted the
European art traditions of his time. Consequently
we see in his pictures of the North-West not the
brilliant sunlight of the high prairie country and
the foothills, nor the pure, intense colour of the
north; we see instead the dull, brown tone of the
studio and gallery pictures of the Middle Europe
of his day. The topography may be North
American but the atmosphere, both physical and
mental, which bathes the scene is essentially
European."[33]

As early as 1877, Nicholas Flood Davin had identified
these qualities in Kane's work as the "influence of the
conventions of the Romantic school." J. Russel Harper
in his *Painting in Canada* points out other specifically
romantic and exotic features of Kane's style:

Kane's is a romantic and idealized world. He
painted the grass of the wildest regions trimmed
like an English greensward. Trading boats
descending the Saskatchewan River have the
dignity of Roman galleys, and buffalo hunts are
like wonderful tableaux on some gigantic stage.
His lithe, graceful horses are sired by some highly
bred blood strain. The stiffly posed warrior
chieftains have a noble bearing. Sometimes he
uses focussing light and at other times decorative
sky effects.[34]

These comments, which could easily be adapted to
describe the work of the early novelists, indicate the
limited fitness of Kane's technique for portraying the
distinctive characteristics of the prairie landscape. Had
Kane's limitations been only in the technical craft of the
painter, they would bear only slightly on the ordinary
pioneer's problem of cultural adjustment, but Kane
appears to have painted the prairie as he saw it. His first
description of the Red River country as he entered it in   25

1846 agrees substantially with his painting of the
prospect near St. Boniface Cathedral. (See Plates 1 and
2) "The country here is not very beautiful; a dead level
plain with very little timber, the landscape wearing more
the appearance of the cultivated farms of the old country
with scarcely a stick or stump on it."[35] This is Kane's
only mention of flat prairie country, and his failure to
see beauty in it, together with his not very apt
comparison with old country farm land suggest that not
only his techniques of expression but his perception had
been shaped by the conventions in which he was trained
and by the landscape he was accustomed to. The settlers
must have been similarly handicapped in their attempts
to see the new land, as one might gather from the
paucity of comment on the topography to be found in
their diaries. Like Kane and the other travellers, they
usually become articulate only after they reach the park
belt, a terrain much nearer to what they have been used
to.

Fiction writers of the Nineteenth Century,
who will be discussed in Chapter II, tended to do to the
experience of the West what the painters did to the
landscape. These early stories, beginning with Alexander
Begg's *Dot it Down* in 1871, are surprisingly varied, but
with few exceptions they all follow recognizable formulae
embellished with a few western details. R. M.
Ballantyne's *Red Man's Revenge* and A. C. Laut's *Lords
of the North*, for example, are high adventure romance
after the manner of Scott or Cooper. J. E. Collins's *The
Story of Louis Riel* and *Annette the Metis Spy* are
sensational romance more nearly akin to the "Dime
Novels" of the American West. James Morton's *Polson's
Probation*, and *One Mistake*, by the pseudonymous
"Zero" attempt the mannered interchange of the
nineteenth-century English novel, despite the fact that
they have pathetically little to work with. In most stories
the real prairie is virtually ignored. Anne Mercier and
Violet Watt, for example, in their *Red House by the
Rockies*, describe the Alberta foothills in the soft tones

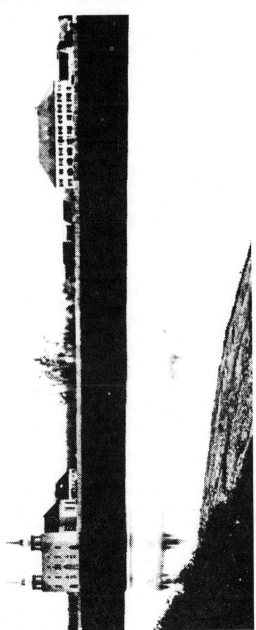

2. Cathedral of St. Boniface, from H.L. Hime, *Photographs Taken at Lord Selkirk's Settlement on the River of the North* (London, 1860), printed in *150 Years of Art in Manitoba* (Winnipeg Art Gallery, 1970), p. 32.

of an English romantic painter—after clothing them tastefully in oak trees. Collins sets Lord Selkirk down (many years too early) in a very exotic Red River Valley: "Here the 'tiger rose,' like some savage queen of beauty, rose to his knees and breathed her sultry balm in his face."[36] More often, as in the stories of Ballantyne and Laut, the prairie is a convenient wilderness against which to pit heroic courage, its hostility personified by the Indians who inhabit it. Like Fenimore Cooper, some of these writers had never seen the plains, of course, but those who had must have been kept, as the painters were, by conventions of their artistic form or by their own habits of perception from giving it any vivid individuality as a setting.

If the limitations of White society's first adjustment to the land had affected only the early fiction, they would have had very little literary importance, since the fiction of the Nineteenth and early Twentieth Century is of mainly historical interest. But the austere face of the prairie has not changed that much since Henry Kelsey first saw it. There were no forests to cut down, and man's structures have done little to interrupt the basic lines of the landscape. And the experience of meeting it from within an alien culture remains at the heart of the literature. Sinclair Ross's Mrs. Bentley is as much an alien to the prairie as if she had arrived by ox-cart a century earlier. The incongruities of that first response to the plains have never been overcome, and their lingering effects can be seen in a century of shifting attempts to come to terms with the land, both in the fiction and in general cultural arrangements. A brief glimpse of the continuing relationship between the fiction and the cultural history of the prairie will be useful for our literary examination of the fiction in succeeding chapters.

One way of explaining the initial inability to perceive the land in settler, painter, and writer is by saying that they needed a way of seeing the land *in relation to man* before it could take on meaningful shape

3. "The Virgin Prairie," wood engraving in George
Monro Grant, *Picturesque Canada* (Toronto:
Belden Bros., 1882), I, 277.

and acquire significant detail. Casting it as a wilderness or as a mere commodity were two inadequate and largely short-lived attempts to do this. What they needed, in effect, was a "myth" in the popular sense of an imaginative pattern which would express their changed relationship to their environment. By the turn of the century the novelists had found one in the "garden of the world" idea, probably borrowed from that earlier phase of western American settlement Henry Nash Smith describes under this heading. It provided the writers with a way of ordering their imaginative perceptions of the prairie, and not surprisingly the natural setting begins to appear more clearly and more substantially in their work at this same time. The first concerted response to the unnamed country in that time of optimism was to what O'Hagan suggests as a glimpse of the first creation. The idea had some plausibility. After the depression of the 1890's the West was emerging into its greatest period of agricultural expansion. The railroads were opening up seemingly unlimited opportunities for grain farming. Cheap land, easy cultivation, and buoyant markets were promising the wheat farmer swift prosperity. Historians as well as novelists spoke of the West in millennial terms.

Some of the settlers and, again, the painters, were ahead of the novelists in adopting the "garden" image of the West. As early as 1880 Nellie McClung's childish expectations were that "We would travel with the sun, until we came to that flower starred prairie where no stone would impede the plough; where strawberries would redden the oxen's fetlocks; where eight-hundred acres of rich black soil was waiting for us. . . ."[37] This illusion was probably the work of the railroads and the immigration department, who would understandably foster such expectations.[38]

The painters, too, seem to have developed this conception of the West considerably earlier than the writers, as the illustrations in Grant's *Picturesque Canada* (1882) reveal. The leading illustration, "Virgin Prairie," probably by the American artist Frederick B. Schell (his

4. "A Prairie Stream," wood engraving in George
Monro Grant, *Picturesque Canada* (Toronto:
Belden Bros., 1882), I, 285.

background may be significant considering the source of the garden idea) is typical. (See Plate 3) The picture represents the flatness of the land and the dramatic prominence of the sky very well, but the bouquet of flowers dominating the foreground and extending beyond the margins imposes a lushness of tone upon an otherwise awe-inspiring but austere prospect. The picture of "A Prairie Stream," (see Plate 4) goes a little further to express the Edenic tone, entwining the trees—themselves of an indefinite species—with traceries of distinctly exotic foliage. The effect of the rounded margin is hard to assess precisely, but it seems to provide a completion to the vision without the need to let in all the bush or prairie which must extend beyond this stream. It has a dream-like self-containment very like the vision of the West encouraged by the text of the book.

In fiction, Ralph Connor's *The Sky Pilot* in 1899 can be taken as the beginning of a trend toward a garden view of the prairie which was to last for over twenty-five years. The lyric praise of farm life voiced by Arthur Stringer's Chaddy McKail in *The Prairie Wife is* typical of what can be found in fiction up to the mid-1920's.

> We're laboring to feed the world, since the world must have bread, and there's something satisfying and uplifting in the mere thought that we can answer to God, in the end, for our lives, no matter how raw and rude they may have been .... And at sunrise, when the prairie is thinly silvered with dew, when the tiny hammocks of spider webs swing a million sparkling webs strung with diamonds, when every blade of grass is a singing string of pearls, hymning to God on High for the birth of a golden day, I can feel my heart swell, and I'm so abundantly, so inexpressibly alive, alive to every finger-tip! Such space, such light, such distances.[39]

This, the archetypal garden, is the most common though not often the most convincing image of the prairie in the stories of Ralph Connor, Nellie McClung, Arthur Stringer, the early R. J. C. Stead, and a host of less popular romancers of their time. Like Eden, their West has no past, only a present beginning when the settler arrives, and a better future. This was, of course, a time of boom and optimism and, for the writers at least, a time of agrarian ideals. The free, independent farmer is in their eyes the most productive citizen and likely to be the happiest and most virtuous because of the ennobling effects of his honest labour and continual contact with nature. Nature is a divine order in almost the eighteenth-century sense, exacting harsh service of man but ultimately beneficent.

The predictable counterpart of this divine natural order is a trivial, corrupt or evil human order, evident whenever the city appears in fiction of this era. The Calgary of Stringer's prairie trilogy or of Stead's *Cow Puncher*, for example, and the cities of Nellie McClung's stories, are areas of exploitation and vice. The raw prairie cities of the boom years did want many of the civilized refinements which are expected to compensate for the lack of wholesome country innocence, but these writers were also responding to the demands of a literary genre. They were producing a variety of sentimental romance which is permeated with a quasi-pastoral assumption that the country is regenerative while the city is sinister and moribund.

The use of this recurrent garden motif in the art and culture generally could be dismissed as simply another way of looking at the prairie without seeing it. To some extent, the imagination is not transforming the given reality but escaping from it. There is no doubt that at this stage the literary imagination was out of touch with certain hard realities of the plains, though no more so than the practical minds that planned the agricultural expansion in the West. The drought years of the 1930's gave sudden and dramatic proof of how dangerous it was to be materially out of touch with the land. Even before that, writers like Grove, Ostenso, and Stead were able to see that the millenial harmony between man and nature implied in the early romances of pioneering was an illusion. At the same time, the garden view of the West did express the basic positive response to the unnamed country as a glimpse of the first creation, and as such it remains a permanent feature of the prairie consciousness. If it obscures the less pleasant effects of isolation and hardship, it does highlight the peculiar inspirational qualities of the land and its promise which are as undeniably real. The garden motif never disappears from prairie fiction, though in many of the later novels it appears ironically, an image for the spirit of precarious optimism which is still typical of the prairie dweller.

The mid-1920's mark a watershed in prairie cultural development. In those years immigration virtually reached its equilibrium. The number of British immigrants who came to the prairies in 1926, for example, was about equal to the number who left.[40] The dream of settlement had, in many respects, been realized. Transportation, communication, and general amenities were improving. Settlers were prospering and expanding their acreage; mechanization was increasing their efficiency; the land was yielding generously except for some areas of southern Saskatchewan and Alberta where it was (ominously) beginning to blow away. Wheat prices were high. Still, there was no millenium of the sort anticipated. A dream had become a prosaic reality. It must have been more than coincidence that in 1925 and 1926 there appeared the three novels usually regarded as heralding a new realism in prairie fiction: Martha Ostenso's *Wild Geese*, Grove's *Settlers of the Marsh*, and R. J. C. Stead's *Grain*.

The techniques of this new fiction encouraged a more thorough representation of the prairie environment and way of life than can be found in any earlier fiction. The novels also show an increasing disillusionment with the romance of pioneering and the naive assumptions underlying it. In the work of Grove, Stead, and Ostenso, as there would later be in that of Ross, Stegner, McCourt, Mitchell and others, there is a realization that the means of physical and economic adaptation to the environment, though initially successful, had not automatically effected a cultural or imaginative adaptation. Rather, they had aggravated the original unfamiliarity with the land into a settled alienation by tending, in D. G. Jones's phrase, to exploit what they should have cultivated. Grove's Abe Spalding is the classic case. He comes from Ontario with a determination to impose an entire way of life upon an apparently featureless tract of land. He succeeds in every measurable way, but suffers in proportion a gradual dehumanization. Here again Jones's analysis is useful when he says that Grove's heroes represent "the arrogant and aggressive masculine logos" of Western civilization which attempts to tyrannize over nature, both external nature and the more spontaneous, irrational aspects of human nature.[41] These are the very aspects Abe cannot cope with in his growing family. Spalding's failure, seen in another way, is a failure of imagination, and one common to many other fictional pioneers. By fixing doggedly upon his own limited vision, he fails to assimilate the realities around him, and those realities when ignored become alien and threatening. At times the prairie becomes for Abe what O'Hagan describes as "the darkness unveiled," the chaos which threatens man's carefully created order.

Among Canadian painters, a spirit akin to that of the prairie realists of the mid-1920's can be recognized in the Group of Seven, but except for A. Y. Jackson and Lemoine Fitzgerald, they had little interest in painting the prairies. This is not true, however, of C. W. Jefferys, who was a forerunner of theirs in the pursuit of artistic nationalism. J. Russell Harper assigns considerable importance to Jefferys's annual visits to the prairies:

His most significant canvases, *Western Sunlight,
Lost Mountain Lake,* and *Prairie Trail* (Art
Gallery of Toronto), were painted from sketches
made on these trips. He sought to discover the
western landscape's real nature— its distant
horizons, the repetition of horizontal lines, subtle
variations of colour in the foliage, and the
clearness of the atmosphere. Later, Jefferys would
preach the gospel of spruce and pine as a theme
for Canadian painters. His vivid interpretations
of the Prairies and his landscapes of other parts
of Canada must have acted as powerful stimuli to
members of the Group of Seven.[42]

The two paintings Harper mentions were done in 1911
and 1912, so again the painters seem to have anticipated
the writers by a decade or more. For all the very striking
realism of Jefferys's work, there is, in these paintings, no
suggestion of alienation or the deterministic worldview
found in the fiction. A nearer analogy to the mood of
the fiction can be found in the slightly later work of
immigrant painters such as Charles Comfort and Alex
Musgrove. Comfort's *Prairie Road* (1925) presents the
sparseness of the land and the domination of the sky
very effectively, creating what might be called intensely
clear air with an opaque sky. Comfort, interestingly
enough, worked for a time with the wood engraving firm
of Fred Brigden in Winnipeg, supplying illustrations for
the Eaton's mail order catalogue, a publication which
must have had incalculable effects on the visual tastes of
prairie dwellers.[43] In Alex Musgrove's *The Prairie
Sentinel* (See Plate 5) the familiar grain elevator appears
to be surrounded by a flimsy and inadequate palisade
which, like the title, suggests a civilized outpost which
feels itself besieged in some indefinite way by the
landscape. Perhaps the intuitions of the painters were
surer. The novelists gradually came to see that the
pioneer is cut off from nature not by an innate hostility
in the land but by his own hostile frame of mind.

5. Alex Musgrove, "The Prairie Sentinel," courtesy of The Bulman Group Ltd., printed in *150 Years of Art in Manitoba* (Winnipeg Art Gallery, 1970), p. 89.

The views of the early realists in fiction might have encouraged a less exploitive approach to the land and prevented some later distress, even of a material sort, had they been widely shared. They do not appear to have been, and their publication in serious fiction was unlikely to spread them very quickly. The average farmer of that era had a grade five to grade eight education and little time for "impractical" men of letters.[44] The relative prosperity of the post-war years could have provided the leisure and the money for general cultural development which obviously lagged behind the physical development of the prairies. Instead, the imaginative failure to adapt to the plains was compounded by economic failure during the 1930's.

The Depression would have been especially disastrous on the prairies under any circumstances, accompanied as it was in so many districts by an almost unrelieved drought lasting from 1930 to 1938. But prairie farmers were rendered more vulnerable to both these dangers by practices of settlement and cultivation developed during the boom years. Many had mortgaged their original homesteads in order to put more land— often sub-marginal land— under cultivation for the sake of a bumper crop which would bring sudden prosperity. The economic depression, the plunging wheat prices from 1930 to 1933, made mortgages insupportable. Their techniques of cultivation, brought from areas of much higher rainfall, made the farmers especially vulnerable to the ravages of the drought. There was no concerted effort to guard against either of these dangers, despite the fact that the Alberta and Saskatchewan governments had both set up commissions to study the problems of dry-land farming as early as 1920, and that by 1926 more than 10,000 farms had been abandoned in Alberta. The topsoil continued to blow through the 1930's until eventually some 18,000,000 acres of farm land were affected and the prairies had lost some 247,000 people.[45]

James Gray, in his *Men Against the*

Desert, describes the long struggle, with the guidance and financing of the Prairie Farm Rehabilitation Administration, to reclaim the desert of the Palliser Triangle. When the PFRA was established in 1935, virtually nothing had been done. To correct the errors of past practices of settlement and cultivation, it was necessary to relocate farmers, returning some land to grass and creating community pastures, to develop farming methods such as strip farming and "trash farming" to conserve moisture, and windrowing of soil to reduce wind erosion. Implements with which to farm the dry prairie, like the discer and the blade cultivator, were developed as well as a new grass to hold the dry pasture lands from blowing away, Fairway crested wheat grass. The previous lack of dry-farming methods and implements is evidence that the settlers knew too little about their land, but there is further evidence that they cared too little as well. It was estimated that only one homesteader in three ever intended to become a farmer.[46] The others hoped to "prove up," sell out, and move on. The land was a commodity. The result of this and similar attitudes was that much of the land was deteriorating through neglect or exhausted by over-cropping before the ravages of drought, hail, rust, and grasshoppers set in. The effects of such mismanagement would have been felt in the 1930's even without the Depression or drought.[47]

The ravages of the Depression and drought years and even the attendant reaction against the land did not set an entirely new direction for prairie fiction. The work of such writers as Sinclair Ross, Edward McCourt, and Vera Lysenko seems rather to complete the disillusionment introduced by the first prairie realists. Especially in Ross's *As For Me and My House*, the most severe of the Depression novels, we see the completed progress of the prairie from beneficent to indifferent to hostile environment. What is new is a strain of desert imagery, with its inevitable suggestion of spiritual sterility extending to characters like Philip and Mrs.

Bentley. Their response to the prairie desert is a turning inward and stiffening of meagre cultural defences against the natural environment. These defences reflect what Northrop Frye has called the "garrison mentality," aptly embodied in the small town, which in prairie fiction is always ugly and spiritually constricting. As a strategy for survival, the garrison culture is here as predictable as it is futile. When you have failed to establish physical or spiritual harmony with your environment, hostility is the only alternative to complete emptiness and unmeaning. In the most extreme imagery of Ross and McCourt there is also a growing implication that the prairie is in some way inimical to the imagination. In *As For Me and My House* and *Music at the Close* the central figures are imaginative people whose potential for artistic expression is apparently stifled by the barrenness of their environment. This defeat would seem to be one final outcome of the challenge to the imagination early observers saw in the prairie—the conclusion to be reached through prairie realism.

It should not be forgotten, of course, that from the 1920's on there is a separate tradition of popular fiction which does not share the tragic outlook of the prairie realists. Just how the two streams of fiction relate to the life of the people on the prairie is difficult to establish, but there is little doubt about what the people read. *As For Me and My House*, when first published in 1941, sold only a few hundred copies.

Developments in painting in the West during the Depression and for the two succeeding decades bore little outward resemblance to what was happening in the fiction. In Winnipeg in the early 1930's, L. L. Fitzgerald and others were starting Canada's first movement into abstract painting, a movement which spread until, during the war years, total non-objectivity characterized the new painting of the prairies generally.[48] After the war, a wave of abstract expressionism spread from Regina—particularly the Regina Art

School under Kenneth Lochhead—"to engulf all but a

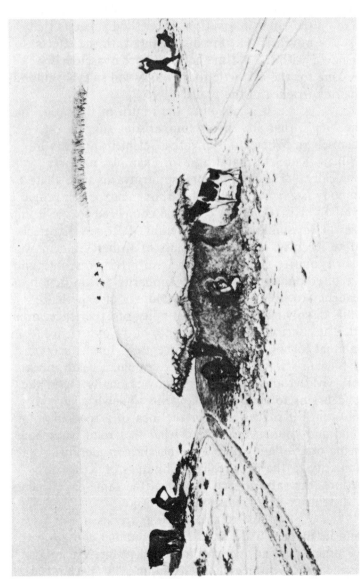

6. William Kurelek, "We Find All Kinds of Excuses," courtesy of the artist and The Isaacs Gallery, Toronto, printed in *William Kurelek, A Retrospective* (Edmonton Art Gallery, 1970), n.p.

few staunch dissidents on the Prairies."[49] When painters move into nonfigurative expression and abandon what can be called the "literary" or "narrative" element of their art, it becomes increasingly difficult to draw useful— or even sane—comparisions with the fiction. That is, direct comparisons, for in one sense the artists' eagerness to take up the latest innovations in method suggests that like the novelists they are dissatisfied with the effects achieved with the old methods and are consciously looking for the aesthetic form which will suitably embody their experience of the prairies.

It is not until the return of figuration in the 1960's, that any direct comparisons suggest themselves. When the "narrative" element appears in William Kurelek's paintings, for example, it works ironically.[50] The familiar prairie farmyards (See Plate 6) embody heavy parables and harbour unexpected religious symbols. His technique could be compared to the ironic uses of verisimilitude in the fiction of Robert Kroetsch. More recently, the water colours of Robert Sinclair with their exquisite drawing and their surprising discontinuous use of colour suggest another similarity to the fiction, a tendency to hold the sensory vividness of experience while dissolving the usual continuity of experience, or of art. The effect is to free the essence of the experience from habitual form and habitual perception. In one sequence of Sinclair's water colours, for example, a road appears very vividly, and at first very conventionally. Then the road begins to shift and change in somewhat surreal ways until it suggests rather the idea of a road in your mind and your memory, and what that road has meant in the prairie landscape. I see here a considerable similarity to the post-realist techniques of Kroetsch's fiction—the same search for form, the same experiments with sensory detail, illusion, discontinuity.

Most of the post-war trends in the West indicate at once a decline in active human contact with the prairie and an increase in detached interest in it as a distinctive environment. The economics of mechanization and marketing have favoured larger farms, turning agriculture from a way of life to an industry. The surviving smaller holdings are often operated by what Wallace Stegner calls "suitcase farmers" who live on the land only during peak periods of spring and fall activity. Small towns disappear as means of communication accelerate, their functions absorbed by cities which, in most respects, are like cities anywhere. Yet at the same time, there is increasing interest in the prairie as a cultural phenomenon, and there are increasing efforts to preserve its past through parks, historical sites, provincial archives, local histories, historical journals, museums, and galleries. Such activities can be recognized as part of a general cultural awakening stirred by urbanization, affluence, and national pride. There are also, for example, more theatres producing Pinter, Beckett, and Albee, but the interest in local cultural and artistic activity is stronger than it has ever been in the prairie. There has not, in fact, been any remarkable increase in the publication of fiction. Book-length fictions set on the prairie have averaged at least three per year for the past hundred years, and do not appear to run much beyond that today. The typical outlook of the more recent fiction does, however, seem to be shifting with the current of general cultural selfconsciousness.

The new environment of urbanization and "agribusiness" in a sense contains the older environment of family farm and small town as part of its usable past. The older environment is now something that can be seen and analysed, along with the attitudes it engendered. Possibly for this very reason contemporary writers have a heightened interest in what Margaret Laurence calls "a coming to some kind of terms with your roots and your ancestors."[51] The present generation of writers are the first who can reasonably claim "roots and ancestors" in the Canadian prairie, and in their looking back, these writers, or at least the best of them, are not nostalgic. They are able to view the prairie environment and their peoples' attempts to adjust to it with new detachment,   43 and they treat the failures of the dominant British-Ontario culture with some asperity. As can be seen in Margaret Laurence's work, there is often sympathy but rarely indulgence for the stubborn pride and short-sightedness of the pioneers.

A parallel trend can be seen in the technique of the novel. The present writers seem more interested in discontinuity in narrative structures, allowing for new collocations of the elements of prairie life. Kroetsch, the most technically adventurous of the group, expresses impatience with "certain traditional kinds of realism,"[52] presumably because he wishes to escape the assumptions implicit in the realistic fiction which shaped an earlier vision of the prairie. He speaks of his own experimentation as an attempt to discover how to write the prairie novel. In effect, the best of the contemporary novelists are dissatisfied with their predecessors' ways of "naming" the new land because it has remained somehow an unknown territory, even for those who have been raised in it. They must find, somewhere amid the dead history and living lies, a vocabulary with which to re-name the old experiences. Kroetsch provides a striking image for the novelist's dilemma in *The Studhorse Man*.[53] His narrator sits in a dry bathtub in an insane asylum, and like the Lady of Shalott, views his subject in a mirror which faces a small window. The absurdity of this narrator's position suggests all the cultural incongruities through which the novelists must struggle toward a clearer view of the prairie experience.

The Nineteenth
Century

Nineteenth-century prairie novelists might have been like
the new-world writer whom A. M. Klein describes in his
"Portrait of the Poet as Landscape" as "the nth Adam
taking a green inventory / in world but scarcely
uttered." But as we have seen, it was not that simple.
Prairie writers have never really enjoyed the freshness of
beginning Klein's metaphor suggests, because they
arrived with the cultural luggage of their British or
Ontario upbringing which they could not or would not
unload. Even the newness typical of the American West
was denied them, because by the time prairie fiction
began in 1871, Canadians had a well documented
historical tradition of hanging onto that luggage, and this
tradition was reinforced by all the familiar structures of
their past society which seemed to have preceded them
onto the plains in the form of missionaries, surveyors,
policemen, and railroads. Rather than Adams, they could
more appropriately be called exiles. Like Margaret
Laurence's Scots pioneers, they came to the West
voluntarily but found they had banished themselves from
the physical centres of the world they still mentally
inhabited.[1]
  The old order remained strong enough
that in most of the nineteenth-century fiction, the writer's
imagination could hardly be said to have engaged the
new environment, let alone assimilated it to an artistic
form. Often the writers did not try; the widest variety of
writings take the form of journals, diaries, and
reminiscences, but there are also over thirty known
volumes of fiction, and more come to light every year.
They include scattered attempts at a kind of
documentary realism, but the most consistent impulses
are toward romantic adventure and—less predictably—
the interplay of manners. The proportions of these types
of fiction reflect fairly closely what was being written in
central Canada during the mid-Nineteenth Century, but
there the conditions were not quite as primitive. The
western writers' unlikely choice of social fiction is a
possible clue to the difficulty the literary imagination was   45

having in coming to terms with the prairie. The writers, of course, were not native to the West, nor for the most part immigrants, but visitors at best, and if their imaginations were stirred by the new land (or by the idea of it) they sought the reassurance of familiar forms in which to give expression to those stirrings. When Agnes Laut, for example, thought of adventure, she thought of Sir Walter Scott, and the result is evident in her *Lords of the North.*

The early fiction also betrays the attitudes and unconscious cultural patterns which hampered the imagination of the colonists in perceiving and assimilating the new environment and made the struggle for survival, physical and imaginative, more severe than it need have been. It would be unwise, of course, to load a great weight of theory on such a frail body of literature, but often the very failures prove the most illuminating in a cultural sense. They are such imperfectly realized fictions that they provide unusually clear examples of the difficulties the colonists faced and strategies they adopted to overcome them. And the attitudes and cultural "sets" evident in the novels are confirmed again and again in the non-fiction written during the same period.

Egerton Ryerson Young, in his mission among the tribes of northern Manitoba, provided some richly suggestive illustrations of the nineteenth-century civilized approach to the West, as it appears in both reminiscences and fiction. In his *On the Indian Trail*, Young recounts his introduction of the Indians to James Evans' Cree syllabics with a simplicity equal to that of the Indians who were first encountering the genuinely magic powers of an alphabet:

> I marked out some simple words such as: 〈〈
> (pa-pa,) ⌊⌊ (ma-ma,) ⟨⌈⌈(oo-me-me, —
> English; pigeon.) I showed them how thus to
> combine these signs into words. This very much
> interested them; but the climax came, when with

the burnt stick I marked ⌐Ó⊃ (Maneto,— English; God, or the Great Spirit.) Great indeed was the excitement among them. They could hardly believe their own eyes, that before them was Maneto, the Great Spirit. He whom they had heard in the thunder and the storm, whose power they had seen in the lightning flash, about whom, with reverence and awe, they had talked in their wigwams, and at their camp-fires—"Maneto!" Here, made by a burnt stick on a rock, visible to their eyes, was that name: GOD ON THE ROCK! It was indeed a revelation. Something that filled, and thrilled them, as I have never before or since seen Indians thrilled.[2]

Young was unprepared for the Indians' reaction; he evidently regarded the native mind as a sort of *tabula rasa*, like the rock, on which he could inscribe the name of the divine. It was partly a lack of understanding of his own culture too, since he would have known very little about how the introduction of phonetic transcription had affected his own civilization or how his awareness had been shaped by growing up in a literate society. To him letters were simply a useful abstraction he was offering the less fortunate as a way to God and, incidentally, to white culture, values, and perceptions. He did not realize how much he was asking them to accept, any more than he understood the culture which he was trying to impose upon them. Though he writes elsewhere about the naturally religious disposition of the Indians, he did not seem to grasp the very concrete wholeness of their relationship with the physical world around them, or the pervasiveness and immediacy of their sense of the divine. Without this understanding of land and people, he readily assumed a virgin formlessness upon which he could impress his abstractions. Meanwhile, his pupils made of his letters something very concrete. Like many other educators and colonizers, Young demonstrated, if he did not discover, that the land and the people had a 47 life and a logic of their own.

Young's *On the Indian Trail* is a useful example because some of the most revealing writing in the early West is not fiction but the journals, diaries, and reports of the explorers, traders, missionaries, and settlers. Some of these writers did attempt fiction, but usually the conscious intention of art led them to forms which obscured more than they revealed about experience in the West. William Butler's *The Great Lone Land* is more poetic than his *Red Cloud the Solitary Sioux*[3] as well as more accurate; Young's own *Oowikapun*[4] is admittedly an encouragement to young missionaries more than a novel, but its homiletic purpose distorts what even Young must have perceived of the land and the life of the natives.

The narratives of the missionaries are in many ways the most instructive. The missionaries had no conscious desire to exploit the land or the people, and they had every reason for wanting to see them as they were, and not simply in relation to white ideas or designs. As a result, they offer the purest evidence of how Europeanized culture shaped and limited men's response to the new land. Young is an extreme example, a product of a settled Ontario upbringing, never at home in the wilderness, though he suffered its hardships heroically. John McDougall, who came to the prairies at the age of fifteen with his missionary father, George McDougall, was an entirely more adaptable man. An accomplished pioneer as well as a missionary, he lived with his charges and was considered by them an Indian as well as a white man.[5] Yet even McDougall carried with him the inevitable luggage of the early education he had been given in civilized schools. In one startling passage in *Pathfinding on Plain and Prairie* he attributes the moral degeneration of the Indians to the buffalo herds and tribal communism. He reasons from a Wordsworthian assumption that the "scene of sylvan beauty" along the Saskatchewan should "give them large, broad and fine views of life and all things." Their religion is false, but also "the great herds of buffalo as abused by man were hurtful to himself, and therefore in the fulness of time the Great Father, in the interests of His children, wiped them from the face of the earth. Tribal communism has always been hurtful to individuality, and without this no race of men can progress" (p. 70).

Aside from what the Wordsworthian approach may have done to his perception of the landscape, these comments reveal some significant things about McDougall. On the one hand it is easy to see why he and the other missionaries were such effective propagandists for the colonization that was to follow them, when a man like McDougall, who was almost as much a hunter and a nomad as the Crees, believed implicitly in the practices and the ideals of the coming colonization. On the other hand, like Young, McDougall reveals the extent to which unconscious patterns of his own culture defined his ability to see the life of the West. Agriculture, individualism, and progress were surely no more than peripheral to his professed religious beliefs, yet they became the main burden of his mission, and must be the only considerations that could lead a humane man to call the destruction of the Indians' food supply a divine, paternal act.

If the missionaries served as propagandists they were themselves the victims of a subtle and pervasive propaganda of the sort Marshall McLuhan and Wilfred Watson discuss in *From Cliché to Archetype*, a propaganda that is environmental and invisible. They had quite naturally been exposed to it all their civilized lives: "The total life of any culture tends to be 'propaganda'. . . . It blankets perception and suppresses awareness, making the counter environments created by the artist indispensable to survival and freedom."[6] The first part of this statement is an interesting reflection on missionaries and settlers. Paradoxically, the white colonizers entering this strange and overpowering environment clung to the forms of their previous

49

environment as the only means of survival, physical or cultural, in the face of apparent chaos. We can see the tendency of these forms to "blanket perception and suppress awareness" indispensable to survival. The latter part of the McLuhan-Watson statement is an interesting way of seeing the failure of the nineteenth-century fiction of the West. The writers, remaining within familiar forms and attitudes, reinforced inappropriate responses to the prairie when genuinely artistic "counter environments" could have freed the imagination to see the new country as it was.

The prose romance should have provided a form adaptable to the opening of the Canadian West, but that adaptation was never made during the Nineteenth Century. It would be easy to attribute this failure to a simple lack of literary talent, but there are other impediments to be found in the attitudes of the writers and in the way they chose their form. To be successful the fiction would have had to be romance of distinctly western aspirations, working out the destiny of the new land in romantic terms. These aspirations were not clearly conceived and too often the romancers used the western setting for the working out of old world or eastern dreams. That tendency was evidently reinforced by their choosing the form too immediately from its use in other contexts, from Scott or Cooper or popular fiction of the American West.

The most blatant examples of this ignorant or casual misuse of the western setting are in J. E. Collins's *The Story of Louis Riel* (1885) and *Annette the Metis Spy* (1887).[7] Collins and his publisher obviously wanted to exploit the popular excitement over the rebellion of 1885; the first of their books, as Collins admits, "occupied me only seveenteen [sic] days."[8] Collins's model could have been sensational popular romance such as the "Dime Novels." His form demanded that there be a hero, a villain and a heroine; southern Ontario sentiment demanded that the hero be Thomas Scott and the villain Riel. Collins created a girl friend for

Scott to provide the love triangle and the motivation for Riel's (a) executing Scott and (b) raising a rebellion. Both of Collins's books portray the most ludicrous sort of hairs-breadth escape adventure, with even an odd gothic touch. Riel, for example, knows a witch in a dismal swamp who holds young women hostage for him. *The Story of Louis Riel* is the more interesting of the two because it was written while the rebellion was still going on, and it dwindles away at the end into casualty lists for the battles of Fish Creek and Batoche. The effect on the reader is like being wakened from a dream. A similar but more powerful effect is produced by the newspaper accounts of Riel's trial bound in at the end of the book. In striking contrast to Collins's own writing, the bare journalistic accounts are so much more moving than Collins's sensationalism that they expose the flimsy contrivance to which they are appended.

The violence Collins does to events and personalities of western history in the process is too copious and too apparent to need detailed examination, but a comparison with Joseph Kinsey Howard's *Strange Empire*[9] (a very partisan pro-Metis history) or even with G. F. G. Stanley's biography of Riel reveals a great deal about the attitudes involved. Collins's books would still have been harmless amusements except for their evident intention to exploit and foment the bitter anti-French, anti-Catholic sentiments widely held in southern Ontario at the time. These intentions are supported by Collins's faintly plausible claims to historical accuracy. In a note to *Annette*, where he is doing a certain amount of confessing, Collins says, "I present some fiction in my story, and a large array of fact. I do not feel bound, however, to state which is the fact, which the fiction" (p. 142). The result is a wilful misrepresentation of the West, catering to an outside audience's prejudices about what was going on there.

The land fares no better than the people at Collins's hands. In the same note he says:

The preceding story lays no claim to value or
accuracy in its descriptions of the North-West
Territories. I have never seen that portion of our
country. . . .
I have, therefore, arranged the geography of the
Territories to suit my own conveniences. I speak
of places that no one will be able to find upon
maps of the present or of the future. Wherever I
want a valley or a swamp, I put the same; and I
have taken the same liberty with respect to hills
or waterfalls. The birds, and in some instances
the plants and flowers of the prairies, I have also
made to order. (p. 142)

It was not Collins's ignorance so much
as his contempt for his subject which made his writings a
disservice to the West and to the people who were going out
to settle in it. By helping to sustain the conception
of the West as a land of harmless adventure or as a property
the righteous must recover from the unrighteous, he
helped to retard the development of any appropriate sense
of the West.
Among the early writers of romance,
Agnes Laut is probably the direct opposite of Collins.
Her intention was to make the early history more
colourful and more attractive for the sake of students,[10]
and her *Lords of the North* (1900) shows evidence of
careful research into the history of the Red River
Settlement and the conflict between the fur companies
which threatened its survival.[11] Promising material for
romantic adventure certainly existed in accounts of the
tactics of the two companies, who ambushed each other's
northern fur brigades, burned each other's forts,
occasionally murdered each other's employees, and
frequently arrested each other's leaders, all with the
colour of conflicting legal rights emanating from London
and Montreal. When Laut sets out to enliven this
material with the appeal of fiction, however, the form
she chooses is a romance of tangled intrigue, reminiscent

52

of Walter Scott's lighter works. Her hero is in quest of a friend's wife and child, stolen away by a mixed band of dishonest Indians, half-breeds, and trappers. Throughout his search he courts a trader's daughter and carries on a deadly but chivalric enmity with a French-Canadian rival. The incongruity of the form is often emphasized by Laut's quite unromantic comments upon the native people. After a Metis foray against the settlers, for example, she says, "Victors from war may be inspiring, but a half-breed rabble, red-handed from deeds of violence, is not a sight to edify any man" (p. 154). After a description of the disastrous confrontation which became known as "The Seven-Oaks Massacre" she comments, "Let us not, with the depreciatory hypocrisy, characteristic of our age, befool ourselves into any belief that barbaric practices were more humane than customs which are the flower of civilized centuries" (p. 341). Since her anti-romantic tone is applied only to the natives and never to the implausibly courtly young lovers Rufus and Miriam, the effect is an essentially old-world, aristocratic romance. Unlike the work of Collins, *Lords of the North* represents an honest encounter with the history of the West, yet it too is a retreat into an inappropriate form. Both the Selkirk Settlement and the nature of Laut's art come into clearer perspective when *Lords*, with its "Norwester" hero is read together with Frederick Niven's *Mine Inheritance*[12] with its Hudson's Bay Company hero and Mrs. A. McLeod's *Cuthbert Grant*,[13] which is a very sympathetic biography of the Metis' leader of the time (significantly, a corresponding Metis fiction is missing). The stereoscopic effect brings into relief the feelings of the contending groups, including the settlers themselves, who were thrown into circumstances which were distinctive if not unique in Canadian history.

Between the negligence of Collins and the care of Agnes Laut can be found a full range of adventure romances, most designed for a British audience and many for juvenile readers. R. M. Ballantyne's *Red Man's Revenge* (1886)[14] belongs with the raft of adventure stories he set in all of the romantic areas of the world, though it enjoys the benefits of Ballantyne's service with the Hudson's Bay Company at Norway House and York Factory from 1841 to 1845.[15] His main characters are nonetheless solidly British, his natives either heathen devils or noble savages, but the land and some local customs are given with reasonable accuracy. W. F. Butler's *Red Cloud, The Solitary Sioux* (1882) is not entirely escapist romance either. It has some of the qualities of an anatomy in Butler's minute detailing of the ways of survival on the prairie—even a kind of Robinson Crusoe appeal—but the plot of Red Cloud's revenge for the betrayal of his father by an unscrupulous trader, the hunts and harrowing escapes, are standard, though here more reminiscent of Cooper than of Scott. The most obviously Cooperesque touches are to be found in Achilles Daunt's *In the Land of the Moose, the Bear and the Beaver* (1885).[16] His Old Jake Hawker is Cooper's Leatherstocking with a dash of Stevenson's Long John Silver. Much of the naturalist's detail in Daunt is probably authentic, but the effect of putting it in the mouth of an ill-created character who never quite belongs is to impose a fatal bookishness on all the woodlore.

John Mackie, writing for a more adult British audience, produced the largest group of adventure fictions of the nineteenth-century prairie West, including *The Devil's Playground* (1894), *Sinners Twain* (1895), *The Prodigal's Brother* (1899), *The Heart of the Prairie* (1899), and later *The Rising of the Red Man* (1904).[17] Mackie evidently cared more about his reading public than about his setting. Although he served in the NWMP from 1888 to 1892[18] he lards his stories with fanciful episodes such as Indian uprisings against the settlers and battles in which the NWMP quite uncharacteristically slaughter several hundred Sioux. He may have taken these sensational episodes from the American West partly because that would be the West his readers were most familiar with.

Mackie also invents lost lakes with mysterious islands almost as freely as Collins would, but in most of his descriptions the flora, fauna, and general terrain are faithfully and often imaginatively described. Like many of the later writers, he had read Butler's *The Great Lone Land.* Not only does he use the expression in his preface to *The Heart of the Prairie,* but he displays something of Butler's ambivalent emotion about the prairie sea. Here, for example, is a sleigh-ride across the Regina Plains area in *The Prodigal's Brother:*

> It filled one with an overpowering sense of the immensity and loneliness of that vast prairie-land; and had it not been for the subdued hiss of the runners over the crisp snow, resembling the steady seething of water past a ship's side, and the jangling of bells, one would have felt that the silence of this land was something appalling—a veritable presence that weighed on the soul like a nightmare, till the victim was fain to cry out to free himself from the spell. (pp. 117-118)

This could be straight Butler, but even so, it is one of the most vivid reactions to the land in the early fiction. In acknowledging the power of the landscape and its demands upon the imagination, Mackie anticipates such later romancers as Connor and Stringer, and to some extent the later realists who are concerned with the "presence that weighed on the soul like a nightmare."

Mackie's books are not devoted entirely to adventure, and this again could have been a response to literary fashion of the time. He provides some description of the strange land, some action, but another of his main concerns is with human interchange on a social level. Here, for example, a crudely mercenary suitor is attempting to ingratiate himself with a Mackie heroine by acts of largess:

"I'd like to please, and I like you to think well of   55

me . . . Hang trouble and expense, I say!"
She was conscious of a sense of disappointment,
but still she knew the danger she was exposed to
by her critical and hypersensitive nature, and
tried to lose sight of much that his speech
implied.[19]

In most of the early fiction the
interchange of manners carries less of the weight of the
book's significance than the adventurous action, but
there is one remarkable exception, a little book entitled
One Mistake, published under the pseudonym "Zero" by
the Canada Bank Note Company of Montreal in 1888.
The heroine-narrator, Miss Nelly Devigne, who describes
herself as "a thoroughgoing flirt," is over from London
for a year's amusement in Winnipeg. The time must be
nearly coincident with the Northwest Rebellion and with
Manitoba's turmoil over schools and provincial
boundaries, but the action is confined entirely to the
drawing rooms and social excursions of the Winnipeg
British community. Aside from its continual love
intrigues, the book constitutes an anatomy of Winnipeg
social life in the 1880's. Miss Devigne makes the rounds
of skating, snowshoeing, and tobogganing parties as well
as teas, dances, and a "musicale" at the Lieutenant-
Governor's (where the people must be asked not to talk
during the numbers).

Miss Devigne's ironic commentary on the
social elite of Winnipeg does not usually produce delicate
nuances of sentiment or a subtle awareness of man as a
social animal. Her tone, instead, becomes supercilious,
mocking, and her revelations obvious and heavy-handed.
This scene from a dance is about as near as she comes to
effective satire:

> Deserted by my cavalier, I ventured to address a
> few remarks to one of Mrs. Grundy's monitors,
> who sat upon my right, but, inadvertently, and
> most indiscreetly, using, in the course of
> conversation, the oldest fashioned term

> descriptive of the two appendages by which rude
> Nature has sustained what brave men dare to call
> our "trunks" (I wonder whom I'm shocking now!)
> this worthy chaperone (first looking everywhere,
> to ensure no male attendance, and evidently
> fearful lest some breeze should bear the sentence
> to an outraged native ear, then, glancing upon me
> with the amused peculiar smile, usually worn
> when gazing on a somewhat shocking picture, in
> a nice retired place) said: "We don't use 'leg' in
> Canada." (p. 71)

Quite incidentally "Zero" anticipates the withering force
of propriety in later prairie fiction.

      What "Zero's" efforts usually demonstrate,
not unexpectedly, is that the texture of Winnipeg
manners in the 1880's is not sufficiently developed to
sustain a revealing or even steadily entertaining fiction. It
is not simply that the social niceties are not refined
enough to be satirized effectively, but that examining the
characters in the glass of London manners fails to reveal
them. We are left with the impression of a London belle
who, like Margaret Atwood's Susanna Moodie, has come
away from the wilderness without quite having learned
what it might have taught her.[20]

      A comparison with Mrs. Moodie is useful
in another way. Nellie Devigne belongs in a long line of
feminine "confessional" narrators in Canadian fiction,
beginning with Frances Brooke's Emily Montague. They
all describe the collision of a cultivated sensibility with
the rudeness of Canadian pioneer society, and usually
their initial attitudes of revulsion or condescending
amusement at their new surroundings undergo a gradual
shift toward acceptance or respect if not identification
with those surroundings. Miss Devigne's first comment
upon the West, for example, is "We spent three days in
travelling through scenes which differed but in their
variety of wildness, one question only arising to the
mind—How mortals could be found to squander years of   57

their existence (I am not capable of the gross flattery which would call it life) amidst those barren rocks and half-charred stumps, or still more naked looking prairie." Later she can remark that "The crispness of the air, the clearness of the night, and the brilliancy of the stars and moon, all struck me as sublime." And it is finally in the rude innocence of the West that this very callous flirt falls in love—the "one mistake" she warns other young ladies to avoid. In prairie fiction the nearest relative of *One Mistake* is Stringer's prairie trilogy, and a line of descent from Stringer's prairie wife to Mrs. Bentley in Ross's *As For Me and My House* is not difficult to trace.

Another of the early novels relying heavily on an interplay of manners deserves some attention. James Morton's *Polson's Probation* (1897)[21] is the story of a young man who comes to Manitoba as a "Farm Pupil" because his inheritance in England is conditional on his avoiding disgrace for five years. Polson's distant cousin and rival for the legacy follows to engineer his disgrace, passing as one Silas Pancrack. He tries unsuccessfully to frame Polson for the murder of an Indian, and must himself retreat to England in disgrace and in the snares of his loathly lady accomplice, while Polson returns with honour, wealth, and the fair maid, Miss Crags. The setting is undeniably rural Manitoba, but Morton imposes upon it a form of English country-house life in which the young men hunt, snowshoe, attend teas, discuss manners and philosophy, and vie politely for the favours of Miss Crags, but never seem to do any farm work. We know from first hand accounts that the Farm Pupil was more often a source of £100 and a free hired man for some unscrupulous farmer.[22] Polson's book belongs to the tradition of the Victorian novel, in that manners and their ironic relation to morals (the villain Pancrack is exasperatingly suave) are very much the subject of the action.

Like *One Mistake,* Morton's book does

not offer a real encounter with prairie life, but it is

significant in several incidental ways. In contrast to his stock characters and his copious and improbable plot, Morton's descriptions of the environment are detailed, particular, and realistic. His narrative of a death in a blizzard, for example, is one of the best before Frederick Philip Grove. *Polson's Probation* also offers a paradigm of the distinctly colonial fiction of the West in which England remains the great good place, and the reward of virtue is to return there in good circumstances. The Northwest is always a kind of "probation," a means of isolating a few British people for scrutiny. This attitude is seen in its most innocent frankness in the charming little stories co-authored by Anne Mercier and Violet Watt, *A Home in the Northwest* (1894) and *The Red House by the Rockies* (1896).[23] When one of their characters says, "Could we not help to build a church here, father? It would be such a blessing to have something to work for, and to leave behind us when we go back to England,"[24] there need never have been any earlier mention of going back. That outcome is implicit in the whole moral perspective of the colonial fiction. The source of the characters' honour, courage, and stamina is their Britishness, and an old world concern for birth and breeding accompanies that pride of nationality. When two of Mercier and Watt's characters appear out of a blizzard, it is said, "That they were English gentlemen was apparent from their first sentence. . . ."[25]

Choosing a type of fiction better suited to an English drawing room than to a sod hut may not have been simply—or even primarily—a literary error on the part of the colonial writers. When you consider a phenomenon like Cannington Manor you can wonder to what extent the writers were faithfully representing a comically inappropriate approach to the prairies. In 1882 Captain E. M. Pierce was given a grant of land by his friend John A. MacDonald to set up an English colony south of Moosomin in what is now southern Saskatchewan.[26] The colony was to sustain itself by growing and processing farm products, but the actual work was to be done by Canadian pioneers. The way of life of the well-to-do principals of the scheme was to be transplanted intact from Britain, "That of an English country gentleman comprising leisure for culture and sport" (p. 3). The only other responsibility they acknowledged was for unpaid service to the community as magistrates and administrators. Their houses suggested the style in which they intended to live. One is described as having "four large reception rooms on the ground floor, as well as kitchen and a large storeroom, with eleven rooms above" (p. 11). Two men were kept busy all winter cutting wood to heat this home. Another of the houses, built of stone, featured an added "bachelor wing." "This, with a separate entrance, consisted of a hall with stairs up to the sleeping quarters for bachelors known as the 'ram's pasture' above the long room with full sized billiard table, so often described—the Beckton brothers in leather chairs by the fireplace, served by a valet, one Harrison, with drinks, and a dozen or more of the happy-go-lucky type of young Englishmen as well as any visiting sportsmen milling around" (p. 14). The young men are said to have "made a real stab at farming," but the farm instructor is quoted as saying, "I was glad when the young gentlemen took up tennis so I could get on with the work" (p. 16).

Tennis, horseracing, and riding to the hounds were favorite sports, but the catalogue of their amusements included: hunting, football, cricket, music, literature, theatricals, painting, philosophical discussions, gourmet cooking, tobogganing, skating, swimming, and sketching parties. They sound, in fact, as though they must have quite wearied themselves with leisure activities. The suspicion that these activities were as much an effort to maintain their identity in the face of the prairie as they were a pleasure is reinforced by the fact that even the typical bachelor's shack contained "a pile of Christmas numbers, silver-framed portraits, school sports trophies, and a view of their home in England graciously encircled by trees" (p. 17). The colony failed, not unexpectedly, partly because an anticipated CPR branch line by-passed it, partly because the men went away to the First World War and never bothered to return. Writers like Mackie, "Zero," and Morton may be seen as chronicling this approach to the prairie— their failures equivalent to the more eloquent failure of the Cannington Manor way of life.

There were some among the earliest writers who, unlike the writers of adventure romance or social fiction, had a strong impulse to document in fiction the new experience of the West. Writers already mentioned, such as Mackie, Butler, and Morton, appear to have seen some aspects of the prairie clearly, but they were always ready to sacrifice the new setting to the old form of their fictions. Some others, such as Alexander Begg, John MacLean, and Kate Simpson Hayes, were evidently not as ready to do this; their stories are inclined to be short and often somewhat formless. An occasional well-wrought short story appears, but most of the works could better be described as "tales." They also tend toward that end of the scale at which fiction blends gradually into reportage.

Paradoxically, one such writer, Bertram Tennyson, was a frequent visitor to Cannington Manor.[27] At times his style exhibits a lyric excess he might have developed from trying to imitate his uncle Alfred, but his *The Land of Napioa* published in Moosomin in 1896[28] includes stories and reflective essays seriously concerned with finding the West as a setting for imaginative writing. His best story is "Blizzard," about a man who dies snow blind and lost in the prairie and in memories of England, but more unusual is his grasp of the problem faced by writers in what he calls "this young hobblede-hoy giant of Canada" (p. 44). He sees particularly the problem of the immigrant writer, remarking that "every man sees in nature that which he brings eyes to see" (p. iv). As though to illustrate his point, Tennyson later presents a prose poem dramatizing a C.P.R. locomotive crossing the West as a new Thor. His sense of an unrecognized heroic grandeur in man's technology confronting obdurate nature anticipates what E. J. Pratt was to do more than a quarter of a century later, but Tennyson's Thor remains alien and artificial.

The only novel-length fiction to offer a realistic picture of prairie life in this period is Alexander Begg's *Dot It Down* (1871).[29] If Begg's impulse to do justice to the Red River Settlement and its people was strong, his story-telling impulse was correspondingly weak. His plot remains a lifeless skeleton, often neglected for digressions about life in the settlement. His Mr. and Mrs. Meredith become slightly involved in the historic controversy surrounding the handover of H.B.C. rights and responsibilities to the Canadian government, but in the end they settle happily. Their daughter Grace dies of a tragic love for George Wade, a man with a past he cannot reveal. Their two sons, Tom and Jack, remain healthy, strapping, and absolutely undifferentiated. Begg, of course, was primarily an historian, and throughout his novel he shows an historian's concern for representing fairly the four interest groups at work in the colony just before the Manitoba Resistance of 1869-70. He describes the Canadian party, the American party, the local residents (including the Metis), and the H.B.C., whose interests seem fairly well identified with those of the settlers. There is a strong sense of the immediacy of history, especially because the book was written when the troubled question of annexation was unresolved. In the last scene, George Wade is returning to the settlement past armed Metis guards posted to prevent the entry of would-be governor McDougall.

"Dot it Down" is actually a minor figure, a Canadian newspaper correspondent who prints slanderous nonsense about the people of Red River. He is a fairly obvious but not very telling lampoon of Charles Mair. The satire was clearly intended to counteract irresponsible reportage, not to antagonize Canadians. Begg's attitude toward Canadian immigration, as well as his overall documentary or journalistic purpose, is evident in the fact that the book ends with a twelve-page "Emigrant's Guide to Manitoba," filled with practical information, including a description of the use of fence wire for farmers who have known only pole fences.

The only significant turn of Begg's plot in *Dot it Down* is the final marriage of his young English gentleman, George Wade, to a Scots half-breed girl. The move is unexpected but not really atypical. One of the most notable features of all the more realistic nineteenth-century fiction is that the native people are depicted more sympathetically and more sensitively than they would be again for several decades. There seems to be a surprisingly close correlation between a writer's imaginative understanding of the land and his sympathy for the native people.

The largest group of stories devoted to Indians and mixed-bloods is in *Warden of the Plains* (1896)[30] where John MacLean not only creates a series of tales about Indians but recounts the Indians' own tales, legends, and myths, as he does in "The Spirit Guide." MacLean was a Methodist missionary in Alberta from 1880 to 1889, and since he wrote non-fiction about the ways of the Indians, his material is probably authentic, and his respect for his subject is evident.[31] As he says, "These people are often called savages by members of the white race, yet they have been taught the greatest respect for all forms of religion, recognizing these forms as methods by which men approach the supreme Power."[32] And MacLean's stories are compelling as well as credible; for all their formlessness, they are rendered in a style of low-key realism reminiscent of Bret Harte. Here, for example, is MacLean's description of a hotel-keeper who harbours a sick wayfarer in "The Hidden Treasure": "He was rough and ready in language and manners, drank freely and gambled and grumbled continually, yet in all the country there was not a more tender-hearted man. He had an Indian wife and several half-breed children, whom he loved intensely and swore at

63

incessantly" (p. 265). It is a pity that MacLean's mastery of dialogue lags so far behind his narrative and descriptive skill. His white characters speak an essentially American wild-west dialect broken into occasionally by a heavy Scots burr. For all that, his stories are as near to "local colorist" realism as anything in his time and place.

The relationship between Indian and White is seen as problematic in much of the early realistic fiction. MacLean's "The White Man's Bride," for example, is one instance of a recurring story about Indian wives abandoned by traders unwilling to stay with them or to take them back to England. Roger Pocock and Kate Hayes both seek out the less obvious aspects of the Indians' plight. Though Pocock was an English adventurer rather than an immigrant, he had a wide variety of experience in the West, including service in the NWMP from 1884 to 1886,[33] and he seems to have responded especially to the tragic or pathetic sentiments aroused by the Indian in a white-dominated world. In his *Tales of Western Life* (1888),[34] "The Lean Man" is a half sardonic half sympathetic story of an Indian who, though not scrupulously honest, is in this case arrested for someone else's crime. After languishing for a time in a NWMP guard room, Lean Man hangs himself with his sash and regains something of his original nobility in this last act of defiance. Another story, "Eric," is suggestive of D. C. Scott's later concern for the confusing heritage of the mixed-blood. Pocock's half-breed is unusually gifted, but because he is ruined by the mistakes of callous authorities, he drowns himself. Pocock's elegy for Eric runs: "There is always one great question about such a man: whether he will find scope for his endowments and master some great art, or drift idly, bearing the rich freight of genius without either helm or sail until a storm arise" (p. 119). It is clear that the half-breed's lack of opportunity to find scope for his genius is the cause of this tragic waste.

Pocock is at his best when presenting the circumstances and feelings of the Mounties he served with. His stories exhibit compassion for the native people more than an understanding of their psychology. Kate Hayes, on the other hand, includes one story in her *Prairie Pot-Pourri* (1895)[35] designed to lead the reader into a peculiarly Indian point of view on what the white man is doing to the native. "An Episode at Clarke's Crossing" is about a Sioux named Peter Larue, or "Daddy Pete" to his granddaughter Tannis. The girl is wooed by a young missionary named Penrhyn, who believes the Indians should have Indian teachers and sends Tannis away to school. There she becomes very thoroughly conditioned to eastern, civilized, White ways. The tragic effects of Penrhyn's liberal and somewhat paternalistic gesture are seen in the destruction of the bond between the girl and her grandfather. Tannis is embarrassed, for example, by the childish and gaudy presents Daddy Pete has proudly collected for her return. When the young minister is recalled by his bishop for becoming involved with an Indian girl, Tannis pines away in the now alien surroundings and eventually wanders off to die. The old man, reduced to senility by her loss, goes in search of her, and in an eerie final scene, walks into the gleaming waters of a moonlit lake imagining he follows her trail. While the ending may be sentimental, a distinctive Indian character is simply and convincingly portrayed, and the complication of motives and their effects does justice to the larger problem of a White culture imposing itself upon the indigenous one.

Miss Hayes's other stories are not as well written, but they all share an evident desire to present the West through western eyes. There is a preference for western ways and an assumption of western values, whether White or native. In "The La-de-dah from London," for example, we are shown the comic ineptitude of an English gentleman travelling to the Northwest with a Canadian farmer. His dialect is unpronounceable, his mistakes and cultivated excesses unforgivable, but in Miss Hayes's world he is able to redeem himself by losing his fortune and marrying a sensible Canadian farm girl. Miss 65

Hayes effects a complete reversal of the moral orientation of the "colonial" fiction.

From a purely literary standpoint, the work of Begg, Hayes, and MacLean is no more accomplished than that of Mackie, Ballantyne, or "Zero," but it shows a certain promise which was not fulfilled in the writing that followed. The early "realists'" documentary impulse might have provided a base from which an authentically western regional literature could have risen, but it did not happen that way, for at least two reasons. First, the writers of the next thirty years did not follow their lead or share their outlook. In particular, their will to document and their sympathy for the land and the native people were lost, as well as their awareness of the incongruities created by imposing Europeanized culture on the life of the plains. Nor did later writers choose to accept a certain formlessness in preference to imposing distorting forms on western life. In most respects, the fiction of the next three decades has more in common with John Mackie's work. During the settlement period, as we will see in Chapter III, writers like Connor, McClung, Stead, and Stringer were too deeply imbued with a popular vision of the West to see very far beyond it. Second, "realists" like Begg, Hayes, and MacLean probably did not speak *for* the people who were settling the West any more than the Mackies or Collins's. Possibly not as much. Writers like MacLean and Hayes seem to have come nearer to speaking for the new land itself, but the Mackies and Collins's probably spoke for a people who were themselves out of touch with the land. Mackie's and Collins's perspective on the settling of the West would not be popular today, but it may well have reflected the state of mind and imagination of the bulk of the settlers.

To judge by surviving accounts, the average pioneer was not very responsive to the land, and had little sympathy for the Indian he was displacing. His strategies for surviving imaginatively were analogous to those of the writers considered here as "non-realists."

66

The settler seems to have thought a little of the romance of the frontier in a general way, while in particulars he hugged the belief that nothing was changed in his surroundings. Lizzie McFadden is in many respects typical of the settlers who have left journals, and two pages from her diary of a migration to Prince Albert in 1879 convey more of the pioneer's state of mind than any explanation.[36] (see plate 7.)

Miss McFadden offers a first response to the prairie all the more eloquent for being almost illiterate. She has some vague sense that the prairie is beautiful, but her "no wood nor water to be got" is strangely similar to what Anthony Henday reported on first seeing the prairie a hundred years earlier. The journey—and the diary—are mainly a struggle to survive and get to the free land over a trying succession of very prosaic obstacles. The trail is well populated, and there is little sense of discovery. The Indians, it later becomes clear, are starving, and that may well have been what they were trying to tell the McFaddens. A few days later Lizzie reports that the Indians' dogs have tried to steal their meat and her father has shot at them but missed. "In the Morning we started away early in the morning as we passed the Indian tents they all came out and laughed at us. . . ." The lack of an intellectual or imaginative framework which will contain even these few incidents is strongly evident. Lizzie McFadden's diary is typical of pioneer accounts in that things seem to happen to her in a kind of vacuum in the new land. Writers like Begg, MacLean, and Hayes could not be said to have spoken for such pioneers, though they might have spoken *to* them with good effect had the circumstances of publishing and distribution been more favorable at the time. Hayes's *Prairie Pot-Pourri*, for example, was published by the Stoval Printing Company in Winnipeg, and it seems unlikely that they would have had distribution facilities to reach much of the population. Such conditions, of course, would naturally prevail until after the pioneer era.

(Friday th 18)
Rained in the morning did
not start till pretty late
started and went through
MacAnnon field and over
a bridge he built and
paid him 90 cents for to
go over had to go over
pretty ruf roads and throu
a bush about a mile
long camped for noon
at a crick it rained all
the morning got some
burries this morning.
seen beautiful fields and
prarie great hills and
dails talked with some
Indians could not under
stand what they say camped o

7. Pages 12 and 13, The Diary of Lizzy McFadden, manuscript: by
permission, from the original in the Public Archives of Canada,
Ottawa.

Pine Creek - Buggy Creek

(Saturday th 19)

Started of early before the
sun was up with out
our breakfast came four
mifes to pine crick had
breakfast and fed the
oxen started again
over hills and hollows
had beautiful roads all
the way had dinner again
at eleven in the middle
of a prarie no wood nor
water to be got seen
some farms camped at
night at boggy crick
made eighteen miles to
day.

(Sunday th 20)

Rested to day very pleasant

The roots of our prairie culture are probably in the diaries of all the Lizzie McFaddens, but in another sense they are in these imperfect fictions, where we can find a surprising number of the themes and motifs which become important in later fiction. "Zero" and the tradition of genteel complaint about cultural deprivation have already been mentioned. A good deal of later fiction, like that of Harold Bindloss, carries on the practice of writing western stories for overseas audiences, with very British assumptions about society and the land. Butler, in his *Red Cloud*, initiates a motif of western journeying which recurs from R. J. C. Stead through Robert Kroetsch. Butler's hero completes his quest at the Rockies with satisfying revenge and material rewards; later writers were to work more sophisticated and often ironic variations upon the theme of westward questing. Even the theme of temperance which was to become so prominent in the work of Connor and McClung is initiated here, especially in Morton's *Polson's Probation*. Silas Pancrack is only one of the villains. The other less explicit one is liquor, which degrades both the poor settlers and the Indians in the story.

These elements appear almost at random, but there is a group of images, best exemplified in the work of John Mackie, which lead directly into the fiction of the first two decades of the Twentieth Century. Mackie develops the fictional Mountie, which Connor, Gilbert Parker, and others were to take up. The press, and particularly the American press, were busily developing the same figure, but it must still be regarded as a literary image—the real mounted policeman was being neglected by writers and Ottawa politicians alike.[37] Mackie's response to the overpowering immensity and loneliness of the West has already been quoted. His approach to the land also prefigures what writers like Connor, McClung, Stead, and Stringer were to do. What seems more directly to anticipate the later writers is Mackie's occasional reflection upon the West as a clarified, simplified model of life. Here, for example, the heroine of his *The Prodigal's Brother* compares the West with her Ontario home: "She had more time to think, she saw a less conventional life; its phases were obvious; her mental vision was cleared so that she could understand aright many social questions that had before perplexed her; and her views of things in general gained in breadth" (p. 76). Mackie offers the beginnings of a view of the West as wide open mental spaces, which was the first view to become popular in fiction. Nothing like a continuous tradition of descent or influence could be argued from these few similarities; it seems more likely that the prairie evokes certain themes and images.

Finally the nineteenth-century fictions are of more permanent interest as examples than as influences. They present the rawest encounter between the white settler and the prairie, and that experience, in one form or another, remains a basic element of the later fiction. They are also the first of a long series of attempts to solve the problem apparent in Lizzie McFadden's diary: the lack of an imaginative framework to point the order and keep out the chaos. These first attempts are weak partly because the novelists, like the settlers, are encumbered by their Europeanized culture. As Tennyson says, "every man sees in nature that which he brings eyes to see." Later novelists, from about the time of Frederick Philip Grove, take this cultural blindness as a theme, but it never ceases to be a problem of the writers themselves.

The Romance
of Pioneering

The early Twentieth Century was the great age of popular
fiction in Canada, a time when a writer like Ralph
Connor could number the sales of his novels in the
millions. In those circumstances it is not too surprising
that prairie writers chose to dramatize the promise rather
than the threat of the unnamed country. They had a
popular audience and they were developing the first
dominant vision of the new land. From the turn of the
century to the mid-1920's the best-known writers,
including Connor, Nellie McClung, R. J. C. Stead, and
Arthur Stringer were all presenting the West in terms
suggestive of a garden awaiting cultivation. This garden
motif in their descriptions is reminiscent of the "Garden
of the World" myth earlier attached to the American
plains, and probably grew out of it. Henry Nash Smith
describes that myth as having ended in bitter
disillusionment during the 1870's,[1] but that would not
keep it from reappearing north of the border. The
Canadian plains were offering a new promise of endless
abundance.

What is more significant for an under-
standing of prairie fiction is that the writers chose the
garden and not the earlier "Frontier Myth" of the American West when they needed a way of ordering their
perceptions of the new environment. The causes and
conditions of that choice are worth examining.

The literary histories on either side of the
border seem in many ways directly opposed, and
comparisons are especially revealing at this early stage,
before the weight of American cultural influence on the
Canadian West tended to obscure the distinctions. On
the American side, Smith says, "The Wild West beyond
the frontier lent itself readily to interpretation in a
literature developing the themes of natural nobility and
physical adventure, but the agricultural West . . . proved
quite intractable as literary material" (p. 211). As critic,
Smith here does an injustice to Willa Cather, Ole
Rolvaag, and a number of other midwestern novelists,
but at this point he is establishing what has typified the

West in the American consciousness, and evidently does not find the midwestern fiction typical. The fiction of the Canadian West, by contrast, developed with the growth of a settled agrarian population and sought slightly different themes from the American. The reasons for this difference are worth some attention because they point to a great deal that is distinctive about Canadian prairie fiction.

The West to be found in English Canadian fiction is rarely a "frontier." If a "frontier" is taken to be that meeting point of advancing civilization and untamed nature, where civilized order confronts unordered wilderness, then there is no reason to expect one, since the frontier era was virtually over by the time the literature began. The fur traders and the missionaries had been operating in the West under what might be called frontier conditions for two hundred years by the time the first western novel, Begg's *Dot it Down*, was published in 1871. When most of the early novelists began to come west with the bulk of settlement from Ontario, Great Britain, and the American Middle West, they came into incredibly rigorous pioneer conditions, but not to the edge of a trackless wilderness. They had the sense of a plain patrolled by the North West Mounted Police, surveyed for settlement, with a railroad stretching out to cross it. They were not on the edge of anything; they were surrounded by something, and they took it to be the civilized order they had always known.

Nor was there much retrospective attention to the frontier condition in the literature. But then, for the most popular novelists, Ontario-born writers like Connor, McClung, Stead, and Stringer, it had not been their frontier. The fur trade had been carried on largely from England and from Montreal, while the main thrust toward settlement, when it came, came from Ontario. The West was never a frontier of Ontario (or Upper Canada) in the sense that the American West was the frontier of that nation as it steadily expanded from the eastern seaboard. Both history and geography prevented such a continuous westward movement. The Canadian West was shaped separately to a greater extent and tied in loosely to Confederation with a railroad (and two armies) as a hinterland or a set of colonies of central Canada. As early as 1946, W. L. Morton described the West's position as a colony of central Canada in his essay "Clio in Canada."[2]

The implications of this manner of development for the literature are interesting. In 1854 an American publicist could say:

> The American mind will be brought to maturity along the chain of the great lakes, the banks of the Mississippi, the Missouri, and their tributaries in the far northwest. There, on the rolling plains, will be formed a republic of letters which, not governed like that on our seaboard, by the great literary powers of Europe, shall be free, indeed.[3]

It would be hard to imagine anyone in central Canada saying this about the early Canadian West. Central Canada was not looking to an advancing frontier to provide its identity or mature its character. There was little demand for a frontier myth in the Canadian consciousness of the time. Central Canada was not, of course, an Atlantic nation seeking independence, but a landlocked nation struggling to maintain its British character. Because the West was hardly more to her than a source of land, markets, and raw materials, the settlers—and the novelists—could not think of themselves as being at the source of historical forces shaping their nation.

As a result, whatever ideals of nationhood appear in the fiction of the early Twentieth Century are attuned to the preservation of an empire which has already asserted its dominion over the land, and which has its centre somewhere else. Frontier values of individualism and egalitarianism are evident, but greatly

74

tempered by faith in a higher, intangible order.

The Garden Myth in Canadian fiction is characterized by an abundance of what might be called "pastoral" imagery and by a more or less explicit moral assumption that nature is regenerative and man and his artificial creations are trivial or corrupt. But it must be remembered that this view of nature does not constitute a main distinction between Garden and Frontier fiction. R. J. C. Stead, in *The Homesteaders*, describes the basic position of man in the prairie-as-Garden:

> It was a life of hard, persistent work—of loneliness, privation, and hardship. But it was also a life of courage, of health, of resourcefulness, of a wild, exhilarating freedom found only in God's open spaces.
> . . . .
> And at night, when the moon rose in wonderful whiteness and purity, wrapping field and ravine in a riot of silver, the strange, irresistible, unanswerable longing of the great plains stole down upon them, and they knew that here indeed was life in its fulness—a participation in the Infinite, indefinable, but all-embracing everlasting.[4]

Stead gives us the romance of pioneering in terms of the infinite, the eternal, and the ineffable; traditionally the terms and concerns of romance. But in Owen Wister's *The Virginian*, in many ways the archetype of frontier fiction, there is a similarly romantic attitude toward man in nature. Here is Wister's description of Medicine Bow:

> Yet this wretched husk of squalor spent thought upon appearances; many houses in it wore a false front to seem as if they were two stories high. There they stood, rearing their pitiful masquerade amid a fringe of old tin cans, while at their very

> doors began a world of crystal light, a land
> without end, a space across which Noah and
> Adam might come straight from Genesis.[5]

The Edenic overtones are, if anything, more explicit in
Wister. The difference in emphasis, however, is
significant. Stead sees the pioneer as taking man's
rightful place in a divine natural order. Wister
emphasizes the conflict between natural and human
order, and if we follow the directions of that emphasis, it
will lead toward the central distinction between typical
American and Canadian fictions of the West. They
present the relationship between man and nature
differently because the Frontier and Garden myths
embody two contrasting visions of *human* order.

Let us compare two bar-room show-
downs, scenes which have outward similarities but which
illustrate the contrasts. The first is from Wister's *The
Virginian*, and if I rely heavily on this novel for my
comparison with Canadian fiction of the early Twentieth
Century, that is because it seems to contain everything—
rustling, lynching, a gun duel at sundown, complete with
a weeping bride. In action and world view it epitomizes
the elements of frontier fiction from Cooper through the
"Dime Novels" to Zane Grey and the movie western.
Wister is also quite explicit about his Western actions
being paradigms for the development of the character of
America as a whole. This scene is at the meeting of the
Virginian with his enemy Trampas. During a poker game
Trampas calls the Virginian a "son-of-a———," at which
the other takes out his gun, and holding it unaimed on
the table, says those memorable lines:

> "When you call me that, *smile.*" And he looked
> at Trampas across the table.
> Yes, the voice was gentle. But in my ears it
> seemed as if somewhere the bell of death was
> ringing; and silence, like a stroke, fell on the large
> room. (p. 29)

Confronted in this way, Trampas declines to "draw his steel," and so the Virginian has righted a wrong, and restored order to the card game. The second showdown is in Ralph Connor's *Corporal Cameron*, published around the same time as *The Virginian*, but set north of the border. Here Connor presents what may be the central archetype of the Mountie, as a slim youngster in a scarlet tunic and pill-box cap who walks into a gambling den where a desperado is flourishing his gun:

> "Put it down there, my man. Do you hear?" The voice was still smooth, but through the silky tones there ran a fibre of steel. Still the desperado stood gazing at him. "Quick, do you hear?" There was a sudden sharp ring of imperious, of overwhelming authority, and, to the amazement of the crowd of men who stood breathless and silent about, there followed one of those phenomena which experts in psychology delight to explain, but which no man can understand. Without a word the gambler slowly laid upon the table his gun, upon whose handle were many notches, the tally of human lives it had accounted for in the hands of this same desperado.
>
> . . . .
>
> "Now listen!" gravely continued the youngster. "I give you twenty-four hours to leave this post, and if after twenty-four hours you are found here it will be bad for you. Get out!"
>
> The man, still silent, slunk out of the room. Irresistible authority seemed to go with the word that sent him forth, and rightly so, for behind that word lay the full weight of Great Britain's mighty empire. It was Cameron's first experience of the North West Mounted Police, that famous corps of frontier riders who for more than a quarter of a century have ridden the marches of Great Britain's territories in the far northwest

77

land, keeping intact the Pax Britannica amid the wild turmoil of pioneer days. To the North West Mounted Police and to the pioneer missionary it is due that Canada has never had within her borders what is known as a "wild and wicked West."[6]

Beneath their comic naiveté, both scenes are simple, unambiguous oppositions of right and wrong, and in each case right is made to prevail not by violence but by the exertion of a somehow uncanny power. Here the differences begin. The Virginian draws the gun with which he will enforce the right, while in Connor's scene it is the man with the gun who backs down. The young Mountie represents the constituted law of the territory, while the Virginian's justice is extra-legal. He speaks of living in a territory where "an honest man was all the law you could find in five hundred miles" (p. 372). And in this showdown, the power which overcomes Trampas and which electrifies the bar-room is a force of personality emanating from within the Virginian himself. The young Mountie is quite pointedly not credited with any special capacities or any personal force beyond a character for being devoted to his duty.

Probably the most significant difference between these scenes is in the source of the justice which is asserted. In Wister's Wyoming, justice is roughly defined by codes of behaviour developed to suit the local conditions of life. As his wise old Judge says, "many an act that man does is right or wrong according to the time and place which form, so to speak, its context . . ." (p. 430). Justice is more particularly arbitrated on the moment, by men like the Virginian. The law, as the Judge says in explaining a lynching, comes originally from the people; when they take it back into their own hands, it is not a defiance but an assertion of the law.

The young Mountie, on the other hand, is merely an instrument of a law which, like the whole system of order he maintains and the whole code of values by which he lives, is created elsewhere. His strength lies in his total acceptance of an authority emanating from a remote centre of empire. One could say that the conception of order in Wister's West is inductive—order is generated from the immediate particulars of experience—while that of Connor's West is deductive—order descends logically from higher precepts to which the individual has no access.

The young Mountie, in his devotion to an unseen order which must be the object of faith rather than reason, epitomizes a more general cultural tendency. Throughout the early fiction there is a hazy identification of the human order of empire, the natural order, and the divine order. A statue in the Alberta Provincial Museum provides a suggestive emblem for the prairie pioneer as he is found in the fiction. All in bronze, a man kneels, holding the bridle of a horse which bears his wife and infant child. The larger-than-life proportions of the statue, the obvious strength of the man, the gazes fixed ahead into the distance, all speak of the romance of pioneering. And there is something redemptive about this new beginning. The grouping of man, woman, child, and patient beast suggests a nativity scene, but in this epiphany what the man kneels before with bared head is a squared mental survey stake with its cryptic notation of range, township, section, and quarter section. This willingness to see the encompassing order as in some way sacred is a strong element in the Garden Myth of the early fiction, and relates it to the spirit of empire in the West which extends from young Henry Kelsey confidently making treaties between Cree and Blackfoot in 1690 to the uncanny devotion of the Mounted Police, to the attitudes of Connor's and McClung's heroes and heroines.

The writers of the early Twentieth Century were prolific, by Canadian standards, and the nature of their fictional garden varied, but some of its consistent features can be isolated. One quality it shares with the frontier of American fiction is a moral simplicity—an

79

innocence which is not necessarily purity but an absence of civilized sophistication. As the wise old doctor in Nellie McClung's *Purple Springs* says, "this big West is new and crude and distinct—only the primary colours are used in the picture, there are no half tones, no shadows, and above all—or perhaps I should say behind all—no background. A thing is good or bad—black or white—blue or red."[7] This is essentially the moral perspective which underlies the fiction of Stead and Stringer too, and in the work of Connor and McClung particularly it is accompanied by the sort of naive social conscience which provides the complex human problems of the West with superficially logical solutions like prohibition, industry, thrift, and simple piety. It is also the moral perspective of most sentimental romance, which was quite predictably the genre in which these writers worked.

The old doctor's contention that there is "no background" refers mainly to the removal of the settlers from their social and family contexts, but it suggests another of the Edenic qualities of the fictional West of this period. It has no past. The land might have been created by the government surveyors. Some of the Mounted Police stories, such as H. E. R. Steel's *Spirit-of-Iron* and Connor's *Corporal Cameron* and *Patrol of the Sundance Trail* depict pre-settlement encounters with the native people, but the popular fiction generally gives the impression that nothing happened until the white settlers arrived. Indian and Metis characters are rare, and like the villains of Connor's police stories, usually degenerate creatures destined for a merciful extinction. This loss of the past can now be seen as a measure of how dangerously out of touch with the land this garden vision of the West was. True, it implied a harmony with nature, but in a millennial perfection, not in the sense of man as a continuing part of the great cycle of life on the plains. The settlers' millennial vision could remain more important than the land under their feet.

It should be noted, too, that the garden

remains solidly British in most of the fiction, despite the
increasing use of the term "Canadian." The novelists and
our popular tradition have been effective enough that we
do not at first question this assumption in the fiction,
though we know that by 1926, in the rural prairies where
the stories were set, only 46.5% of the people gave their
racial origins as British.[8] In the fiction we find some
lighthearted raillery at the English remittance man or the
green farm pupil, but the essentials of the "Canadian"
nationality are assumed to be the English language and
the British cultural tradition. Like the Indians,
"foreigners" (immigrants of non-British origins) can
sometimes be amiable creatures, but are usually
distasteful if not vicious. There are few exceptions.
Edward McCourt gives Connor undeserved credit for a
broadminded treatment of the middle-European
immigrant in his *The Foreigner* published in 1909.
McCourt contends that Connor describes the Slavic
community of North Winnipeg "with sympathy and
understanding based on acute observation and instinctive
Christian charity,"[9] without apparently noticing the
heavily condescending tone. Here, for example, is
Connor's description of how the typical Slavic immigrant
reacted to prosperity:

> . . . he rapidly sloughed off with his foreign
> clothes his foreign speech and manner of life,
> and his foreign ideals as well, and became a
> Canadian citizen, distinguished from his
> cosmopolitan fellow citizen only by the slight
> difficulty he displayed with some of the
> consonants of the language.[10]

There may be acute observation behind such comments,
but there is also enough smugness to evoke the worst
connotations of the term "Christian charity." McCourt
notes that Connor allows his hero Kalman to emerge
from a sinister, sub-human slum "to win the heart and
hand of a beautiful Anglo-Saxon girl—no less than the

daughter of a peer" (p. 74). What he overlooks is that Kalman is prepared for this apotheosis by being purged of his foreignness, symbolized by the death of his bomb-throwing nihilist father. The balance of Connor's sympathy for ethnic minorities can be seen in the comments of his benevolent missionary, Parson Brown, who says, "'These people here exist as an undigested foreign mass. They must be digested and absorbed into the body politic. They must be taught our ways of thinking and living, or it will be a mighty bad thing for us in Western Canada' " (p. 255).

To judge by the fiction, Connor voiced no more than the popular conviction—and the intentions of the public school system, for that matter[11]—but there is an occasional exception. E. A. W. Gill's *Love in Manitoba* is a story of a Scandinavian community in the "Grove" country of northern Manitoba, written in 1911, but in a style of low-key realism uncommon at that time. There is wisdom and sympathy in Gill's treatment of the English and non-English characters alike, and a stringent wit in his rejection of bigotry. He includes a comic racist, the postmaster, Old Man Dawson, of whom it is said that when a Swedish settler is on trial, "He hinted darkly that, by the time the trial was over, the Pope o' Rome would be seriously compromised; the Swedes were 'furriners'; 'furriners,' in default of evidence to the contrary, were clearly 'Romans,' and every 'Roman' is the accredited agent of the Pope and the devil."[12] Gill's most worthless character is Roland Vale, an effete young English farm pupil, his most worthy is Jim Hardie, a Canadian farmer. His villain, unfortunately, is an Indian, but in most respects Gill's outlook is a good deal more liberal and more appropriate to the mixed population of the West than Connor's solidly British assumptions.

It would be misleading to ignore the more general exceptions to the garden view of the prairie in this period. The Great Plains of North America were then a resource for international story-tellers who might have little or no contact with the prevalent Canadian

sentiments of the day. The English writer Harold
Bindloss, for example, set at least nineteen of his novels
on the Canadian prairies, and at least four of these were
published in Toronto as well as in New York and
London. Though they usually include some romantic
adventure, these novels do nothing to idealize their
settings, as we can see from this description of a young
immigrant's first glimpse of the prairie:

> Spring, I was told, was very late that year, and
> the plains rolled before us to the horizon a dreary
> white wilderness streaked by willow-swale, with at
> first many lonely lakes rippling a bitter steely-
> blue under the blasts, while crackling ice fringed
> their shores.[13]

Bindloss was probably a more capable craftsman than
any native Canadian writer of the period, and he had
spent enough time in the West to make his settings
authentic with real observed detail (something Connor
did not always manage), but he never seemed to find in
the prairie any distinctive spirit of place. His stories
remain English adventures in a strange land, and the
same could be said of Ridgwell Cullum, another English
adventure writer who set at least eight of his novels on
the Canadian prairies, of which at least four were
published in Toronto as well as in New York and
London. Cullum was more strenuously devoted to
adventure plots than Bindloss and less scrupulous about
fidelity to the landscape, but evidently wanted the prairie
to be more than a backdrop. As early as 1914, in his *The
Way of the Strong*, he fictionalizes some of the social
and economic fabric of the prairie, including the
workings of the Winnipeg Grain Exchange and labour
unrest on the railroads, matters which were
conspicuously absent from the idyllic fiction which
claimed most people's attention at the time.[14] Bindloss
and Cullum were actually no more careless about the
history and geography of the prairies than Canadian

adventure writers such as Bertrand Sinclair, Gilbert Parker, William Lacey Amy with his endless "Blue Pete" detective stories, or Hulbert Footner with his strange private geography of the plains. Footner's prairie sometimes extends as far as Great Slave Lake, and for some reason he has Prince George where Edmonton ought to be. The foreign writers differed from the more prominent native-born writers largely in that they did not develop a distinctive vision of the prairie West.

It might at first appear that the exceptions bulk larger than the rule, but most of the fiction shares some of the assumptions of the garden West. The adventure stories share its moral simplicity and optimism; the novels of pioneer life usually share the belief in a beneficent natural order. The novels which must remain as clear exceptions are those few treating realistically the problems of settlement and the morals and manners of the pioneer communities. In addition to Gill's three novels, they include H. H. Bashford's *The Manitoban,* Laura Salverson's *The Viking Heart,* and Will Ingersoll's *The Road that Led Home* and *Daisy Herself.* Some of these writers, like Gill and Ingersoll, were local colourists, legitimate forerunners of the realism which R. J. C. Stead was to bring to public attention in *Grain,* and also the founders of the continuing popular tradition I will discuss in Chapter VI. There are even rarer instances of novels devoted to an author's concern over social issues, like Francis Beynon's *Aleta Dey* and Douglas Durkin's *The Magpie.*

These groups of "exceptions" I have described contain no neglected masterpieces, but they make interesting reading beside the novels of Connor and McClung. Like the work of John MacLean, Alexander Begg, Roger Pocock, and Kate Hayes in the Nineteenth Century, they are in some ways more earnest and more honest than the more popular "garden" fiction, but they were not the centre of literary attention or the most typical expression of their society at the time. In effect, they did not establish the direction in which the stream of prairie fiction was flowing.

That was established by the more idyllic fictions, and the figures who inhabit the fictional garden are worth describing, because they are the bases of some of the central archetypes of prairie fiction. The most characteristic, though not the most numerous, are the Mounted Policemen, ministers, and school teachers, suggestive of the secular, sacred, and cultural aspects of the encompassing order. Connor, as we have seen, defined the fictional Mountie, though variants can be found in the work of Bindloss, Cullum, Parker, Amy, James Oliver Curwood, S. A. White, and many others during the same period. The Mountie actually had unique literary potential as a national culture hero, but what became of it will be seen in Chapter VI. Connor also gives us the figure of the minister in his creation of young Moore in *The Sky Pilot*. The minister, like the Mountie, had appeared in nineteenth-century fiction but had never been developed into a memorable character. Moore is superficially alien, unsuited to the West:

> He was very slight, very young, very innocent, with a face that might do for an angel, except for the touch of humour in it, but which seemed strangely out of place among the rough, hard faces that were to be seen in the Swan Creek country.[15]

He is clearly all that is missing from the West in a broadly spiritual sense, all things aesthetic, ethereal, and somehow feminine. His purpose is to set up a church, but also to civilize the West. He must contend with all that is crude, vulgar, and brutal in the raw settlements, and he must do it in a manly way. At first Moore is met with ridicule, but here he presents an interesting contrast with Owen Wister's eastern narrator. While Wister's "tenderfoot" can win only a conditional acceptance among westerners, and that by learning the ways of the West, Connor's "pilot" convinces the coarse ranch hands of the value of his eastern cultivation. He wins their respect by being a better baseball pitcher, and he outfaces a saloonful of scoffers in the same way the young Mountie quiets a roomful of gamblers. The contrast is characteristic of the Canadian vision of order.

In a Connor story, the reformation of the half-wild westerners is inevitable. The effect is romantic, sentimental, and didactic.

Nellie McClung's Pearly Watson is the prototype of the school teacher in prairie fiction. Mrs. McClung devotes practically no attention to Pearly's teaching, but then the fictional prairie teacher is commonly seen more as a general cultural force in the community. Pearly does not, in fact, become a teacher until the third book in which she appears, but she is engaged in good works and moral crusades from her first appearance in *Sowing Seeds in Danny* in 1908.[16] Like the Mountie and the minister, the teacher is against drink, brutality, and idleness, but for slightly different reasons. In the fictional garden, her particular role seems to be as guardian of the virtues of decency, human compassion, and respect for the "finer things in life," virtues which seem particularly threatened by the freedom and disorder of the West. Since they are threatened chiefly by male weakness, it is appropriate that Pearly and her creator are crusaders for women's rights. The simple didactic message of Mrs. McClung's stories is a call for prohibition and female suffrage, which are assumed to be the solutions to all social abuses, including war.[17] Pearly leads the "Band of Hope" (a gathering of school children assembled to swear they will never touch liquor), she saves neglected wives from their tyrannical husbands, and in *Purple Springs* she leads the women to a dramatic overthrow of the provincial government. In McClung's writings, as in Connor's, there is the implication that what is needed is a marriage of East and West, with the civilized East softening and humanizing the virile but intemperate West. The troubled domestic life of this marriage is portrayed very well—the values of the teacher are essentially eastern—but the reconciliation she insists upon is not very convincing. Little Pearly is too obviously an instrument of Mrs. McClung's didactic purpose.

What remains of permanent value in Nellie McClung's writings is the tone of pragmatic anti-romance which occasionally wins out over the sentimentality that mars much of her work. This anti-romantic tone dominates the first half of her first book, *Sowing Seeds in Danny*, which was written before she saw her fiction primarily as a useful means of moral instruction.[18] Her first gently ironic sketches could have provided Leacock with a model for his *Sunshine Sketches*. Like Leacock, she exercises a whimsical yet deftly satiric wit in arranging a few type-characters to embody the essence of a small Manitoba town. Mrs. Burton Francis, for example, is full of philanthropic zeal but hopelessly adrift in her theories about sowing the seeds of virtue in the hearts of the poor. After showing her beleaguered charwoman Mrs. Watson, who is the mother of nine, a book called *The Beauty of Mother-hood*, she enters in her diary: "Dec. 7, 1903. Talked with one woman to-day *re* Beauty of Motherhood. Recom-mended Dr. Parker's book. Believe good done" (p. 8). Mrs. McClung, in these first hundred pages of her work, was a worthy forerunner of W. O. Mitchell as a prairie humorist, and the poems Pearly writes could be set down anywhere in Paul Hiebert's *Sarah Binks:*

> The little lams are beautiful,
>   There cotes are soft and nice,
> The little calves have ringworm,
>   And the 2-year olds have lice!

> It must be very nasty,
>   But to worrie, what's the use;
> Better be cam and cheerful,
>   And appli tobaka jooce. (p. 221)

Unfortunately Mrs. McClung chose rather to follow the spirit of these verses than to develop the human comedy they represent. The last half of *Sowing Seeds* is unbearably maudlin.

Considering the social history of the prairie provinces, it is not inappropriate that Mountie, minister, and teacher should have become central archetypes in the fiction. They were not merely symbols developed to express the writers' sense of a beneficent imperial order. Mounted Policemen, we know, were commonly working in isolated detachments, closely integrated with their small-town and rural communities and expected to provide much more than police services. Because of the nature of the prairie settlement they often remained not only the symbolic but the practical presence of government and larger civilization in remote centres until very recently, when the smaller communities themselves began to disappear. Teachers similarly became involved in other phases of the social organization of the prairies. You find them everywhere in local histories. When the farmers began their first successful organization to secure fair treatment by the grain-handling interests, the Territorial Grain Growers' Association in 1902, one of the most prominent members was E. A. Partridge, a homesteading school-teacher who went on to become the first chairman of the farmers' grain marketing company.[19] William Aberhart was a high school teacher, and what is probably more significant, the innumerable local study groups through which his Social Credit movement built its power before entering Alberta politics were commonly organized by local teachers. Nellie McClung was herself a schoolteacher before she carried her moral teachings into the more public arenas of women's organizations like the Women's Christian Temperance Union and finally into politics, where she became a member of the Legislative Assembly of Alberta in 1921. Ministers have been equally prominent ever since the missionary days of legendary figures such as Albert Lacombe, James Evans, and

George and John McDougall. Ralph Connor himself, as
the Reverend Charles Gordon, became not only a local
power but an international figure through his services to
the League of Nations.[20] J. S. Woodsworth, the father of
the Cooperative Commonwealth Federation party, was
ordained a Methodist minister and had come to the West
as the son of a missionary in 1882. Aberhart, again, was
both teacher and minister of his fundamentalist
Prophetic Bible Institute in Calgary. The impression one
eventually gathers is of the pervasive interconnections of
the institutions of church, state, and even commerce. In
1917, for example, the churches declared an annual
"Grain Growers' Sunday" to promote the farmers'
cooperative grain growers' associations.[21]

This interlacing of institutions, like the
writers' choice of the Mounties, ministers, and teachers,
speaks of the general anti-revolutionary tendency of the
society this literature expresses. Even in the area of
comparatively radical politics the people seem to have
preferred leaders in some way identified with the
institutions of the older culture. The Social Credit
theories of Major Douglas were, after all, imported from
Britain, and so were the models for the farmers'
cooperative associations which led eventually to the
founding of the C.C.F.

The figures logically at the centre of the
garden of the West, the pioneers themselves, are best
represented by R. J. C. Stead in a succession of his early
novels from *The Bail Jumper* in 1914 to *Neighbours* in
1922. They are at the centre, but do not, like the
Mountie, the minister, and the teacher, *represent* the
intangible order of the garden. This may be why it is in
the portrayal of the pioneers that we see a good deal
more evidence of the weaknesses which would eventually
discredit the whole garden myth, in fiction as well as in
fact. Stead shows us an array of the dangers besetting
the pioneer's vision of "participation in the Infinite,
indefinable, but all-embracing everlasting" on the plains.
Stead's second novel, *The Homesteaders,* could be taken   89

as the central romance of western settlement. His main
characters, John and Mary Harris, are ideal pioneers. He
is an Ontario school teacher, fired with ambition, strong,
poor, and proud. She is gentle, equally idealistic, a little
romantic, but strong in her softer woman's way. They
settle in 1882 in an area Professor A. T. Elder identifies
as near Cartwright, Manitoba, where Stead himself grew
up, and their life "of courage, of health, of resourcefulness" earns them a prosperous farm over the next
twenty-five years.

It would seem that the ideal is being
realized, but Stead shows that success is fatal to the
ideal. For Harris, the "unanswerable longing of the great
plains" has become an insatiable desire for more land.
We see him after twenty-five years, brutalized by work
and crass ambition, negligent of all the finer traits of his
own character and of the human needs of his family:

> Harris did not know that his gods had fallen, that
> his ideals had been swept away; even as he sat at
> supper this summer evening, with his daughter's
> arms about his neck, he felt that he was still
> bravely, persistently, pressing on toward the goal,
> all unaware that years ago he had left that goal
> like a lighthouse on a rocky shore, and was now
> sweeping along with the turbulent tide of
> Mammonism.[22]

Because of the change in John Harris, his household
assumes a pattern which will reappear again and again in
the work of Grove, Martha Ostenso, Arthur Storey, and
others. It includes the "prairie patriarch" filled with the
righteousness of his own purpose, but in fact a land-
hungry, work-intoxicated tyrant. The farm women are
subjugated, culturally and emotionally starved, and filled
with a smouldering rebellion. Stead rescues his characters
from this unwholesome situation by the use of another
recurrent motif, the journey westward toward the
mountains. While the daughter, Beulah, goes West in the

90

proper spirit, seeking more abundant life, Harris goes in search of the greater gains to be made in land speculation in the opening province of Alberta. He is under the influence of the villain, Hiram Riles, who is completely characterized by the description of his journey west: "Riles found the journey westward a tiresome affair. His was a soul devoid of enthusiasm over Nature's wealth or magnitude, and the view of the endless prairie excited in him no emotion other than a certain vague covetousness" (p. 164). The quest leads only to a melodramatic intrigue in the foothills of the Rockies, but like so much of the westering in prairie fiction, it is an episode in the inevitable journey toward disillusionment and self-discovery. Harris is brought to his senses and regains his original ideals.

In Stead, a response to the land, not as property or power but as "Nature," is a reliable index of character, and the land as setting is responsive to man in an elemental and romantic way. Crucial scenes of emotional turmoil are commonly answered by storms, as when Dennison Grant is deciding he must lose the woman he loves for the sake of her child, or when Raymond Burton in *The Bail Jumper* is taking flight at the cost of both his desire and his sense of honour: "But to the fugitive the threatened storm meant nothing. The warfare of the elements could tear no deeper than the warfare of his soul."[23] At this stage in his career Stead was not always as subtle as he might have been. Similarly, passion has its reflection in material fires, and water is closely associated with love and the softer emotions, with all that is regenerative and with the mysteries of femininity. If some of Stead's elemental imagery is laboured, his water imagery develops gradually into an organic function of his setting in the last two novels, *The Smoking Flax* and *Grain*. Stead was again working with a vein of imagery which would continue into later prairie fiction. It seems that water, like wind, is a rich imaginative resource on the great dry sea of the plains.

91

Stead's novels also include the theme of a marriage of East and West, of culture and vigour, which can be followed from John Mackie to its ironic exposure in Robert Kroetsch's novels where the relationship is shown as an exploitive one—more a statutory rape than a marriage. Stead expresses the need for this marriage in the cultural degeneration of his ideal pioneer, John Harris. The one-time schoolmaster, after too long in the West, is even reduced to speaking barbarous non-standard English. In *The Bail Jumper*, Burton loves the refined, eastern girl, Myrtle Vane; Dave Eldon in *The Cow Puncher* improves himself for the love of Irene Hardy, the daughter of an eastern doctor; Jane Lane in *Neighbours* refuses to accept the narrator, Frank Hall, until he has broadened his mind with readings in English literature; Cal Beach in *The Smoking Flax* brings eastern sensibilities to bear on the barren conditions of the western farm wife. The marriage is usually effected, and that is in keeping with the generally robust, optimistic tone of Stead's early novels.[24]

For the image of the pioneer woman, we can turn to Arthur Stringer, whose presentation of her is psychologically fuller and deeper if not more plausible than Stead's. Stringer also envisions a marriage of East and West, but from the female point of view. In his prairie trilogy[25] the narrator, Chaddy, is an eastern socialite who at first responds rapturously to the prairie as garden and to her strong, taciturn Scots-Canadian husband, Duncan McKail. But here, as in Stead, Mammon is the false god that leads McKail away from his wife. Duncan becomes crass and insensitive, eventually forsaking the farm for a somewhat sordid and vulgar life of real estate speculation in Calgary.

Stringer in his prairie trilogy may also have made direct contributions to Ross's *As For Me and My House*. His Chaddy McKail, along with Carol Kennicott in Sinclair Lewis's *Mainstreet*, may have provided an early model for Mrs. Bentley. There is no evidence that Ross ever read Stringer; the characters touch only at a few points. Yet if one considers some other details of Stringer's prairie trilogy, one cannot easily believe that the similarities are pure coincidence. Chaddy begins a letter in *The Prairie Wife* which soon turns into a diary very like Mrs. Bentley's. The stories are both in the tradition mentioned earlier of the confessions of a refined sensibility exposed to the rudeness and cultural sterility of the pioneer West. While at first Chaddy's attitude and disposition are optimistic and frivolous, as the trilogy progresses she begins to sound more and more like Mrs. Bentley. Entry after entry begins with something like "Duncan, it's plain to see, is still in the doldrums. He is uncommunicative and moody and goes about his work with a listlessness which is more and more disturbing to me," or "Dinky-Dunk is on his dignity. He has put a fence around himself to keep me at a distance."[26] There are even times when, like Philip Bentley, he retreats to his study. The McKail marriage deteriorates into the same sterile tension we find in the Bentley household, and the woman's possessiveness is implicated in both situations. When Chaddy finds Duncan in California at the end of a tragic love affair, she says "He looked leaner and frailer and less robustious than of old. But in my heart of hearts I liked him that way. It left him the helpless and unprotesting victim of that run-over maternal instinct of mine which took wayward joy in mothering what it couldn't master."[27] Mrs. Bentley is more subtle, but admits early in her diary to a similar impulse toward Philip: "He's a very adult, self-sufficient man, who can't bear to be fussed or worried over; and sometimes, broodless old woman that I am, I get impatient being just his wife, and start in trying to mother him too."[28]

Like the Bentleys, the McKails have their outside romantic interests. His is the pale young schoolmistress, Alsina Teeswater, whom Chaddy drives from the house because Duncan has seduced her. She has a superficial resemblance to Judith West, though unlike Judith she does manage to go to the city and win 93 the man. Chaddy's first outside interest is non-serious—a gaunt and gauche young scholar named Gershom Binks, who knows everything but understands nothing. He offers, on every occasion, bits of useless pedantry such as the fact that the piano "was really evolved from the six-stringed harps of the fourth Egyptian dynasty."[29] Unlike Paul's etymologies in Ross's novel, Gershom's pedantries do not reveal his emotions or his character beyond the superficial fact that he is helpless in the western setting. In general, the similarities between Stringer's fiction and Ross's are interesting mainly as they reveal how much more Ross can do with a technique or with an image that has virtually become a cliché.

While much of the early twentieth-century fiction dramatizes the various temptations in the garden, none really raises the possibility that the garden ideal is a dangerous illusion in itself. Nellie McClung comes close to raising it in *Painted Fires* in 1921. Her title itself is intended to mean "illusions," but Mrs. McClung is writing specifically about the illusions of a "foreigner." Her heroine, Helmi Milander, is a spirited Finnish girl, wholesome and virtuous, but at times wilful and passionate, by far the most attractive of Mrs. McClung's women. She emigrates with a vision of the New World derived from a sentimental post-card her aunt has given her entitled "Auntie's Garden." Helmi in Winnipeg is led into trouble by her idyllic impression of the New World, but is able to escape farther west, and her flight from evil is again archetypal. As she rides the train west, "She wondered, if one kept on going, going, going, would every disagreeable thing fall away, every sin and every sadness?"[30] It seems at times as though Mrs. McClung is offering Helmi as an image of the general western illusions of the time, but the plot denies the implications of her imagery. After cruel misfortunes Helmi finds her happiness, settled in the foothills on the banks of "English River," well within the boundaries of the larger western illusion.

There is further evidence—more intrinsic

if slightly more tenuous—to suggest that the Garden Myth was an inadequate imaginative conception of prairie life, that it induced a fiction too chaste, sunlit, and superficial to assimilate all the dark, spontaneous and unruly impulses the prairie has been conveying to the imaginations of men from the time of the earliest travellers. For all the sublime faith in order, spiritual and temporal, which underlies Connor's sentimental plots, for example, there appears unexpectedly in his writings a latent anarchic power, emanating from the land and taking the form of unregenerate natural man (or woman). The ultimate test of Moore's success, for example, is winning the faith of Gwen, the young daughter of "The Old Timer" of Swan Creek. She is a complete child of nature, wild and firey as her own streaming red hair, wilful and wicked in an outwardly asexual way. In some sense she is the spirit of Connor's West. She can be won over only after a riding accident confines her permanently to bed, when only the "Pilot's" Christianity can save her from despair. Connor was so pleased with this episode that he published it separately as *Gwen, an Idyll of the Canyon* in the same year as he published *The Sky Pilot*.[31] The canyon, a deep cleft in the prairie grown up with lush, exotic vegetation (an image of submerged sexuality which mercifully seems to have escaped the good minister) becomes a symbol for the spiritual beauty that can grow out of physical pain, and one which Connor later used as a kind of parable in his sermons.[32]

Once the "Pilot" has Gwen safely confined to her bed, he makes frequent visits to what is referred to as "Gwen's canyon" in order to tell her how beautiful and soothing it is. Here is Connor's description:

> As we went down into the cool depths the spirit
> of the canyon came to meet us and took The
> Pilot in its grip. He rode in front, feasting his
> eyes on all the wonders in that storehouse of
> beauty. Trees of many kinds deepened the

shadows of the canyon. Over us waved the big elms that grew up here and there out of the bottom, and around their feet clustered low cedars and hemlocks and balsams, while the sturdy, rugged oaks and delicate, trembling poplar clung to the rocky sides and clambered up and out to the canyon's sunny lips. Back of all, the great black rocks, decked with mossy bits and clinging things, glistened cool and moist between the parting trees. From many an oozynook the dainty clematis and columbine shook out their bells, and, lower down, from beds of many-coloured moss the late wind-flower and maiden-hair and tiny violet lifted up brave, sweet faces.[33]

The "Pilot" emerges from this rather suggestive experience saying "That does me good. . . . This was Gwen's best spot." The kind of idyllic retreat Connor is attempting to create is evident from the vegetation he uses, importing elm and oak trees from his native Ontario, and cedar and hemlock from the mountains, but the sexual suggestion remains with the canyon through the story. Gwen is later patronized by Lady Charlotte, a grand, cultured, eastern lady whose great sorrow is that she is childless. In the same spirit of apparent innocence, Connor has Gwen ask Lady Charlotte if she has a canyon too, to which the lady replies, "and there are no flowers, Gwen, not one, nor seeds, nor soil, I fear" (p. 249).

The humour of the situation (whether conscious or not) is less significant than the sexual energies associated with the land through Gwen, which come through clearly even if they are not specifically intended. It is not simply a matter of Connor's naiveté. In Arthur Stringer's *The Mud Lark* the suggestions of displaced sexuality become equally comic. His hero is so wedded to the land, he sleeps in a back room with his prize seed wheat rather than with his bride, whose jealousy becomes explicitly sexual: "During a lull in the rain I could even sniff a vague aroma from that mistress of his, a soft and earthy and seminal smell from the sleeping acres of green that stirred and swayed voluptuously in the humid darkness."[34] The identification of woman with the land is not uncommon, of course, but the way in which Stringer and Connor lose control of their imagery suggests the inadequacy of their type of fiction in dealing with the more elemental and instinctual areas of experience. American frontier fiction of the time was no less chaste, sexually, but with its adventure and violence, and especially its cult of individualism, it made room for the expression of a good deal more of what is dark, irrational, and passionate in man and his relation to his surroundings.

The Garden Myth was not merely too sunlit and superficial for good fiction. It encouraged a dangerous cultural tendency. For the settlers, the assumption of a land contained within familiar cultural patterns which were ultimately divinely sanctioned obscured the fact that their relationship to environment had changed or needed to change from what it had been in Britain or Ontario. The attractions of the myth could make them forget that it was only precariously in touch with the realities of the new environment, which had still to be reckoned with. The reckoning was reached most dramatically in the drought years of the 1930's, but the physical hardships were only part of it.

Equally important was the connection between the garden myth and the spirit of empire, with its tendency to impose the culture of the dominant Ontario-British minority on the West. This connection engendered some of the most harmful and persistent of the cultural anomalies that have plagued the West. Long after Connor's *The Foreigner* has been forgotten, the prairie school child of German or Ukrainian extraction is still being presented with English literature to study as his own. It is neither his nor his ancestors' nor the literature of the place or the people about him but the literature of the ancestors of a minority of his

97

companions. What Wallace Stegner once said about
learning in his small-town Saskatchewan school that
history and geography extended no farther West than the
Great Lakes is still an almost universal prairie
experience.[35] The emotional and psychological effects of
confinement within an alien cultural environment on the
prairie are not understood in the fiction of the early
Twentieth Century, but they are prominent in later
novels, including those of Grove and Ross.

As a phase in the struggle of the Canadian
imagination to humanize the new environment and
assimilate it to an artistic form, the garden myth, taken
by itself, had immediate advantages. As I said earlier, the
writers needed a way of seeing the land *in relation to
man* before it could take on meaningful shape and
acquire significant detail. The garden myth must have
been serviceable to a degree because descriptively the
land does begin to emerge during this period with more
convincing particularity. There is even a beginning,
especially in the work of Stead and Stringer, of the
development of archetypes which will later help the
prairie novelist's imagination to a better representation of
the distinctive life of the prairie people. There is also
evidence of the slow growth of the type of realism which
characterizes the fiction from 1925 onward. From the
beginning Stead was developing the descriptive
techniques that matured in *Grain* (1926). This passage
from *The Bail Jumper* (1914), for example, could easily
be attributed to the later Stead—or to Grove:

> Suddenly a shape loomed through the grey mist
> of the night. The horses lurched back upon the
> double trees, their trace-chains clattering with the
> slack. The shape took form; a frightened team
> were seen plunging in the deep snow by the
> roadside; the vehicles interlocked.[36]

In such isolated passages, there is economy, rhythm,
movement, and a sense of sound in the language as full

as Stead ever achieved. And the minute circumstantial realism found in parts of *The Smoking Flax* would lead quite logically to the perceptions and the conclusions that follow in *Grain*.

Further, if the garden world was a far /from adequate unifying imaginative conception of the prairie, the idea of an Eden-like place has never entirely disappeared from the fiction. It remains an underlying assumption in the popular tradition of prairie writing, and in the more seriously "literary" novels it has its place as an ironic image of human illusions, like Doc Murdoch's lush garden in Kroetsch's *The Words of My Roaring*, or Neil Fraser's naive dream of the Peace River Country in *Music at the Close*. It seems to be one of the poles of the prairie imagination. Kroetsch, in his *Alberta*, describes the people as "locked between dream and nightmare," and the dream is as real and as essential as the nightmare.[37] The fiction of the early Twentieth Century, then, may have remained too naively within a dream of the West, but it reflected certain very real and enduring qualities of the prairie mind, and it is richly revealing of the culture which has provided the unseen environment of that mind.

Prairie Realism

Historian W. L. Morton describes the 1920's in Canada
as Janus-like, facing back to a rural agricultural past and
forward to an era of urban industrialization.[1] By the late
1950's that industrialization is an accomplished fact in
the minds of Canadians as well as in the cities of
Canada. In the years between, the machinery for
industrialization exists and yet rural agrarian ideals
survive for a generation or more. On the prairies in
particular, the mid-1920's are the turning-point Morton
describes; settlement is more or less complete, and the
process of industrializing agriculture has just begun. In
literature the following transitional period produces an
accomplished realistic fiction of rural prairie life. The
novels of Frederick Philip Grove, Sinclair Ross, and
Edward McCourt come immediately to mind, but it
should be remembered that the literary metamorphosis is
no faster and no more thorough than the social transition. While prairie realism is the distinctive development
of the period, there exists, from the 1920's onward, a
separate popular tradition, to be discussed in Chapter VI,
which shows a strong continuity with the sentimental
romances of Connor and McClung.
          Both traditions share a mounting
skepticism about the romance of pioneering, but the
newly developing prairie realism quite predictably
favours a darker view of prairie experience than the
popular tradition of sentimental comedy. If not a tragic
view—and Grove for one did refer to his view as tragic—
it at least conveys a painful sense of the human failure
and waste, weakness and suffering in prairie life. The
world it depicts is fallen, and not to be sentimentally
restored to a garden state. It must be redeemed by
suffering and sacrifice, like the death of Abe Spalding's
favorite son Charlie, or of the pale young mother Judith in
As For Me and My House. This realist tradition is of
particular interest, not only because it includes most of the
best fiction of the period, but because it demonstrates the
next phase of the imagination's struggle to accommodate
the prairie experience.

In 1925 and 1926, three significant novels of the West were published: Frederick Philip Grove's *Settlers of the Marsh*, Martha Ostenso's *Wild Geese*, and Robert J. C. Stead's *Grain*. Commonly the three are mentioned together because they are assumed to have brought realism to prairie fiction, but as usual, the meaning of the term "realism" is uncertain. The three writers have little in common stylistically. What they do share is a recognition that in spite of material progress, the English-speaking settlers remain spiritually alienated from the land. Their work is both a decisive sign of disillusionment with the romance of pioneering and an admission that man has found no honest imaginative conception of the prairie that can place him in harmony with it.

Grove's treatment of the new theme develops from *Settlers* through *Our Daily Bread* (1928) and *The Yoke of Life* (1930) to *Fruits of the Earth* (1933), where he creates the most complete image of the new awareness. The central figure of the work, Abe Spalding, learns how much he has paid for his material prosperity in spiritual emptiness. In a chapter entitled simply "The Prairie," Abe attempts to understand his surroundings for the first time, and finds the experience disquieting:

> He had looked down at his feet; had seen nothing but the furrow; had considered the prairie only as a page to write the story of his life upon. His vision had been bounded by the lines of his farm; his farm had been floated on that prairie as the shipwright floats a vessel on the sea, looking not so much at the waves which are to batter it as at the fittings which secure the comfort of those within. But such a vessel may be engulfed by such a sea.[2]

The original problems of the settlers are all here, in this image. Abe fails to apprehend the natural surroundings;   101 instead he imposes an imaginative order brought with him; the prairie retaliates by making him feel dislocated, unconnected, threatened. The main difference from earlier fictions is that Abe is made aware of his failure. The imaginative failure becomes, with Grove, an explicit theme. Much of the best fiction in the period of prairie realism, including the work of Ross and McCourt, explores the varied, complex nature of this alienation from the land.

Grove, Stead, and Ostenso are especially interesting as originators of this period of prairie realism because they differ so sharply in their ways of representing man's alienation. Stead is the only one whose techniques would fit consistently into any definition of realism. This may sound surprising after Stead's earlier romances, but not if we consider *The Smoking Flax* (1924).[3] There he develops the techniques of circumstantial realism evident in his earliest work to the level he will need to create the oppressive circumstances of Gander Stake in *Grain*. The two novels are actually interwoven, sharing characters and events, but with points of view different enough to change the emphasis and the perspective in which we see those events. It is as though Stead had needed the earlier novel to discover that his real subject was not the romantic transient Calvin Beach, but the prosaic Manitoba farm boy, Gander Stake. Stead's is a patient, almost dogged fidelity to the daily circumstances of prairie life which work inexorably to stunt the growth of his hero, just as Gander's ill-fitting trousers induce a permanent hitch in his walk. But Gander remains more comic than pathetic in his deformity; he limps because he wants to wear a belt, like a man, and he is personally narrowed to the limits of the farm because he chooses a man's work over a child's growing up.

The tone of *Grain*, too, keeps Gander more comic than pathetic. Stead introduces an ironic distance between the reader and his hero, in the tradition of realists since Fielding. The tone is carefully established in the first paragraph of the novel:

> Perhaps the term hero, with its suggestion of high
> enterprise, sits inappropriately upon the chief
> character of a somewhat commonplace tale; there
> was in Gander Stake little of that quality which is
> associated with the clash of righteous steel or the
> impact of noble purposes.[4]

The "somewhat commonplace tale" has come to the
prairie to dispel the romance of pioneering, and Gander
of course is of the unheroic generation after the pioneers,
but there are still questions of heroism and purpose and
romance hovering around the action of the novel.
Gander cannot share the romantic urge to go to war, and
so he loses his girl, Jo Burge, to a friend who returns as
a wounded hero. Gander himself is called "hero" for
saving a boy's life on the threshing machine, but his chief
heroism is demanded in helping his friend back to health
and relinquishing his claim to Jo Burge. Stead's irony
does not produce a denial of the romantic but a tension
between the commonplace and the romantic.
On the surface it would seem that Gander
is a very prosaic son of the soil, alienated not from the
land but from society in all its aspects which he identifies
sarcastically with the drill sergeant's order to "form
fours." Certainly Gander, by becoming involved in farm
work at a very early age does miss out on most of the
socializing activities of childhood, and quite willingly, as
Stead says: "If he was being robbed of his childhood he
was content to be robbed, for in its place he was being
given manhood before its time. When he saw other boys of
his own age going to school he regarded them with pity
and contempt" (p. 59-60). The manhood Gander wins is
presumed to be in harmony with the soil, and Stead
describes his hero in that way: "Gander was a farmer
born and bred; he had an eye for horses and a knack
with machinery; the mysteries of the self-binder he had
solved before he was nine" (p. 40). The phrase "an eye   103

for horses" has a very precise application to Gander, who is without any impractical sentiment for them, and the emphasis is appropriately on machinery, which becomes the soul of Gander's farm life. Conspicuously Stead makes no mention of the land itself, and there is no evidence in action or description that Gander has any attachment to the soil, any sense of the rhythms of the seasons or any response to the beauties of his surroundings. When Stead once refers to Gander as being close to nature (p. 120) and once says that "all his instincts were rooted deep in the soil" (p. 79), we must take what he says on faith. It is not until the young city girl, Jerry Chansley, has pointed it out to him that Gander notices the prairie sunset: "She had said the sky was beautiful. For the first time Gander watched it—and wondered" (p. 151). Stead's partial misunderstanding of his own hero may be instructive; if Gander is an example of what it has come to mean to be "deeply rooted in the soil," then the people have lost even the conception of harmony with their surroundings.

Gander's nearest approach to loving the land is his love of exerting power over it through machines. Romantic sentiments which might have attached to the land or a woman are caught up in the power of machines. When Gander has his first ecstatic glimpse of a steam engine, Stead says "although Gander was a boy not touched by the romance of books here was something that stirred him deeply—the romance of machinery, of steam, which at the pull of a lever turned loose the power of giants!" (p. 54). The mention of the giants of folk-tale suggests that Gander lives in a mechanical mythology, a new imaginative environment in which the power is not in the land or the elements but in machines under man's exclusive control. He evidently has no further need for the garden vision of a benevolent natural order. What this love affair with machinery does to man's relationship to the natural processes of the land is explored again more explicitly in Grove's *Fruits of the*

Earth, and may, in fact, be the central theme in the

fiction of this period. We can see its effects on Gander's instincts for human love in his progress with young Jo Burge. At times the rivalry of girl and steam engine seems a fairly equal one; at the first mention of his opportunity to work as fireman on a threshing outfit, "Gander's heart thumped again, but with an altogether different emotion. If the thought of Jo Burge could make that heart quicken its beat, so too could the prospect of firing a steam engine" (p. 98). But the steam engine wins out, and though it should be clear from a number of incidents that Gander has been emasculated by the machine, Stead's supposed remedy for this condition is to send him into town at the end of the novel to work as a mechanic, as though the urgent necessity were to get him off the land. Gander had never really been on the land; the machine had always been between him and the soil. Stead does not seem to have been aware of this, even when he has Gander's father innocently remark, "you'd think farmin' was an industry, instead of a pursoot" (p. 86). Ironically, an industry is precisely what farming is becoming as Gander grows up.

The effect of mechanization, of farming becoming "an industry instead of a pursoot," is, in classic marxian terms, to further alienate prairie man from the land. This process in turn affects the relations of the people involved and even their basic humanity. Stead says that the Stake family "hid their sentiment from each other and held it a weakness to show any sign of family affection" (p. 63). Kreisel discusses this type of emotional repression as a universal effect of having to conquer a harsh land,[5] but here the family relationships are further demoralized by mindless concentration upon production, upon farming as industry. In *Smoking Flax* Stead explains the resultant plight of the farm woman left to do all the domestic work which supports the family, but in *Grain* he finds a more expressive way, in an image of Mrs. Stake when Gander unexpectedly offers her a little kindness. Gander's impulse springs from the same meeting with the 105 city girl which brought him to see the sunset for the first time. The mother does not know this, and becomes rather waspish about the strange girl when she finds out. Our subsequent loss of sympathy for her only emphasizes the painful vividness of this first impression of the woman and her son:

> In the garden to the west of the house he saw his mother working, her form doubled over in a gingham dress faded drab with age. He felt a sudden surging in his heart toward his mother. He shuffled over to her, down between the rows of currant bushes greening with their spring foliage. She did not hear his footsteps in the soft earth; she was bent over, setting out cabbages.
>
> "Couldn't I do that?" he interrupted her. She looked up quickly, her sharp eyes piercing him as though she suspected some kind of treachery. She could not recall that Gander ever before had offered her a service. He was playing a joke on her. But he held his ground steadily.
>
> "I thought you were busy with the car," she parried.
>
> "Through with it. Could help you a little, if you like."
>
> "Why—why—Willie?" Her old face began to twist. It recalled the day he gave her the twenty-dollar bill.
>
> "That's all right, Mother," he said, with strange gentleness. "I'm goin' to give you a hand. I'm goin' to help you, once in a while."
>
> Still with misgivings, she showed him how to set out the tender plants. (p. 150)

The image of the mother is especially poignant, appearing as it does in the spring, in the garden, among the tender growing things. When we reflect upon the garden image of the prairie in Stead's early work, the irony is massive, hard even to grasp. Whether or not Stead was aware of it, he could not have found a better way of exploding the prelapsarian image of the farmer as innocent, ennobled by his contact with nature. Both of his characters here are fallen enough, but especially the farmer. Paradoxically, it is Gander who is not at home with growing things other than cash crops and must be shown how to plant a cabbage. If Stead means the ending of his novel to be hopeful—and it would seem out of character for him not to—then he must not have recognized that it was, so to speak, the machine in the garden which caused this fall. For Gander at least, the machine is the visible cause of alienation from the land. Stead in a less doggedly realistic mood might even have recognized the possibilities of the steam engine breathing fire and drawing its sinuous train of cars as a kind of mechanical serpent.

Martha Ostenso could be said to approach the condition of man on the prairie from the opposite direction to Stead. Like *Grain*, her *Wild Geese* has been described in such phrases as "uncompromising realism"[6] but the realistic fidelity to circumstantial detail is the least remarkable feature of the style and is in some degree misleading. Take the initial scene of waiting for Caleb to come home; the suspense is quite plausibly created right down to the sound of Lind Archer's chair: "The Teacher sat quietly in the low red plush rocker, listening to the springs of it exclaim as she rocked to and fro."[7] For two and a half pages the imminence of Caleb is felt in the nervous apprehension of the whole family even more than in the direct references to his bullying ways by the one rebellious daughter, Judith.

> Then the door opened. At first, Caleb seemed to be a huge man. As he drew into the centre of the kitchen, Lind could see that he was, if anything, below medium height, but that his tremendous shoulders and massive head, which loomed

107

forward from the rest of his body like a rough
projection of rock from the edge of a cliff, gave
him a towering appearance. (p. 13)

The detail of the household has been circumstantial, but
Caleb, when he appears, is a creature of romance. The
period of expectation, while we weigh the implications of
the other characters' attitudes toward him, allows Caleb's
looming figure to grow without the constraint of any
visible, finite description, and when he is finally
described, it is in imprecise but superlative adjectives—
"huge," "tremendous," "massive," "towering"—and with
an equally expansive simile, "a rough projection of rock
from the edge of a cliff." Caleb is in this way given the
larger-than-life dimensions of a romantic villain, and in
spite of later apparently realistic detail such as his
"weedy, tobacco-stained moustache," he retains that
stature through the novel.
      Whatever Ostenso's early advocates have
said about her realism, the power of *Wild Geese* resides
in this romantic characterization. Ostenso gives us dark
romantic symbols acting out the subconscious drama of
man's relationship with the land in contrast to Stead's
daylight rendering of the pressures of common
circumstance on those committed to the land. Ostenso's
characters are richly evocative—Caleb, Judith with her
"great, defiant body," who "stood squarely on her feet,
as if prepared to take or give a blow" (p. 11), and minor
characters like Fusi Aronson, described as "somehow
lonely, as a towering mountain is lonely" (p. 31). From
the success of *Wild Geese* it is evident that romantic
plotting and characterization could not have been what
kept Connor and McClung out of the first rank of
western novelists. And on the prairie, of all places, with its
precarious balance of dream and nightmare, romance in
one form or another is bound to continue showing its
value as a way of capturing subjective experience. The
earlier romances had just been too superficial,

sentimental, and moralistic to reach what was going on

between the settlers and the prairie. The new fiction seemed "realistic" regardless of technique because the authors were now engaging this elemental relationship between man and land. *Wild Geese* could be seen as a demonic counterpart to the idyllic romances, a wholesome antidote because it grants the true power to some of the dark forces in human and external nature.

The characters in *Wild Geese* are dark because man's relationship with his environment is distorted, but like Stead, Ostenso does not seem to realize why the settlers are alienated from the soil. She presents her northern Manitoba people at odds with the land ostensibly because they are enslaved to it and it is a harsh master. The tyranny of Caleb is the tyranny of the land, and Ostenso describes him as "Caleb, who could not be characterized in the terms of human virtue or human vice—a spiritual counterpart of the land, as harsh, as demanding, as tyrannical as the very soil from which he drew his existence" (p. 33). The young people from civilization, Lind Archer and Mark Jordan, can free the victims of his tyranny because they can understand and articulate the condition of the people. Lind, from whose point of view most of the story is told, describes to Mark what is wrong with the Gare household: 'They all have a monstrously exaggerated conception of their duty to the land—or rather to Caleb, who is nothing but a symbol of the land' (p. 78). Such a suspiciously authorial comment amounts to a serious lapse in plausibility unless we take Lind to be an intensely bookish young woman who would go around talking about people as symbols. Ostenso intrudes to impose this convenient identification between the tyrant and the land. Caleb, of course, is literally blackmailing his wife Amelia with the fact that Mark is her unacknowledged illegitimate son, and through her he can reduce the children to almost inhuman subservience. His only opposition is from Judith, who says she hates the land and talks openly of going to the city.

By this point it should be apparent that a   109

great deal rests on the uses of the term "land." There are inconsistencies in Ostenso's symbols which betray uncertainty or equivocation in her statement of the relationship between man and the land. Judith is to be set in opposition to the "land," yet she is everything earthy and elemental. She is once described as "the embryonic ecstasy of all life" (p. 33). And if the earth itself were a denial of life, then it would never admit of this sort of description: "A softness was unfurling like silk ribbons in the pale air, and the earth was breaking into tiny warm rifts from which stole a new green" (p. 25). And Judith is closely identified with the earth beyond Caleb's farm. Her communion with wild nature alone in the woods is very sensual:

> Not knowing fully what she was doing, Judith took off all her clothing and lay flat on the damp ground with the very waxy feeling of new, sunless vegetation under her. . . . Oh, how knowing the bare earth was, as if it might have a heart and mind hidden here in the woods. The fields that Caleb had tilled had no tenderness, she knew. But here was something forbiddenly beautiful, secret as one's own body. (p. 53)

As this passage suggests, Judith also embraces the wild nature within her, allowing her hatred to flare up against Caleb and meeting her lover with a pure animal ferocity. Caleb, on the other hand, is to be identified with the "land," yet he is a man whose every feeling is repressed, who is said to fear "things out of man's control" (p. 53), and while Judith is fruitful in the natural way, pregnant before she and Sven elope, Caleb is beyond fertility, a sterilizing influence keeping his children on the farm and driving off any suitors.

There are two senses of the term "land" which must be distinguished here. Judith can be identified with the land in the sense in which we have been using the word, land as natural environment. Caleb

can be identified with the land only in the sense that
"land" is a human construct, property, a means to
power. Where Judith represents communion with the
land, Caleb represents power over it. The two act out the
conflict, central to so much prairie fiction, between the
impulse to work in harmony with nature and the impulse
to dominate and exploit it for gain. Grove later includes
both the cultivator and the exploiter in one character,
Abe Spalding, but it is typical of the simplistic moral
world of romance that in *Wild Geese* the two are
separate, their conflict external and visible.

Ostenso sets up two patterns of allusion
which support the interpretation of Caleb as oppressor of
the land. Amelia stands in a painful opposition between
the old, mean, ugly Caleb and the young, refined, and
noble Mark Jordan, who must never learn of his
illegitimacy. Her love for young Jordan who arrives in
the spring is suggestive in itself, as is the opposition of
young and old, but when we are told that hateful Caleb
succeeded to Amelia's hand after Mark's father was
gored by a bull, we begin to suspect the submerged
presence of a cyclital vegetation myth such as that of
Venus and Adonis. Three times the older Jordan is
mentioned: "The man who had been gored to death by a
bull on his own farm in the distant south had taken
Amelia's soul with him" (p. 20), "The son of Amelia and
big Del Jordan, who was gored by a bull" (p. 59), "He
[Mark] wore his clothes with such an air, sat in the
saddle like a soldier. . . . And his father had been gored
by a bull . . . after everything. . . ." [ellipses Ostenso's]
(p. 87). These are virtually the only references to
Amelia's first lover. The suggestion of Caleb as the boar
of winter reinforces his role as a sterilizing force,
overthrown by the influence of the young Adonis,
Mark Jordan.

The second allusion is to the Old
Testament Caleb. Gare is the most complete embodiment
of that central archetype of prairie fiction, the prairie
patriarch. He is an absolute temporal leader of his   111

family, a tyrant, but he also pretends to a divine
commission to carry out his purposes, like the patriarchs
of old. We know this hypocrisy masks only greed and a
lust for power. Caleb will not allow the rest of the family
to attend Church, but "Before dinner on Sunday it was
the custom for the family to assemble in the sitting-room
and hear Caleb recite the sermon that had been delivered
at Yellow Post church" (p. 41). Predictably he takes
advantage of these occasions to reinforce his own power
with the sanction of the word of God. The choice of the
names Caleb and Jordan adds interesting overtones to
Gare's role as patriarch. When Moses selected men from
all the tribes to cross the Jordan and spy out the land of
Canaan, Caleb was the one who urged taking possession
of the land immediately; "Let us go up at once and
possess it for we are well able to overcome it" (Numbers
14:30). Others, fearing the struggle, sought to give the
land a bad name, calling it "a land that eateth up the
inhabitants thereof" (Numbers 14:32). Ostenso may not
have intended Caleb's death in the muskeg as an instance
of the land eating up the inhabitants thereof, but she
certainly presents Caleb as one seeking a promised land
at all costs.

Caleb's way of doting upon his land is
revealing. At night he walks out alone with a lantern to
inspect it, as Judith says, "to assure himself that his land
was still there" (p. 18). He obviously sees land not as
something he lives with, or from, or upon, but as
possession, almost as though it were moveable property
which someone might steal. His land-hunger evidently
includes no love of the soil; he delegates all the detailed
farm work to Amelia and the children, and he exhausts
his land just as he overworks his family. His compulsion
to master the land in an exploitive way is exactly
paralleled by his need to master his wife and his very
naturally rebellious daughter. And here Ostenso gains
some advantages by setting the domineering masculine
will against a female opponent. Caleb takes what is
112 clearly a perverted sexual pleasure in imposing his will

upon Judith, trying to break her spirit, make her yield entirely to him. At the same time, the part of his farm which focuses his desire for land is his flax crop which he regards with a furtive sexual appetite:

> Caleb would stand for long moments outside the fence beside the flax. Then he would turn quickly to see that no one was looking. He would creep between the wires and run his hand across the flowering, gentle tops of the growth. A stealthy caress—more intimate than any he had ever given to a woman. (p. 119)

Nowhere in prairie fiction is there a more definite identification between the land and woman and the whole unconscious world of impulse and desire. Caleb, like any number of other prairie patriarchs, must conquer all these; his arrogant conscious will must be unchallenged by the spontaneous and irrational, even at the cost of losing touch with all nature including his own. D. G. Jones, in his chapter "The Dictatorship of Mind" in *Butterfly on Rock*,[8] explains that European man has in this way alienated himself from his natural surroundings by his unrelenting efforts to subjugate these unruly elements inside and outside himself. While Jones does not apply his idea to *Wild Geese*, it is this very drama of repression and its consequences Martha Ostenso presents so effectively in Caleb and his family, and could have presented even more powerfully had she not apparently misinterpreted her own symbols.

Ostenso inadvertently provides an example of the cultural incongruities we have been discussing. Like her heroine Lind Archer, Ostenso brings the light of culture to bear upon this primitive, inarticulate community, but because it is an inappropriate culture, it leads her to identify the villain Caleb with the land. What follows from that identification is the type of well-intentioned blunder we come to expect of the official bearers of culture on the plains: Miss

Archer and Miss Ostenso move Judith, who is elementally bound to the land, into the city. It is hard to imagine
this passionate young amazon being happy in the urban
domestic environment to which they consign her. Ostenso
finally offers us a splendid intuition weakened by a
faulty conscious grasp of what she has sensed.

Grove seems to have understood the
conditions of man's alienation from the land which Stead
and Ostenso sometimes revealed only inadvertently. The
dehumanizing effect of operating the farm as an industry,
for example, which Stead only imperfectly grasps. Grove's
Abe Spalding is made to become gradually aware of as
his farm expands. The strong, dark bond between the
land and man's inner life, evident but unexplored in *Wild
Geese*, Abe senses more clearly if less movingly in the
passage quoted in the early pages of this chapter. In all
his prairie novels, from *Settlers of the Marsh* to *Fruits
of the Earth*, Grove sees that the main drama is not
between man and external nature—though his characters
frequently misunderstand it to be—but within man,
between his conscious will and his own nature.

External nature in Grove is only potentially hostile. In his short story "Snow," for example,
the sun looks down from an "indifferent sky"
on the death of young Redfern, and the characters are
ground in the teeth of an indifferent fate. The stricken
mother's last remark, "God's will be done," is the final
irony upon a world of cold mechanism.[9] Naturalistic
assumptions of this sort actually inform very little of
Grove's fiction, however, and Grove explicitly repudiates
Zola as a pseudo-realist and his naturalism as pseudo-
science.[10] In *Fruits of the Earth*, when Abe discovers that
his great brick mansion is beginning to erode away by
imperceptible stages, his remark that "the moment a
work of man was finished, nature set to work to take it
down again" (p. 134) supposes a totally different
universe, working by design, actively opposed to man's
will—that is, if man pits his will against nature's, and
initially Grove's heroes do. Niels Lindstedt is introduced

in a classic posture of defiance to nature in the first few
words of *Settlers of the Marsh*: "On the road leading
north from the little prairie town Minor two men were
fighting their way through the gathering dusk."[11] Like
many of Grove's sentences, this has at first an opaque
quality which is worth penetrating. Somewhat later a
snowstorm begins, but at this point in their journey there
is nothing specific against which the men are fighting—
just the dusk, the north, the beginning of November, the
wilderness.

That is a fair image of the struggle with
nature in Grove. Both Niels and Abe Spalding are well
suited to the tangible part of this contest, and the fact
that both men win material success with comparative
ease is a sign that Grove did not want to cloud the issue.
It is the intangibles in nature which league with the inner
nature of man to defeat him, and both men neglect the
intangibles. The outward struggle with the land can even
become an escape from the more perplexing human
problems. When Niels, for example, cannot bear to test
his dream of marriage by asking Ellen Amundsen, it is
said that "a sort of intoxication came over Niels; work
developed into an orgy" (p. 67). At this point and
elsewhere in the action, the real struggle with himself is
neglected, the real dangers of personal disintegration
toward which Niels drifts are ignored.

External nature is a fair opponent, and
man could presumably prove himself in the stress of his
encounter with it. In Grove's world a strong man can
win; what matters is how he wins and what the struggle
does to him. Very early in *Settlers* Grove gives us an
image to suggest the dangers of this struggle. As Niels
and his friend Lars Nelson walk together into the
blizzard, "Both would have liked to talk, to tell and to
listen to stories of danger, of being lost, of hairbreadth
escapes: the influence of the prairie snowstorm made
itself felt. But whenever one of them spoke, the wind
snatched his word from his lips and threw it aloft" (p.
16). The men are typically isolated in their struggle, for 115

throughout the novel communication in the harsh
northern life is sparse, fragmentary, not just unfulfilling
but dangerously unilluminating. The more Niels struggles
to master his environment, the more isolated he becomes.
The same could be said of Abe Spalding. Even Abe's
involvement in local politics is only apparent human
interchange, ultimately isolating him still further.

What the struggle can do, not only to the
communication between men, but to a pioneer's
humanity, is partly illustrated in the contrast between the
Amundsen and the Lund households in *Settlers*.
Amundsen's farm is a model of human order carefully
asserted; Lund's is haphazard, reflecting both a concern
for human comfort and indulgence of human weaknesses.
It seems to include the wrack of broken and betrayed
dreams, typified by the ornate but worn-out furniture
and clothing which inadequately serve the needs of the
Lunds. This last especially is repugnant to Grove's fresh,
idealistic young hero. "Niels could not help contrasting the
shabby, second-hand, defunct gentility of it all, and the
squalor in which it was left, with the trim and spotless but
bare austerity of Amundsen's house. It struck him how
little there was of comfort in that other home: Ellen's
home! And yet, how sincere it was in its severe utility as
compared with this! Amundsen's house represented a
future; this one, the past: Amundsen's, growth; this one,
decay" (p. 31). Two entirely different approaches to life
are made visible. The Lunds' dreams have been betrayed
by an easy-going acceptance of the good and the bad in
people, including old Lund himself; the struggle with the
land seems to be a losing one, and to the young Niels,
full of his own fresh visions, it is depressing, as it would
have been to the young Abe Spalding. Amundsen, on the
other hand, is willing to sacrifice anything to the
fulfillment of his purpose, including the children he left
in Sweden, and his wife who must suffer pregnancies and
self-induced abortions to remain productive on the farm.
Amundsen is a prairie patriarch a good deal like Caleb
Gare, as harsh and demanding, as hypocritically pious,

as sterilizing, and like Caleb he is killed by nature, crushed under the ice he must haul for water in winter. His lack of harmony with nature is also suggested by this shortage of water. On the Amundsen place Niels and Nelson dig for several days without striking water, while on the Lunds' they find abundant water only a few feet below the surface. And ultimately it is the Lunds who manage to endure, yielding to fate yet clinging to their humanity. The novel does span some seventeen years of life on the marsh, and as Niels grows to accept all of himself he also grows to value the Lunds and their acceptance of life; Abe Spalding is another of Grove's ambitious men who must suffer through the same growth toward acceptance.

In the struggle with the land, the way in which the pioneer seeks to impose his will has everything to do with his spiritual or imaginative harmony with the land. Niels's giant strength is a thing of nature itself, and as long as he works in a state of innocence, he appears to enjoy a kind of harmony with nature. Niels works with his own hands, to expunge the memory of his mother's humiliating servitude in the houses of the rich in Sweden. Abe Spalding does not have any such motive, and here a series of distinctions between the two pioneers begins and should not be overlooked. Abe is from a small farm in Ontario which would have allowed him a respectable living, but no scope for ambition. He comes West to find a "clear prospect," meaning not only totally arable land, unencumbered by debt, but unobscured vision and unimpeded progress. "Well, he would conquer this wilderness; he would change it; he would set his own seal upon it! For the moment, one hundred and sixty acres were going to be his, capable of being tilled from line to line!" (p. 22). His will is militant, to "conquer," and imperialist—the first quarter will suffice only "for the moment." Abe is another prairie patriarch, a little less sinister than Amundsen or Gare, a little less hypocritical, but with the same overweening ambition. Though Abe too is a physical giant, his strength can by   117

no means compass his aspirations. He is caught in a
chain of logic which will lead him to the worst kind of
alienation from the land, mechanization:

> Conquest of the landscape depended on ways and
> means of speeding up the work . . . . What was
> the solution? There was only one: power farming
> as it was called: machinery would do the work of
> many horses and many men. But Abe liked the
> response of living flesh and bone to the spoken
> word and hated the unintelligent repetition of
> ununderstood activities which machines
> demanded. Yet sooner or later he must come to
> that; he would have to run the farm like a
> factory; that was the modern trend. . . . (p. 41)

Like a factory. Because of his ambition to conquer the
land, Abe inevitably undergoes the depersonalizing
effect of mechanization, the alienating effect of industrialization.

It is not surprising that Grove, living as he
did at the height of the mechanical age, concentrated on
mechanism, both as theme and as imagery in much of his
fiction. The imagery is most obviously developed in
Master of the Mill where the mill itself becomes an
image of cosmic forces. In *Settlers*, Niels is not directly
implicated in mechanization—he is an earlier pioneer
than Spalding and he is also non-Anglo-Saxon, which
may have something to do with Grove's way of relating
him to machines. At the same time, there is a strain of
mechanical imagery running through this novel of
Grove's. At the prospect of having a machine come in to
dig his well, Amundsen, for example, discharges Niels
and Nelson. And in the end when Niels returns from the
penitentiary, his sense of the deterioration of the marsh
district is emphasized by the number of automobiles
around. The only time Niels is himself identified with
machinery is when his inability to recognize his situation
with Clara Vogel is driving him mad. When Niels cannot

face the moral dilemma of his marriage, he retreats to the security of his implement shed where he paces among his machinery. As his preference for machinery grows, his relationship with animals deteriorates. In his last winter of bush work when Niels works like a machine it is said "Towards the end of winter Niels's relationship to his horses became completely demoralized" (p. 165). The term seems to have its full literal meaning of having lost a moral basis. He treats his horses without consideration and they respond like slaves—or machines. And when he is finally overbalanced by the inescapable assertion of his wife's whoredom, when he sets out on the blind path to her murder, his state is described in mechanical terms. "His muscles tightened and remained tight. It was as if a powerful spring inside of him had been tightly wound and then arrested by some catch, either to snap under the strain or to unroll itself in the natural way by setting some complicated wheel-work into irresistible motion, grinding up what might come in its way" (p. 186). True, Niels is also described as a wounded animal seeking its lair, but the mechanical image is remarkable because it is rare and is typically associated with unhealthy states. It further emphasizes the conflict between nature and mechanism which runs through Grove. And like the inexorable logic Abe Spalding is caught up in, it emphasizes the autonomous quality of mechanism, which does not extend the will of man but captures it. Only in a diseased state does the human will ally itself with mechanism against nature.

A suspicion of mechanism might be expected of all the prairie realists at a time when industrialization threatened the agrarian life about which they wrote, but oddly enough Ostenso says little about it, while Stead seems to have been quite taken with the romance of machinery. Grove was the only one to see the machine as a natural metaphor for impersonal forces which drive man away from his ideal self. In this respect Stead was more a product of his time; the machine together with the social and economic machinery which 119 shape men's lives in an industrial society were until the mid-1920's accepted by the prairie people as though they were part of the divine plan of progress. Far from seeing them as any threat to agrarian ideals, the farmers who banded together to protect their way of life with grain growers' associations were eager to adopt some of that machinery by forming corporations to market grain and other commodities. They evidently believed in the economic machinery as another means to the millennium they envisioned in the garden of the West. As late as 1918 the members of the Saskatchewan Grain Growers' Association are said to have looked forward to a time when "Locals will own their own breeding stock, assemble and fatten their own poultry, handle and ship their eggs, operate their own cooperative laundries and bakeries, kill and cure meat in cooperative butcher-shops for their own use—have meeting places, rest rooms, town offices, libraries, moving-pictures and phonographs with which to entertain and inform themselves. To stand with a hand on the hilt of such a dream is to visualize a revolution in farm and community life—such a revolution as would switch much attraction from city to country."[12] This "dream" was evidently the corporate extension of the garden myth, a prelapsarian view of the business world. Developments in industrialization and commerce would bring about a slow end to the agrarian West, but only men like Grove saw it plainly. His Abe Spalding is again a classic pioneer, living personally the social history of his era and becoming disillusioned not only with machines but with the social and political machinery of his community.

Grove also offers us a more complex and problematic moral universe than either Stead or Ostenso. He says, "We do not, in life, meet with heroes and villains . . . ,"[13] and this tells us a good deal, not only about the mimetic level at which Grove chooses to work, but about the moral shading of character in his novels. At the beginning of *Settlers*, for example, the incidents could easily have generated heroes and villains. Old

Sigurdsen turns Niels and Nelson out into a blizzard at gunpoint. In *Wild Geese* the same inhuman act—turning the brothers of Fusi Aronson out in a storm—is one mark of the blackness of Caleb's villainy, yet Sigurdsen develops into a sympathetic character and the closest friend of Niels. Grove's denial of the black and white morality of hero and villain is part of his rejection of earlier romantic fiction, but here it is especially significant because one of Niels's fatal weaknesses is a need for such moral absolutes. He has come to Canada where he believes life is simplified and he can be brought only slowly and painfully to see that no moral question is ever simple and that no human being can escape being implicated in the sins of humanity.

Grove can create a more complex world than Stead's or Ostenso's because he commands a greater range of technique. The circumstantial realism which Stead developed to good effect, Grove managed with greater precision. The most obvious examples appear in the essays in *Over Prairie Trails*. At the same time, Grove could explore the shadows of desire and dread which heighten the characters in *Wild Geese*. Grove called himself a "realist," but the term broadens as he discusses it. He holds that realism is "a matter of literary procedure, not choice of subject," but he rejects Zola's naturalism. In his essay "Realism in Literature," Grove says "Shakespeare was a realist; but his realism has very little to do with accuracy in such externals as the historic or social costume. Art is not a matter of facts and figures. 'The aim' said Lowell, 'of the artist is psychologic, not historic truth.'"[14] And in pursuit of that "psychologic" truth Grove sometimes enters those areas of radically subjective experience usually considered the province of romancers. The whole symbolic structure of *Settlers*, for that matter, with its light and dark females, its questing, death and rebirth patterns, could profitably be explored in romantic terms.

For particular techniques, Grove's creation of two crucial scenes in the novel is worth examining. The first is when Niels innocently comes to ask for Ellen's hand. The scene is her garden, which for Niels has become an idyllic spot; the time is just before a summer storm, and throughout the scene, which is unusually sensuous, vivid, and lyric for Grove, nature seems to respond to the rising emotions of the two, who both know what is to come. Even Niels somehow senses the tragic issue of his errand, but suspense is built up. A little later in the scene, after the passage quoted here, the narration shifts to an immediate, breathless present tense:

> As they crossed the yard, imponderable things, incomprehensible waves of feeling passed to and fro between them: things too delicate for words; things somehow full of pain and anxious, disquieting anticipation: like silent discharges between summer clouds that distantly wink at each other in lightning.
>
> The air, too, was charged; its sultriness foreboded a storm. Yet, there was not a cloud in the upper reaches of the atmosphere; only at the horizon there lay, in the far north-west, a white bank which above the dark cliff of forest, showed a rounded, convoluted outline, its edge blushing with a golden iridescence.
>
> The slightest breeze ambled into the clearing from the east, scarcely perceptible, yet refreshing where it could be felt.
>
> Between the two, as the silence lengthened—between man and woman, boy and girl—the consciousness arose that the other knew of the decision which was at hand: it was almost oppressive. Some step was to be taken, had to be taken at last: it was a tragic necessity no longer to be evaded . . . . (p. 94)

The nature imagery is all pathetically attuned to the people; the emotions run to subjective absolutes, "imponderables," "incomprehensibles" (ultimately inexpressibles); the two figures are generalized as "boy and girl" so that the present tense, when adopted, creates a timeless archetypal drama of youth. In the corresponding later scene of their meeting after Niels's marriage, Clara's murder, Niels's prison term, a similar idyll is enacted in subdued tones, with tempered judgments, shades of feeling, so that the romantic urgency of the first flush of their love is replaced by the sober tones of a circumspect maturity.

With the range of his style—not all of which fits comfortably under the term "realism"—Grove generates a full experience of man's engagement with external nature and its relation to his own internal nature. In *Settlers* particularly he may have found one of the rare combinations of techniques which capture at once the insistence of brute circumstances on the plains and the dreams of the pioneers, and which respond to both the threat and the promise of the unnamed country. To say that Grove has taken man's alienation from the land as his major theme would be misleading. His vision of man's relationship with the land is far more complex and ambiguous, but it is consistently a denial of the earlier simplistic view of man in the garden, the romance of pioneering. Grove recognizes that man's will to assert himself over the land is not simply a corruptible impulse, as Stead had seen it, but in itself an arrogant if not blasphemous denial of nature.

The progress of realistic fiction during the three decades dominated by what I call prairie realism was not, of course, as simple as this rather single-minded description would imply. Some minor realists, like Allen Evans, could be said to echo the work of Grove. Evans's prairie tyrants are related to Grove heroes, but they are much cruder creations. Herman Miller, in *Dream Out of Dust* (1956) for example, about sums up his aesthetic values in his objection to landscaping the farmstead: "Trees takes plenty space."[15] A larger group of women writers resemble Martha Ostenso in the dark power they ascribe to the land and the accompanying strong romantic elements in their novels. Vera Lysenko in the first half of her *Yellow Boots* (1954), for example, depicts a peasant people darkly wedded to the soil and to the mysteries of the seasons. Nell Parsons in *The Curlew Cried* (1947) presents a typical romantic image of a civilized woman's fear of the darkness of the land when her eastern heroine is brought to her bridegroom's farm: "Opposite the farmyard a dark bluff rose to dominate the scene. It stood aloof in shadowed frowning silence, as if it knew some bitter secret from the past of the passively violent land."[16] This suggestion of something mysterious as well as sinister is common in this group of novels. Gladys Taylor's *Pine Roots* (1956) is similar in this respect, though as the title suggests it is set just beyond the prairie in northern Manitoba.

In less romantic novels the land is portrayed as harsh and potentially sinister but in no way mysterious, though it can resemble a creature of sentience and will. These novels include the rural half of Flos Jewell Williams's *New Furrows* (1926) and all of Sheila Russell's *The Living Earth* (1954). The most accomplished of the group is Christine Van der Mark's *In Due Season* (1947), which begins on the prairie and moves north to the Peace River Country. There a strange reversal of the familiar patriachal order of prairie fiction takes place. The pioneer woman, Lina Ashley, throws off her amiably shiftless husband and applies herself ruthlessly to succeeding on a bush farm, partly at the expense of her family and her less forceful neighbours. Lina's humanity can be seen to deteriorate as she prospers materially until she resembles the coarse, work-intoxicated tyrants found in so many prairie novels. Lina grows into a grim harmony with the harsh spirit of the northern land, which is very powerfully evoked in Van der Mark's descriptions. A similar emergence of female power can be seen less distinctly in Russell's and Taylor's novels, and the same tendency becomes general in post-war fiction from Ross, McCourt, and Mitchell to Margaret Laurence.

Not all writers of realistic prairie fiction in this era can be identified with any distinct conception of man's relationship to the soil. Harold Loeb's *Tumbling Mustard* (1929), for example, is a novel of undeniable psychological and circumstantial realism about a young man who faces his own weakness of character in a variety of ways. The action takes place during a land boom just after the turn of the century in the Medicine Hat area, and the setting has an authentic feel to it, but the novel generates no strong sense of man as either alien or native to the land. He simply drifts over it. A more extreme example is the rather intellectually pretentious novel for which Bertram Brooker won the Governor General's award in 1936. *Think of the Earth* is its title but not its tendency; the action could have been set on the fringe of anywhere. Frederick Niven is an altogether more substantial contributor to prairie fiction who does not belong in the main stream of prairie realism because his attention is not on the land but on the people and their history. He brings to prairie writing a foreign preoccupation with time rather than space. In his *Mine Inheritance* (1940) and *The Flying Years* (1935) the West becomes a series of historically connected events in a setting often vividly described but never established as a considerable determinant of the history through which Niven's characters move.

Wallace Stegner, in his *On a Darkling Plain* (1939), presents a more complex relationship between man and the land. He does not show man as alienated from the soil, nor does he imply that union with nature is necessarily a desirable goal. His hero Edwin Vickers comes more or less empty-handed to homestead a quarter section of bald prairie in southern Saskatchewan, but we know from his letters to friends in Vancouver that he is a romantic poet at heart.[17] His faith undergoes a very believable change, too. Wounded in the Great War, he is totally cynical about man and his motives, and hopes to disengage himself from his kind entirely, but he finds he cannot throw himself on the

125

bosom of mother nature. Not, at least, where her bosom is so hard and flat. He cannot stand being alone with nature indefinitely, and he cannot avoid becoming involved with his neighbours and their slightly simple 18 year old nature-child. Ina, who plays with dolls, is both a living counterpart of Vickers' naive romanticism and a practical warning against the dangers of cultural deprivation. The nearby town stricken with the influenza epidemic of 1918 draws Vickers inexorably, like a whirlpool, but there he learns that regardless of how despicable the reasons for man's endeavours, the essential worth is in the struggle and the uglier the conditions, the better the qualities of human spirit revealed.

Despite the cataclysmic events of the 1930's the fiction about that decade is as much a completion of the moral questioning begun by earlier realists as it is a reaction to the terrible years of depression and drought. One of Mrs. Bentley's early conceptions of her place on the prairie sounds very like the fulfillment of Grove's prophecy that "such a vessel may be engulfed by such a sea." Mrs. Bentley says, "There's a high, rocking wind that rattles the windows and creaks the walls. It's strong and steady like a great tide after the winter pouring north again, and I have a queer, helpless sense of being lost miles out in the middle of it, flattened against a little peak of rock."[18] Whatever protection that ill-conceived vessel of human order afforded has been lost, the vessel sunk and the survivors left clinging to the small, treacherous island of the prairie town. Mrs. Bentley suggests more than the depression lot of personal poverty and despair; there is a threat of utter annihilation, darkness, and unmeaning. This is a good existentialist image too, and that may be part of the growing appeal of *As For Me and My House.* The drought and depression of the prairie can provide a type of man's ultimate isolation and loneliness.

If the fiction of the 1930's brings full circle the movement from the garden myth to nature as 126 inimical to man, it also introduces new elements.

Drought and dust storms produce inevitable imagery of the desert as distinct from the earlier wilderness. Where a wilderness is chaotic and threatening, a desert is barren and suggests a spiritual emptiness which is not a feature of the earlier fiction, however grim it might become. The overtones of a waste land barren through the sins of the people haunt some of Ross's stories, and there does seem to be a need for some kind of sacrifice. The victims are more weak than wicked: Judith West in *As For Me and My House*, Ellen in "The Lamp at Noon," Eleanor in "Not By Rain Alone." The same could be said of sacrificial victims in McCourt's novels: Neil Fraser in *Music at the Close* (1947), Norah in *Home is the Stranger* (1950), Dermot in *Walk Through the Valley* (1958). Possibly the bitterness of the 1930's brought out the need for human sacrifice. Man clearly has had a responsibility for his disharmony with nature; the world which had been disordered in Grove's fiction is now beyond remedy. It demands ritual atonement.

There is also a growing recognition that the shapes of man's own culture isolate him from the land and contribute to this spiritual emptiness. The farmers at Partridge Hill are the hardest hit people in Ross's novel, yet they are grimly, doggedly continuing in the hope that the land will come back. Philip's portrait of Lawson testifies to the strength of the farmer's endurance. The townspeople are the most forlorn people in the desert, and those lost between, people like Philip and Paul who have been isolated from the land by a little education, now belong nowhere. It is a final, full recognition that man's culture has kept him from placing himself imaginatively in the land.

Neil Fraser in McCourt's *Music at the Close* is another forlorn figure, the nominal owner of farm land, but enamoured of the life of the mind and incapable of developing any relationship whatever with the land. He would rather speculate on grain futures, or rent out the farm and travel, or neglect it and dream of moving to the "promised land" of the Peace River

127

Country. What Neil imagines (and perhaps McCourt did too) is that some bond or harmony with the land had once existed but had been lost. Of his Uncle Matt, Neil says "he had loved the land with an inarticulate, single-minded intensity."[19] Given the story from Neil's point of view, we have little evidence of any such love; Neil's belief in it is significant mainly in confirming its absence in himself. Being such a creature of illusions, Neil easily gives in to disillusionment and bitterness toward the land, but his wife Moira brings him back to reality: 'It's not that the land is sour, Neil, and you know it. It's just that it's neglected, only half-cultivated. It's our own fault that we're in a mess, not nature's' (p. 185). Neil's farm is a visible example of the desert—both physical and psychic—which can be created by man's failure to adapt culturally to the plains.

To revert to Grove's sea metaphor, we appear to be getting fiction in which the vessel, the pioneer farm, has been engulfed by the prairie sea, and in its place man clings to culture or the town, which is seen as an island, but as Mrs. Bentley says, "a rocky, treacherous island." Throughout *As For Me and My House* it is evident that the town does more to constrict than to support or protect the people. It is a false refuge. In this respect the failure of the town explodes the pioneer faith in an encompassing intangible order which was the basis of the fiction before the 1920's. The cultural order is life-denying because it is false, like the pettiness and bigotry of the town reflected in the false fronts of the stores, and false because it is unnatural on the social circle, Mrs. Bird, describes herself as an "expatriate" from England, though she has never been there (p. 21). Mrs. Bentley describes one of Philip's sketches which catches the town's quality of incongruity.

> Another little Main Street. In the foreground there's an old horse and buggy hitched outside one of the stores. A broken old horse, legs set stolid, head down dull and spent. But still you

feel it belongs to the earth, the earth it stands on,
the prairie that continues where the town breaks
off. What the tired old hulk suggests is less
approaching decay or dissolution than return.
You sense a flow, a rhythm, a cycle.

But the town in contrast has an
upstart, mean complacency. The false fronts
haven't seen the prairie. Instead they stare at each
other across the street as into mirrors of
themselves, absorbed in their own reflections.

The town shouldn't be there. It
stands up so insolent and smug and self-assertive
that your fingers itch to smudge it out and let the
underlying rhythms complete themselves. (p. 69)

A failure of the imagination is obviously a major factor
in this disharmony between man and his surroundings.

Yet however petty and despicable the
town, Mrs. Bentley concedes that she needs it as protection against the emptiness of the desert:

We've all lived in a little town too long. The
wilderness here makes us uneasy. I felt it first the
night I walked alone along the river bank—a
queer sense of something cold and fearful,
something inanimate, yet aware of us. A Main
Street is such a self-sufficient little pocket of
existence, so smug, compact, that here we feel
abashed somehow before the hills, their
passiveness, the unheeding way they sleep. We
climb them, but they withstand us, remain as
serene and unrevealed as ever. The river slips
past, unperturbed by our coming and going,
stealthily confident. We shrink from our
insignificance. The stillness and solitude—we
think a force or presence into it—even a hostile
presence, deliberate, aligned against us—for we
dare not admit an indifferent wilderness, where
we may have no meaning at all. (pp. 99-100)   129

In this passage, as I have said, Mrs. Bentley provides the first recognition in prairie fiction that man creates the hostility he confronts. It adds an entirely new dimension to the view of man's alienation from the land. It is the condition Frye has described as the "Garrison mentality," in which the people, feeling their culture threatened by the vast indifference of the wilderness, huddle together, stiffening their meagre cultural defences and projecting all their hostilities on their surroundings. The effect, as we can see in *As For Me*, is to isolate people not only from the surrounding hostile nature, but from each other and in great measure from their own elemental natures. It is, as Frye and D.G. Jones point out, a condition common in Canadian literature, but it is especially appropriate to the prairie at this point where man's failure to establish imaginative harmony with the prairie has been aggravated by a failure of his apparently successful physical adaptation to the plains.

Prairie realists represented man as spiritually alien to the
plains, isolated and alone in a still unnamed country
because he had transformed the prairie with his hands
but not with the power of his heart or his imagination.
Imagination is central to the realists' view of man's
failure to adapt to the plains. For artists the fate of the
creative imagination is always an especially sensitive
indicator of how well man is thriving in his natural and
cultural environment, and the realists represent the
imagination as caught between a mechanistic culture and
an intractable land. The region was settled, of course, at
the right time to inherit extremely dreary ideals of
progress, bound up with industrialism and its inevitable
mechanistic philosophy, and the prairie was a hard land
to capture imaginatively. But the explicit images of man's
imaginative vision and creative efforts are in this body of
fiction so consistently darkened by futility that they
suggest a large-scale failure of the collective imagination
in its work of humanizing the new environment.

    Not surprisingly, the house becomes one
of the most prominent symbols, representing man's first
cultural and imaginative assertion as well as his most
immediate defence against his environment. The number
of unfinished, ruinous, or incongruous houses in the
fiction implies a very elementary failure of the imagination. As Grove puts it, rather heavily, in one of
his essays, "We have not yet crystallized our attitude to
life into architectonic symbols; perhaps we never shall."[1]
The house, as "architectonic symbol," is often the
embodiment of a larger dream, and therefore closely
related to recurrent figures of dreamers, visionaries,
sensitive children, and artists. In the fate of these figures,
as we will see, some of the prairie realists suggest not
only the imagination struggling with the prairie but an
essential hostility between the two: the prairie remains
intractable, the imagination is stifled by its harshness.

    Each of the novels which mark the
beginning of prairie realism, *Grain, Settlers of the
Marsh,* and *Wild Geese,* contains a similar house, one

131

that is identified with human ideals in some way, but
becomes a mocking reminder of the neglect, failure or
defeat of those ideals. In *Grain* the promised house
which is to dignify Mrs. Stake's service on the farm is
delayed so long that it comes to represent betrayal more
than concern for human values. In the East, Jackson
Stake had promised his bride "a frame house with lath
and plastered walls and an upstairs," but it is said that
"Gander was driving a four-horse team before the ribs of
his father's frame house at last rose stark against the
prairie sky."[2] By this time the family is beginning to
disperse, and they do not, in any case, know how to inhabit
the more pretentious house. The priorities of humane and
materialistic values are emphasized when Jackson cannot
use the old house for a granary: "It is one thing to live in
a house with rotten sills, but quite another to risk the
year's harvest in it" (p. 85). The atmosphere of the Stake
household is almost inimical to the imagination. What
happens to young Gander is essentially what happens to
the spirited colt he breaks to the plow: "discipline soon
ground the imagination out of his soul as it does to other
beasts of burden besides horses, and already he accepted
straining on his traces as a distasteful but inevitable
procedure" (p. 118).

In *Wild Geese* the new house is a minor
recurring motif, the preoccupation of the plodding eldest
son, who is described as a "stumbling dreamer, forever
silent in his dream."[3] This dream of a house is the only
sign we have of stifled potential in Martin. He is a
builder at heart, and his conception is grander than
Jackson Stake's: "The dream grew to a desire that crept
into his hands. His hands grasped the good, enduring
lumber, the plaster, the fine laths, the shingles, the panes
of glass, the stones for the foundation and the chimney
of the New House. . . . There would be a verandah
facing the main road such as he had seen on the houses
pictured in the mail order catalogue" (p. 92). It is a
measure of Caleb's villainy that he will not think of
132   building anything but a barn, and it is another sacrifice

to monetary values. In both of these novels, as in many others, the imagination could hardly be said to contend directly with the prairie. It is sacrificed to something in the people themselves, their will, their avarice, their need to subdue the prairie.

Houses in Grove's novels play a larger part. In *Settlers of the Marsh*, when Niels brings Clara home as his wife, she refers to his house as "the famous White Range Line House."[4] Its fame has spread partly because the house is remarkable in itself. The most imposing in the district, with a kitchen and four rooms fifteen by eighteen feet, Niels's house is part of a grand vision, meant to embody visibly his dream of plenty and domestic comfort. When Ellen will not marry him and complete the dream, the house becomes a hollow mockery, and when the horror of his marriage to Clara grows upon him, the house becomes a demonic parody of his dream. It is totally inhabited by the deathly life of the woman he identifies with sin, and Niels avoids it as much as possible, sitting and staring at it from the security of his implement shed: "He entered his house only when it could not be helped. . . . But he stared across at it, with unseeing eyes, at that big house which he had built for himself four, five years ago . . . . For himself? No, of that he must not think. . . . That way lay insanity" [ellipses Groves's] (p. 149). The woman is a caricature of the wife Niels had hoped for. The house, like his dream, has been profaned; Niels cannot tolerate the fallen woman in his house any more than he can admit human imperfection to his dream.

Grove's other novels make further use of houses. In *Our Daily Bread*, the term acquires its extended meaning of family or dynasty as John Elliott nurses his patriarchal dream of gathering his children about him. His cultural assertion belongs to the familiar category of imposing blindly upon the plains a social order brought from another tradition. It does not fit, and Grove uses the decay of the actual house as an image of the decay of the old man and his dream.[5] The grand house in *Fruits of the Earth* is more celebrated because Grove himself has drawn attention to it. In an author's note to the book, and again in *In Search of Myself*, he describes an almost derelict farm from which sprang one of the germinal ideas for the novel:

> This farm was such as to suggest a race of giants who had founded it; but on inquiry I found that it was held by tenants who tilled a bare ten per cent of its acreage. In a barn built for half a hundred horses they kept a team of two sorry nags; and they inhabited no more than two or three rooms of the outwardly palatial house.[6]

The house again speaks of dynastic or patriarchial ambition, but specially in this picture of its decline it shows the vanity of human presumption which haunts Grove's entire novel. Abe's house is in some sense a blasphemous assertion, not just against nature but against God—a Tower of Babel. And like the houses in *Grain* and *Wild Geese* it is delayed so long that it comes to represent the neglect of human values for the sake of ambition. For Ruth, who has wanted "comfort, not splendor," it is too late. Like the Stakes, the Spaldings are ill at ease with luxury: "They sat in the dining room; both had sat too long on straight-backed chairs to feel at ease in an arm-chair."[7]

In Ross's *As For Me and My House,* the house is more than ever a cultural expression, not of a doubtful dream but of a certain nightmare. "The house huddles me," Mrs. Bentley says, "the walls disapprove."[8] And the house does seem capable of both sentience and will. It is the culmination of a strain of house imagery in a number of ways: first in acquiring a life of its own, remarkably strong for all the shabby meanness of the place; second, in being an accomplished cultural assertion—not of the Bentleys, who are only transients, but of the prairie culture and especially the small town with all its hostility to its natural surroundings. It has

134

been said earlier that the settler's thoroughness in making a formal rectangular world from the "elegant undress" of the prairies was to have unfortunate physical, social, and psychic consequences. The "House of Bentley," both literally and figuratively, is one of the diminishing squares produced by the geometry of the culture. In a similar and related way, the settlers' implicit faith in the unseen, intangible order, evinced in the earlier fiction as a garden myth, descends ultimately to the sort of repressive, life-denying order which this house represents to the Bentleys. On a rare occasion when Mrs. Bentley buys some steaks to celebrate receiving some of Phillip's back pay, she feels in the house itself the disapproval of all the little towns they have served in, all dominated by their Mrs. Finleys and their gods of propriety:

> . . . there was a curiously unsympathetic stillness through the house. I wanted to celebrate, and the walls disapproved. They seemed to be concentrating on me, trying with all their will power to restrain me to propriety and decorum.
> Every few minutes the windows gave a little rattle of deprecation. Even the smell, the faint old exhalation of the past—it seemed sharper, more insistent, seemed trying to tell me that this is a house of silence and repression and restraint, that it is stronger than we will ever be, that its past will not be mocked. (p. 58)

In his discussion of architectonic symbols, Grove offers the example of Roman architecture as imaginative assertion of a relationship to the world: "The Roman palace expresses the feelings of the householder of its time; it expresses the *human reaction* of its builder to his surroundings: constant fear and constant watchfulness."[9] It is interesting that this example should occur to Grove in a discussion of the West. Although visually the parsonage in Horizon is undistinguished, to Mrs. Bentley it expresses emphatically the view of the 135

Roman householder. Yet like the cultural order it
expresses, the garrison mentality as it has been called,
the house does not protect. It leaks rain, it leaks dust
and drafts, it stands too near the sidewalk and all the
unsympathetic ears of the town. It keeps nothing out but
it holds the Bentleys in, like live bait in a trap.

At the same time that the house is a
microcosm of the town and the threatening world
outside, it is a mirror of the Bentleys' own stifling
personal condition. The "House of Bentley" is a rather
uncertain structure. In the passage quoted above it is
apparent that Mrs. Bentley projects her own fears upon
the stillness of the house. Like the "force or presence"
she thinks into nature, the repressiveness of the house is
further evidence that we create our own fetters, both
collectively and individually.

Houses, of course, are everywhere in the
slighter fiction of the period. In Barbara Cormack's *The
House* (1955), for example, the threads of several lives
are passed through one small house on the prairie; in
Vera Lysenko's *Westerly Wild* (1956), Marcus Haugan's
house, at once sinister and inviting, becomes a sort of
prairie version of Rochester's house in *Jane Eyre*. These
and the minor uses of houses in the work of better
writers need only be acknowledged as examples of what
we are examining. They attest to the development of a
core of essential images of prairie life. It would seem to
be from Ross's use of the house as complex social and
personal image that later house imagery descends. There
are the great brick houses of Margaret Laurence's
Manawaka, for example, with their ponderous imported
traditions. In Kroetsch's *The Studhorse Man*, the
madhouse from which Demeter writes may owe something to the senseless constrictions and incongruities
of the Bentley house. The fact that it is a madhouse may
also say something about the Bentleys' kind of garrison
culture as a vantage point from which to view the prairie
experience.

Just as in Grove's novels the pioneer's

vision is expressed in the house, the house is linked to
the protagonists of the imagination. Grove's inspiration
coming from a derelict house suggests an impression
which grows as one looks more carefully at the imagery
of the prairie realists. The house is ruinous, its grandeur
only suggestive of the size of man's presumption and of
his failure. The same can be said of other images of
man's imaginative vision on the plains: the visionaries,
artists, sensitive children, all speak of the failure of
imagination. The artists are frustrated like Philip
Bentley, the visionaries self-deluded like Niels Lindstedt,
the children misled like Len Sterner. The dominant
culture of the new land seems to be represented,
paradoxically, by a cluster of domestic images suggestive
of ruin: the derelict house, the failing patriarch, the
stifled mother, the frustrated artist, the culturally starved
child, all seem nearer to an end than a beginning.

Grove's pioneers, of course, are a distinctive group and a particularly expressive one. The
"race" for which he claims to be a spokesman includes
only those who "feel the impulse of starting anew," those
for whom "order must arise out of chaos; the wilderness
must be tamed."[10] They should be distinguished from the
ordinary pioneer who came West mainly for economic
advantage. Grove describes men of unusual spirit,
imagination, and vision, and their impulse to start anew
and make order arise out of chaos is both their strength
and their weakness. As we have seen in Chapter Four,
Abe Spalding's vision of Spalding Hall dominating the
prairie, John Elliott's patriarchal vision of generations
growing up around him, Niels Lindstedt's vision of
domestic purity—all tend to blind the visionaries to what
is happening around them. Had they not been so blinded
they might have had a better grasp of the realities of
their lives, but they would have been smaller, less
significant men. To Grove they embody the central
dilemma of the pioneer condition.

Niels Lindstedt is the most subtle and
complex of these visionaries, and an understanding of his 137

character and of the action of *Settlers of the Marsh*
depends upon a recognition of the sequence of his
visions. They first appear at the very beginning of the
novel when Niels and Nelson are battling a snowstorm:
"A vision of some small room, hot with the glow and
flicker of an open fire, took possession of Niels" (p. 17).
This is a prototype upon which Niels's later visions are
built. He has come to Canada because he wants to begin
anew, to expunge the memory of his mother's humiliating servitude in Sweden. Here he believes that life is
simplified, and his simple dream of success and domestic
happiness can be fulfilled. This is the usual form of
Niels's vision:

> . . . a vision took hold of Niels: of himself and a
> woman, sitting of a mid-winter night by the light
> of a lamp and in front of a fire, with the pitter-
> patter of children's feet sounding down from
> above: the eternal vision that has moved the
> world and that was to direct his fate. (p. 36)

The elements of warmth, security, love, and generation
are for Niels clothed in innocence and purity and
watched over by his mother. They are threatened, it
appears, by the allure of Clara Vogel who brings out low
and disgraceful impulses in him. It is said that when
Niels is with Mrs. Vogel "his chastity felt attacked" (p.
52). The virginal Ellen Amundsen is the woman Niels
expects to complete his dream, but her feminine
qualifications are mainly negative. She is demure, chaste,
even cold. The vision itself is essentially a denial of Niels's
own creatural impulses and in effect, of all warm, living
imperfect humanity. No real woman belongs in it, as
Niels at one point realizes: "True, he had seen in his
visions a wife and children; but the wife had been a
symbol merely. Now that he was in the country of his
dreams and gaining a foothold, it seemed as if individual
women were bent on replacing the vague, schematic
figures he had had in his mind. He found this intrusion

strangely disquieting" (pp. 39-40). The inhuman abstraction of Niels's vision is in one way merely childish, but later it has serious consequences. It implies an intolerance of human imperfection, a naive black and white morality, which leads Niels both to marry and to murder Clara Vogel.

There is a version of the dream which includes Clara as the partner, but the tone is changed, as well as some features of the scene; there is no pitter-patter of children's feet, and the two do not sit on either side of the fire. "He was crouching on a low stool in front of the woman's seat; and he was leaning his head on her" (p. 56). There are suggestions, though Grove does not elaborate on them, of sorrow, but also of greater physical intimacy, and of submission to an almost maternal care. The faint suggestion of Niels's mother is curious, since Clara looks to him "like sin" while his mother appears to him as a vision of reproving purity, but Grove seems to have juxtaposed the two deliberately. They are not as far apart as Neils imagines when he turns for support from Clara's tempting to the vision of his mother:

> He longed to be with his mother, to feel her gnarled, calloused fingers rumpling his hair, and to hear her crooning voice droning some old tune. . . .
> And then he seemed to see her before him: a wrinkled, shrunk little face looking anxiously into his own.
> He groaned.
> That face with the watery, sky-blue eyes did not look for that which tormented him: what tormented him, he suddenly knew, had tormented her also; she had fought it down. Her eyes looked into himself, knowingly, reproachfully.
> [Grove's ellipses] (p. 55)

Niels, of course, does not suddenly know any such thing.   139

What he sees in his mother's eyes is his own self-reproach at being sexually stirred by Clara. While he has begun to grant his mother enough humanity to feel his temptations, he does not at this stage understand the look on his mother's face. He will first have to accept his own humanity, and in particular his own sexuality.

If the novel had ended, as some would like it to end, at the murder of Clara, then Niels's character would have been left in this state. The novel would have been about a rather unusual little tragedy of innocence rather than about the always tragic necessity of being disillusioned, of falling from innocence. Having it confirmed that he has married a whore and then killing her teaches Niels nothing essential about humanity, but the total experience, including the need to return and take up life again, does lead him to a qualified acceptance of man in his fallen state, as we can see from two strangely related incidents in the novel.

The first, quite early in the novel, is during the illness of Old Sigurdsen, who has become something of a father to Niels. The old man rambles in his sleep, and fragments of his past drift to the surface:

> Tya. . . . Yo, she laugh . . . and she turn her hips. And her breasts. . . . Hi . . . tya. And she bite! Sharp teeth she had, the hussy. . . ." [sic]
> And this decay of the human faculties, the reappearance of the animal in a man whom he loved, aroused in Niels strange enthusiasms: as if he could have got up and howled and whistled, vying with the wind. (p. 84)

Niels is repelled by the animal in Sigurdsen as he is by the animal in himself, yet his instincts respond sympathetically. Nothing could seem further from his visions of his mother than the senile sexuality which survives in Sigurdsen's delirium, yet the memory of this scene eventually merges with a vision of his mother. It can only happen much later, after Niels's tragic marriage and prison term.

> The vision he saw was that of the homely
> face of his mother. Yet, her features were strangely
> blurred; as if, superimposed on them, there
> appeared those of another; and at last he recog-
> nized these as the features of the old man,
> of Sigurdsen, his neighbour whom he had loved.
> Long, long ago, in another such vision,
> his mother had looked at him reproachfully,
> seriously, warningly.
> And the old man, in the wanderings of his
> decaying mind, had betrayed to him some corner
> of his subliminal memories. . . .
> These two, in vision and memory, seemed
> to blend, to melt together. Both looked at him, in
> this new vision, out of one face in which, now
> his, now her lines gained the ascendency. . . .
> The wistful face of his mother relaxed in a
> knowing smile: yes, such was she who had borne
> him. . . .
> The old man's face took her place: he was
> moving his lips and muttered, "H'm . . . tya."
> [Grove's ellipses] (p. 210)

Sigurdsen suggests both sexuality and creatural decay,
the two things Niels could not accept, in others or
himself, and here they are incorporated into Niels's
guiding vision. The mother's face relaxing into a
"knowing smile" is on the one hand a sad falling away
from the ideal of purity it has been to Niels, but on the
other hand it is a measure of Niels's acceptance of himself
and life. This composite vision is the clearest evidence we
have that Niels has been matured and not simply
subdued by his experience of seventeen years. Critics
such as Saunders would not interpret the last part of the
novel as an unnecessary "happy ending" if they had
attended carefully to the sequence of Niels's visions. The
ending, in fact, encompasses a much larger tragedy than 141

the murder of Clara—the inevitable fall from innocence.[11]

      Niels's life is central to Grove's treatment
not only of the immigrant imagination but of the pioneer
imagination generally. It also embodies the central
insight which shapes all of prairie realism. Niels is
misled, in a sense, by the "virgin" land into believing he
can begin anew and impose order upon chaos in a way
he cannot do. Thus the imagination is drawn out,
pursuing a freedom which does not exist. When Niels
thinks of moving further back into the bush, Grove
applies to him almost the same words he uses later in *In
Search of Myself* to describe his "race" of pioneers:

> He looked upon himself as belonging to a
> special race—a race not comprised in any limited
> nation, but one that cross-sectioned all nations: a
> race doomed to everlasting extinction and yet
> recruited out of the wastage of all other
> nations . . .
>   But, of course, it was only the dream of
> the slave who dreams of freedom. . . . [Grove's
> ellipses] (p. 119)

Grove's visionaries are inevitably tragic. If they lose their
struggle with nature, like Kolm in *The Yoke of Life,* they
are destroyed; if they win, like Abe, they become
obsolete as pioneers and therefore meaningless. And as
idealists they are virtually committed to failure. As Grove
says, "it is one of the fundamental tenets of my creed
that an ideal realized is an ideal destroyed."[12] The
imagination, committing Grove's pioneers to dreams and
visions in this way, is as much a destructive as a creative
force. Taken a step further, it becomes the morbid
sensitivity and self-destructive power of young Len
Sterner in *The Yoke of Life.*

      While Grove's visionaries are a race apart,
it is difficult to separate many of the dreamers, artists,
and sensitive children in prairie fiction. Often they

coincide as they do in McCourt's Neil Fraser, who does not progress from one to the other but remains all three until his death. There are, however, some distinctive features of the relationship each type of character develops with the prairie. The sensitive child is depicted as an alien in an environment specifically hostile to his sensitivity.[13] Consider Grove's Len Sterner, David Torey in Arthur Storey's *Prairie Harvest* (1959), Eric Barnes in Eggleston's *The High Plains* (1938), Lilli Landash in Vera Lysenko's *Yellow Boots,* Charlie in Grove's *Fruits of the Earth* and others too numerous to mention. The child is culturally deprived, usually unable to get even rudimentary schooling without great difficulty, and a stranger to literature, art, and good conversation. Or, worse still, he may be driven to empty observance of the forms of an incomprehensible culture, like young Tom's piano lessons in Ross's "Cornet at Night." Without help at home, the child often has an ally, a teacher or some other bearer of culture who represents the unimagined possibility of escape from the cultural desert, who provides the child with ideals and sets him in pursuit of them. Lilli has the Scottish teacher who helps her to escape from virtual slavery, Eric has the disreputable old geologist who stirs his imagination and eventually provides the money for his escape, and Charlie Spalding is a favourite of old Mr. Blaine, the school teacher. The child's mentor can, at the same time, breed illusion, as the romantic ne'er-do-well Charlie Steele does for Neil Fraser, or by awakening in the child an intellectual life, set him in tragic pursuit of impossible goals, as Mr. Crawford does for Len Sterner. Since the culture bearer does commonly bear an alien culture into the prairie world, he is therefore a disruptive force. This much the prairie realists saw of their problem, but they usually saw the disruption as salutary for the child because the prairie way of life threatens to stifle the young imagination. Ross's "Cornet at Night" isolates the child's anguish briefly and poignantly. There the child's artistic imagination is identified with the beautiful but forlorn   143

note of the cornet played in the immense prairie night by
the impractical young man who is so hopelessly out of
place in the life of the farm. Our pity is not for the
young man, who has chosen, but for Tom, who cannot
choose.

Dreamers in prairie fiction are commonly
tried by the hard realities of prairie life and found
wanting. All the less successful men of imagination in the
fiction—Philip Bentley, Len Stèrner, Neil Fraser—have
the taint of the ineffectual dreamer about them, but
McCourt provides the most extensive study of dreamers.
As R. G. Baldwin says in his article on McCourt, the
main question in the novels is "the place of dreams and
the imagination and romantic aspiration in the world of
reality," and to McCourt the prairie represents the most
uncompromising reality. His primary concern is with
"sensitive people who are experiencing the ordeal of
coming to terms with the land or being crushed by it."[14]
Michael Troy in *Walk Through the Valley* is probably
the only one of McCourt's romantics who successfully
comes to terms with the land. Walter Ackroyd in *Fasting
Friar* does not really have to, though for him, as for Neil
Fraser and for Norah Armstrong in *Home is the
Stranger*, the landscape carries that age-old threat to the
imagination sensed by Butler in 1870. For Ackroyd his
prairie university seems to stand "in fortress-like
isolation, beleaguered by sinister powers of which the
prairie was the visible expression."[15]

When Neil Fraser comes from Ontario as
a boy, the prairie depresses and frightens him. When his
imagination is kindled by romantic books given to him
by the alcoholic remittance man, Charlie Steele, it
blossoms in romantic fantasies totally inappropriate to
his surroundings. He tries to impose these fantasies upon
the prosaic people around him, like Charlie and his
friend's sister Helen: "When Guinevere and Launcelot
rode together they looked for all the world like Helen
Martell and Charlie Steele."[16] Neil's imagination is
obviously not transforming his surroundings but escaping

from them, and instead of abandoning his fantasies as he grows up, Neil creates a continual succession of them. Each stage of his life is robbed of any chance of success by the fantasies it occasions: his infatuation with Moira Glenn, his trip to the university to become a scholar poet, even his return to the farm. "Neil returned to the farm with grandiose schemes half-formed in his mind. The price of wheat was high; all signs pointed to its going still higher. Neil was now in full control of the farm, and half the proceeds were to be his. With any kind of luck he could clean up in a very short time" (p. 135). The not unexpected result is that Neil loses everything in speculations on the grain market.

When Neil finds Moira again after Gil Reardon's death, she makes a choric comment upon his life: "Neil, why don't you try living in the real world for a while? It's more honest—and more heroic" (p. 168). And Neil does try. He returns to the farm in mean, almost desperate circumstances, and he even declares his determination by burning his attempts at writing. But for Neil love is not enough; the temptations of the imagination are too great. When the drought dries up the prairie, he dreams of a Promised Land in the Peace River Country.

> His imagination had leapt over three hundred miles of prairie and parkland to the cool banks of the smooth-flowing Peace, so unlike the turbulent, yellow Saskatchewan, where his acres stretched through miles of woodland and pasture and wheat field, and where his green and white colonial house, standing on a rising point of ground, commanded a magnificent sweep of water stretching into remote, purple distances. (p. 183)

A house is again a prominent part of the dream. When Neil goes to war at the end of the novel, it is with the appearance of escaping rather than facing the challenges 145 of life. And as he lies dying, he sees his death very clearly as a solution to the problem of his living on to disappoint Moira, his son, himself. His reflection that "His death was the only justification for his having lived at all" (p. 217) has the same mawkish quality found in his earliest fantasies. Neil is still the little boy dying heroically to save Helen Martell from stampeding cattle and savouring the pathos of his own funeral.

Neil would presumably have been a dreamer in any environment—we have no evidence that the prairie caused his imagination to turn in that direction, but the monotony of prairie life and the absence of "ghosts," as McCourt puts it, probably drive Neil deeper into his fantasies. At the same time the prairie as McCourt describes it is a setting to test the dreamer severely. The fate of Norah Armstrong in *Home is the Stranger* is a clearer demonstration of this paradox. Norah is an Irish war bride attempting for her husband's sake to accept the newness, rootlessness and rawness of the prairie. She is associated with two of the typical images of the imagination, houses and water. Jim Armstrong's house expresses only the prosaic limits of the farm life to which she finds herself confined. She conceives a fascination for the old, ruinous Anderson house because it suggests both romance and tragedy. There is a third house, the new house Jim intends to build and which becomes a focus for their temperamental differences. Typically Norah would have it down by the river while Jim wants it up on the prairie nearer his work. In general Norah feels pitted against the prairie without adequate support, and when she is left alone in a blizzard her courage fails her. Desperate for protection, she yields to the romantic Irishman who has been trying to seduce her, and in her demoralized state, allows the baby to die in the storm. Norah is not totally defeated even then. The first sign of her recovery in the hospital is her refusal to go away to the coast. She will atone by facing the challenge of the prairie. Her victory, modest as it seems, is not convincing, but it does clarify McCourt's

146

recurrent theme of dreamers failing because they will not face the prairie.

McCourt is probably the only writer to make the landscape itself so threatening. The power of this landscape over the imagination is implicit in his stories, but he is always more conscious of its terrors than of its beauties. What Ackroyd says about the landscape could have come from any of McCourt's novels: "'It's beautiful, yes,' he said 'but sinister. You feel so unprotected somehow. As if there's nothing between you and all the evil in the universe.' "[17] Here is O'Hagan's "darkness unveiled" with a vengeance; the unknown is hostile; the openness is equated with exposure, not freedom; the artist's naming, like the rest of his culture, is a ritual, a spell to ward off all that evil. McCourt can never be completely identified with his characters who see the prairie as totally inimical to the imagination. He acknowledges in characters like Neil Fraser the imagination's share in the failure of harmony between man and land, but he never seems to recognize the transplanted culture he so admires as having a part in that failure.

We must divide artists from mere dreamers in prairie fiction somewhat arbitrarily because the artists usually fail, and when they succeed we suspect the authors themselves of dreaming. In Salverson's *The Viking Heart* (1923), for example, Balder becomes a musician, Elizabeth a fashion designer, but their successes are part of the obvious wish-fulfillment which so weakens the latter half of the book. Lilli Landash in *Yellow Boots* rises to fame as a singer, but again the purpose of her success is so obvious we cannot believe in it.[18] More convincing are those who never demonstrate conclusively that they are artists, like Edwin Vickers in Stegner's *On a Darkling Plain*, who must give up his romantic fantasy about solitude and nature and seek involvement with very prosaic humanity.

Stegner's imagery of prairie isolation suggests a vacancy extending to an eventual dissolution 147

of human understanding, to madness or idiocy. Grove in
The Yoke of Life (1930) exhibits darker more demonic
possibilities of what the creative imagination can do to
itself in isolation. The total disjunction between the
idealized world of Len Sterner's adolescent imagination
and the world he must encounter day by day leads
eventually to a monstrous conviction of sin and guilt
which he can overcome only by destroying himself and
Lydia, around whom he has created an image of purity.
Len may be only a dreamer, but his imagination's
uncanny power to transform his surroundings is evidence
that he might have been an artist in other circumstances.

Just as the imagination seems threatened
in this fiction by the dry sunlit prairie, it is more
comfortably associated with water. There are easy
associations we could expect in any fiction. Stead, for
example, had long been using water as the element of the
emotions when he wrote *The Smoking Flax* and *Grain*.
In these novels it is slightly associated with the
imagination when Calvin Beach begins making his living
by writing after he moves to a cottage by the lake. One
way of associating water with the imagination may have
special significance for prairie fiction. William New, in
his article "Sinclair Ross's Ambivalent World" notes that
in *As For Me and My House* "the recurrent water
images seem to accompany an inability to come to terms
with reality."[19] He refers directly to such scenes as Mrs.
Bentley's walks in the rain by the railroad, but his
observation might be extended to a number of prairie
artists and dreamers. Norah Armstrong, for example,
walks in the rain; she also sits by the river with Brian
Malory, her romantic escape from prairie wifehood. Norah
dreams of losing her child in water, and she does lose her
child in snow through her inability to face the harsher
realities of the prairie environment. It is by the river that
Neil Fraser's hero Charlie Steele takes his life, talking
wistfully about "the setting sun and music at the close."
Len Sterner has a life-long attraction to Lake Manitoba,
148 and it is there he consummates his destructive dream,

taking Lydia on a quiet voyage along the shore, which seems to be a purification of the spirit for the sacrificial death in the tide-race of the narrows at the top of the lake.

The water imagery in *Wild Geese* is mixed. The lake has a strong connection with the rich imaginative and spiritual life of the Icelanders. The water of the northern lake country to which the half-breed Malcolm goes is part of a dream of escape from the only reality Ellen has known, though ironically her refusal of Malcolm is a failure to face the reality of Caleb's tyranny. The association between water and imagination is one which carries over into contemporary prairie fiction. Margaret Laurence's Hagar Shipley, for example, takes her dream of freedom to the old fish cannery by the sea. The dreams of Kroetsch's heroes are linked with rain and rivers, and one of the conspicuous ironies upon his narrator Demeter in *The Studhorse Man* is that he sits writing in a dry bathtub. Water imagery in the work of Laurence, Kroetsch, and Wiebe will be examined in Chapter VII.

It is remarkable how often we return to *As For Me and My House* for the culmination of a theme or a vein of imagery. The figure of the artist and many of the implications of being an artist are all drawn together in the complex fabric of Mrs. Bentley's diary. She herself is, of course, the undeniable artist of the novel, though she may mistake her main talent. Her piano playing may, as she admits, have become wooden, but her diary is an artful creation. True to the confessional form, she structures her experience intellectually to uncover the meanings she wants to reveal, though the process, fortunately for the reader, is not completely under control, and we see beyond her declared intentions.

Philip is the artist about whom we are most concerned—because Mrs. Bentley invites us to be and because he appears to be stifled in his art. He lacks Mrs. Bentley's facility for living in the pettiness and bigotry of little prairie towns and in the pain of his own hypocrisy because, however he may deny it, he is viscerally connected with these towns, as Mrs. Bentley says:

> He grew up in one of these little Main Streets, rebelling against its cramp and pettiness, looking farther. Somewhere, potential, unknown, there was another world, his world; and every day the train sped into it, and every day he watched it, hungered, went on dreaming.[20]

From this Mrs. Bentley draws the mistaken inference that Philip belongs somewhere else, when his present indecision confirms that as a result of his childhood he belongs nowhere. That is, unless he should manage to go back and recover his roots as a culturally deprived child of the prairie. Mrs. Bentley's own relationship to the prairie is explicit: it threatens her, or at least she thinks a hostile presence into it. As a result, she does not realize how ambivalent Philip's feelings are toward these towns through which they pass. She is puzzled by the way he draws the false fronts in one of his endless sketches of a prairie main street: "False fronts ought to be laughed at, never understood or pitied. . . . They ought always to be seen that way, pretentious, ridiculous, never as Philip sees them, stricken with a look of self-awareness and futility" (p. 4). Philip is caught internally in the trap of these small towns, and his art shows it, however he may mouth theories of dispassionate form in painting. An understanding of these sketches and of the depth of Philip's feeling of implication in the sins of the small town might have given Mrs. Bentley a surer understanding of her husband.

      Seeing the prairie child in Philip, we can feel uneasy about his move to the city, even though Mrs. Bentley engineers it as a means of freeing the artist in her husband. As artist Philip may draw more from the prairie than his wife suspects, and here we must explore another facet of the well-considered question of Mrs. Bentley's reliability as narrator and as character judge. At least initially she sees the prairie not as inimical to the artist but as a challenge: "I used to think that only a great artist could ever paint the prairie, the vacancy and stillness of it, the bare essentials of a landscape, sky and earth, and how I used to look at Philip's work, and think to myself that the world would some day know of him" (p. 59). The vast simplicity of forms which she later interprets as a kind of faceless malice, is first a challenge to the creative imagination. She seems to be articulating the central paradox of the imagination on the prairie from the time of W. F. Butler to the present. Later she quotes Philip's remarks about the artist fulfilling himself "'when he looks into a void, and has to give it life and form'" (p. 112). At least to an inexperienced eye, the prairie is more like a void than any other landscape, and the artist, as hero of the imagination, must give it form so that it will not become the threatening chaos Mrs. Bentley sees.

We do not know that Philip actually has the talent to be this "great artist," but at times Mrs. Bentley sees it in him: "I've been sure right from the beginning—sure that there's some twisted, stumbling power locked up within him, so blind and helpless still it can't find outlet, so clenched with urgency it can't release itself" (p. 80). The only unclenching of that power we are shown is during the vacation at the ranch, which is admittedly not bald prairie, but not far from it. It is not foothills country, as it is sometimes carelessly assumed. Since the trees are "scraggly little willow bushes that Philip describes contemptuously as 'brush,'" and the mountains are "four or five hundred miles west," these hills are in mid-Saskatchewan, probably on the Qu'Appelle or South Saskatchewan River. Philip, working appropriately by the water, releases more aspects of himself into his painting than he has done for years. The picture of Laura's horse, for example, is not just a concession to popular taste as Mrs. Bentley

implies; it is a celebration of something more spirited
than the dying horses in his mainstreet sketches, and
Philip's willingness to seek recognition is a further
coming out of his "clenched urgency." The urgency is
still there, but on the ranch it seems to encounter its real
object. Mrs. Bentley remembers "the day he sat bare-
headed in the sun up against the problem of putting
eternity into his hills" (p. 107).

It is hard to escape the conclusion that
Philip's strength as an artist is released by the land, just
as his strength as a man is released by Judith West, the
girl from the land. The day Mrs. Bentley realizes Philip
has been different at the ranch, "bigger somehow, freer,"
(p. 107) she conceives her determination to get him out
of the ministry—but not in the direction of that river.
Back to the city, where *she* came from. The move
promises to be another in the sequence of well-
intentioned misunderstandings which have made up the
Bentley marriage. The new cycle beginning with the new-
born Philip should, logically, initiate a new set of
misunderstandings.

If we are to judge by the action and the
imagery rather than by what Ross's narrator tells us, then
Philip's example would suggest that the prairie challenges
the imagination rather than stifles it. If Philip is stifled, it
is by social forces, and Mrs. Bentley seems to be Delilah-
like delivering him into the power of the Philistines.
Another necessary inference is that the challenge of the
prairie has not been taken up; the "great artist" of whom
Mrs. Bentley speaks has not come forward.

The weight of critical activity bearing
upon this question of the imagination stifled by an
overwhelming environment would suggest that it is at the
heart of prairie fiction, just as the problem of the
frustrated artist is sometimes argued to be at the centre
of Canadian literature as a whole. It may be the central
question at least for the realists we have been examining,
but I am not convinced that the problem has been clearly
articulated in the criticism. The tendency of the

transplanted culture to isolate and confine the individual has not been clearly recognized; the emphasis has all fallen on the hostile environment. For that reason my interpretation of Ross's novel may at first appear perverse. I am insisting that the plight of the imagination is to be blamed not so much on the environment as on a long cultural tradition of inadequate response to it, which is something later writers like Margaret Laurence and Robert Kroetsch are quite explicit about, and something Ross demonstrates, intentionally or not, in *As For Me and My House.*

The tragic pattern of life as outlined by Grove and Ross is obviously only one side of the prairie experience just as the menacing aspect of the landscape is only one of its faces. In its elusive power the prairie remains dream and nightmare, glimpse of creation and darkness unveiled, and both are acknowledged not only by the generation of writers who follow the prairie realists but by the popular novelists of their own time. In the next two chapters I will examine the ways in which these groups counterbalance the tragic view of the realists.

Adventure Romance
and Sentimental Comedy

The ascendancy of the tragic view of prairie life outlined
by Grove and Ross has been largely the work of critics
and the academic community over the past twenty years.
Novels like *Settlers of the Marsh* and *As For Me and
My House* were all but forgotten until they were revived
by McClelland and Stewart's reprints and subsequently
taught in university courses and written about in
journals. Ross's novel, for example, sold only a few
hundred copies in the original and was not reissued until
it appeared in the New Canadian Library series in 1957,
while Nellie McClung's *Sowing Seeds in Danny*, first
published in 1908, was into its seventeenth edition by
1947 and was still being reprinted in 1965. The central
"tradition" of prairie fiction, then, can be considered a
strongly academic one after the 1920's. Until recently
when they began writing about Margaret Laurence and
Robert Kroetsch the critics confined their attention fairly
narrowly to the prairie realists. And their choice is not
difficult to explain. With a laudable partisan spirit they
were looking among their writers for someone not only
of cultural or local importance but of literary merit
which could be recognized beyond his own region.
Realism during the 1950's was the most critically
respectable thing for a novelist to be practicing, and this
may further explain why some critics called their
favourite authors "realists" even when, like Martha
Ostenso, they were writing powerfully romantic fiction.
        The novelists who have become known as
prairie realists did seem to share the dark view of life
advanced by other realists of the day. The type of fiction
which grew popular with American writers such as
Hamlin Garland, Frank Norris, Theodore Dreiser, and
Sinclair Lewis, with its scrupulous attention to
circumstance and its underlying naturalistic assumptions,
was well adapted to portraying man as a fated victim of
a hostile environment. It did not lend itself as well to
celebrating the modest triumphs of the human spirit in
adversity. It is impossible to find a thorough-going
naturalist in Canadian prairie fiction, but literary

convention undoubtedly played a role in developing the stark image of the prairie from Grove onward, as it did in determining which prairie fiction would be taken as central by the critics.

It is equally clear that the "dark" tradition included most, though not all, of the best fiction written about the prairie from the 1920's to the 1950's. The most remarkable exception is the work of W. O. Mitchell, who is acknowledged as a major prairie writer yet whose work has received little attention aside from finding a place in general studies. Ross's work, for example, though only one of his novels and a collection of short stories are considered worthwhile, has been treated in at least eight substantial articles and a book about him has recently been commissioned in the Twayne World Authors Series. Grove's work has brought forth over two dozen articles and five books, while Mitchell has been the subject of only two articles and two published interviews. It is not only that Mitchell's strength is not in the kind of intricacy which compels critical exegesis; it is probably because Mitchell is difficult to place. He belongs to the generation of the prairie realists, and his techniques are in the broad sense as "realistic" as theirs, yet he does not share their tragic view of prairie life or their sense of man as alienated from his environment. The few critics who have paid attention to Mitchell have seemed ill at ease with the buoyant tone of his novels, partly because they have not been sensitive to the conventions within which he is writing. Mitchell writes comedy—and very serious comedy—about prairie man.

Obviously we cannot go on trying to appropriate Mitchell to the "dark" tradition simply because he is a "serious" artist. Yet his *Who Has Seen the Wind* is the nearest we have to an enduring classic of prairie fiction: a novel read for almost thirty years by people who were not paid to read it, and respected by academic as well as popular critics. The success of this novel, quite aside from the inherent limitations of prairie realism, would be a compelling reason for looking

155

beyond the critically accepted tradition at the other
fiction being written about the prairies in the same
period. I am tempted to distinguish this body of fiction
as the "popular tradition," but the phrase can only be
understood with qualifications. Most of these novels did
not achieve a wide popularity, and most were not
produced in a calculated effort to appeal to the tastes of
a mass audience. They are "popular" in the sense that
they do not seriously challenge popular values either
literary or moral. In this respect they contrast with the
work of the realists who were painfully conscious of the
human cost of such popular ideals as progress and
success. Most of these novels were probably written
without a conscious sense of a tradition, but they did
preserve a strong continuity in spirit and substance with
the earlier work of Connor and McClung at a time when
the realists were reacting strongly against that variety of
sentimental romance. Since no one tradition could
include writers as diverse as William Byron Mowery,
Wilfrid Eggleston, and W. O. Mitchell, it will be useful
to distinguish two broad streams of fiction according to
type or genre. The larger and less accomplished consists
of adventure romances of the sort written by Mowery,
Harwood Steele, and S. A. White. The better developed
stream consists of a form of sentimental comedy with
roots in the earlier sentimental romances but with a more
sardonic view of man. What the two have in common
stems from an underlying view of man in relation to the
prairie. Where the realists saw man alienated from his
environment in a fallen world, whese writers held open the
possibility of restoring man's harmony with nature and
of redeeming the wickedness of the world.

      The majority of the adventure romances
involve the Mounted Police, and the Mountie stories
deserve attention because they constitute the nearest
approach we have to a popular art form of the Canadian
West analogous to the American Western. They were
often written for a popular audience and produced in
quantity. Although many were published outside Canada

and many more were too ephemeral to find their way
into major libraries until recently, my own researches
have already turned up some 150 volumes of fiction in
which Mounties play a prominent part. Not all of these
are adventure stories, not all are set in the West, but
most of them are. Sometimes as many as twenty of these
would roll from a single pen, as in the case of William
Lacey Amy's interminable Blue Pete stories. As John
Cawelti explains in his *The Six-Gun Mystique*, popular
fiction of this sort is more than an escapist pastime.[1] It is
that, but it also has a cultural significance beyond its
literary merit, partly because its creation is formulaic
rather than original. He suggests that in modern civilization the mass media and the popular arts have assumed
important functions performed by game and ritual in
older, more cohesive cultures. The formula Western,
in addition to being a kind of game participated in
"for a sense of group solidarity and personal enjoy-
ment and recreation" serves as an acceptable way
of expressing symbolically certain latent motives which
could not otherwise be faced, particularly urges toward
aggression and violence. Most important, it has the function of "articulating and reaffirming primary cultural values."
It is impossible to do justice to Cawelti's analysis in
fewer words than he devotes to it, but for our purposes it
is sufficient to see that the Western formula ritually reaf-
firms the values of progress and individualism by re-
enacting the triumph of civilized order over a savage
wilderness. In the most familiar plot the frontier town,
or civilization, is threatened by savagery in the form of
Indians or outlaws and is saved by a hero who exists
between the two worlds. The hero has the civilized
conscience of the townspeople but the mastery of violence
and the freedom and mobility of the savages. He insures
the assertion of law and order at whatever cost to his
own freedom and love of the wilderness. He is evidently
a simpler descendent of the Daniel Boone or Leatherstocking character described earlier as embodying the basic
tension between the urge to tame the virgin land and   157

the urge to preserve its wild freedom.

A hero like Jack Schaefer's Shane or the Lone Ranger would have been historically inappropriate to the opening of the Canadian West, but the Mountie hero had unique possibilities for a popular literature of the West. As I pointed out in my comparison of Connor's young policeman and Wister's Virginian, the Mountie embodied most of what was distinctive about the early Canadian West. In particular, he represented that faith in an encompassing order which was vaguely conceived to be at once man-made, natural, and divinely sponsored. The formula would have to be different, of course, and would give less satisfying scope to latent aggressive and violent urges, but it could be equally effective in ritually affirming popular ideals of progress and uniquely Canadian conceptions of order. And the game would be just as absorbing, since the historical Mountie was certainly as heroic and adventurous as the cowboy, gunman, or mountain man of the American West. What is equally important to the cultural ritual is that he represented the West as the Canadian people conceived it to be. However wild or rebellious the West might become, they preferred to see it as a haven of peace, order and good government, watched over by a colonial policeman in a red coat: solid, anti-revolutionary, visible proof that order would continue to be something which descended deductively from higher levels of government and society.

The history of the Mounted Police in the West and the North provides endless raw material for adventure romance which would be consistent with the "primary cultural values" Canadians would want reaffirmed ritually. The most familiar anecdote involves a single policeman walking into a camp of armed savages and arresting the chief's son for horse stealing, but for the ideal example I would like to shift briefly beyond the prairie to the men who fought their way through howling snowstorms to establish customs posts in the White and Chilkoot passes in February of 1898.

Of these I especially like the men of Inspector Belcher's detachment who could not fit into his small, leaky customs house:

> Because of the hut's limited size, the rest of the Chilkoot detachment stayed in tents on Crater Lake, battered by a hurricane-force wind and driving snow for ten days non-stop. The conditions were appalling. Attempts to fetch firewood from the nearest source of supply seven miles away had to be abandoned because it was dangerous to move more than a few feet away from the tents. Those containing the supplies were blown down and the others were only kept upright by teams of men taking it in turn to cling grimly to the support poles. To make things even more intolerable, the water began to rise on top of the frozen lake; soon the tents were six inches deep in water, blankets and bedding were saturated and the police crouched on sleighs above the water level trying to snatch some sleep. But on 26 February, the first fine day after the storm, the Union Jack was hoisted and Customs collections began.[2]

Who else would suffer such hardships in order to stop a stream of bewildered goldseekers in the middle of a frozen wilderness and exact customs duties for a government several thousand miles away which was paying them seventy cents a day to supervise one of the richest gold rushes in history? There is something emblematic, something richly, comically, tragically Canadian about such episodes. They illustrate why the Mountie as hero was never understood by a Hollywood film industry accustomed to the kind of heroics Cawelti analyzes. The Mountie is a hero of self-denial rather than of self-assertion, and the possibilities of that style of heroism were latent in some early images of the Mountie, at least in the Canadian fiction.

Those possibilities cannot be seen clearly until we recognize that there have actually been three contending images of the Mountie in fiction. The first to appear was the British Mountie, found as early as 1888 in Roger Pocock's *Tales of Western Life* and later in the work of John Mackie, G. B. Lancaster (Edith Lyttleton), R. W. Campbell, Harold Bindloss, Ridgwell Cullum, and other British adventure writers. He is usually a young adventurer, the black sheep of a good family, losing himself temporarily in the colonies. At the same time, he has the responsibilities as well as the privileges of his class, including a duty to uphold the flag of empire. For him, the empire is the cause to be served, and social caste is the true basis of authority in doing it. The British Mountie declined along with the English market for romantic tales about the farther flung reaches of the empire, but he died hard. He is to be found as late as 1944 in stories printed in *Blackwood's Magazine* as "Experiences in the Life of Dr. H. G. Esmonde Told by Major George Bruce."[3] There he is still doing his colonial duty in the wilds of northern Canada, and falling into what sound suspiciously like East Indian tiger traps in the bush. Such survivals emphasize the fact that the British Mountie was never clearly distinguished from any other colonial soldier on police duty.

The Canadian fictional Mountie, as defined first by Ralph Connor is obviously related to the British. He has strong imperial ties, as we saw in Connor's description of the youngster in the bar room, but he seems more supported by the empire rather than supporting it. He is civil and well-mannered, but gentility of birth is not important; he carries no personal authority by virtue of his birth or anything bred into him. Even physically he may give no impression of personal force, yet he can ride into a howling mob and arrest his prisoner without unholstering his gun because he upholds the law by moral rather than by physical force and by a power which flows out of his selfless devotion to a remote ideal of civilized order. The

Canadian Mountie can be found in the stories of Gilbert
Parker, Harwood Steele, R. Dyker, Walter Liggett,
Amos Moore, and a few contemporary novelists such as
Rudy Wiebe and Ken Mitchell.
    The American image of the Mountie is
again superficially similar, but profoundly different to
the Canadian and British. James Oliver Curwood's *Steele
of the Royal Mounted* provides an example as early as
1911. "Private" Philip Steele is tracking murder suspect
William de Bar across the frozen North.[4] In a chapter
significantly entitled "The Law Versus the Man," they
meet at the absolute end of their resources, fight to
exhaustion and then agree to postpone their dispute until
they have reached shelter and food. In gallantly saving
Steele's life, de Bar is rising above the purely official,
legal differences which separate their common humanity.
By agreeing to allow de Bar a fair fight for his freedom,
Steele is setting aside his duty to the law for his private
sense of fair play. And in Curwood's story, this is right,
because these men are depicted as *larger* than the law—
mere law, blindly imposed from a distance must yield to
justice as arbitrated by the individual conscience on the
spot. Curwood is giving us essentially the morality of the
U.S. frontier, one diametrically opposed to the spirit of
the NWMP. In effect Curwood populates the North with
U.S. Marshals in red tunics. This image of the Mountie
is to be expected in Curwood and lesser known
American writers such as George Goodchild and LeRoy
Snell, but Canadian writers also seem to have taken up
the Western formula. William Byron Mowery's and
Ralph Kendall's Mounted Policemen can often be found
pursuing justice outside the law in a very uncharacteristic
way. William Lacey Amy's hero, Blue Pete, is a mixed-
blood and a reformed rustler who is effective in police
work because like the Western hero he exists somewhere
between the rigid law of the police and the savage world
of Indians and outlaws. The Canadian fictional Mountie
usually stands between civilization and savagery only in a
physical sense; in spirit he is detached from both—above 161

or beyond—and almost as abstract as a principle.

Writers like Amy and later James Beardsley Hendryx, who wrote mainly of the Klondike, took not only the heroes but the basic action of the Western, which is equally inappropriate to the Mountie and the society he represents. The Western hero resolves the conflict between civilization and savagery by a salutary, almost surgical, application of violence which tilts the balance of power in favour of civilized law and order. By reaffirming masculinity, individualism, and the inevitability and superiority of progress he may articulate "primary cultural values" of American society, but his actions could never express the spirit of the Canadian West. The Mountie hero resolves the conflict between civilization and savagery too, but in a different way—not by using violence but by denying it. Consider him at his most typical, say, in the character of Connor's Corporal Cameron preventing the Blackfoot Confederacy from joining the Northwest Rebellion in *Patrol of the Sun Dance Trail* or Harwood Steele's Hector Adair in *Spirit-of-Iron* censuring an armed camp of Indians for interfering with the arrest of a horse-thief, or Rudy Wiebe's Inspector Lief Crozier in *The Temptations of Big Bear* asserting his will in the face of the massed tribes of Big Bear's Plains Cree, fired up after the last great Thirst Dance. In these nerveless confrontations with superior force the Mountie traditionally convinces the savages of at least three things: that the civilized values he represents are so important an individual life is not to be considered beside them; that they are strong enough to have raised him above the threat of violence; that the coming of those values is so inevitable that it need not be enforced by him. In effect, he resolves the conflict by persuading the savage side that no conflict is desirable or even possible. Where the Western hero is in some sense a mediator between the savage and civilized factions, the Mountie is more in the nature of an arbitrator, expressing aptly the Canadian sense of order as a thing imposed deductively.

Despite the Canadian Mountie's potential for a native popular literature, it was the American image that won out in the public imagination. The mid-1920's to the mid-1950's saw not only the growth of prairie realism but coincidentally the heyday of the Hollywood movie, and both of these events may have contributed to the decline of the Canadian fictional Mountie. Hollywood very quickly took the Mounted Policeman to its celluloid bosom. Rudolf Friml's celebrated musical, *Rose Marie*, for example, appeared in a silent version in 1928 starring Joan Crawford. The dozens of serials and feature-length films about Mounties which followed included *McKenna of the Mounted* (1932) with Buck Jones, *Rose Marie* (1936) with Nelson Eddy and Jeanette MacDonald, *Susannah of the Mounties* (1939) with Shirley Temple, and *North-West Mounted Police* (1940) with Robert Preston and Gary Cooper.[5] What novelist could hope to compete with the image making power of the screen or with the appeal these stars had for the popular imagination in that era? Since Hollywood naturally favoured an Americanized and glamourized image of the Mountie, it is not surprising to see that image increasingly dominating the fiction.

At the same time, the more accomplished writers of Western Canada who might have offset the trend by developing the indigenous version of the Mountie were inclined to avoid an image that had been overheated by the glamour of Hollywood. Especially in an era of determined "realism" there seemed no place in serious fiction for a glamourous policeman, and admittedly, it is hard to imagine a scarlet-coated Rider of the Plains breathing the air of Sinclair Ross's Horizon. Edward McCourt was the only prairie realist to cast Mounted Policemen even in minor roles.

The Mountie was partly a victim of his own success and of the vague myths which it inspired. He became a property of an international entertainment industry, part of somebody else's popular culture. He   163 was also a victim of Canada's own cultural history. From about the time of Hollywood's rise it has been apparent that Canadians preferred to buy their popular culture from the United States where it was produced commercially for export rather than grow their own. This preference, ironically, has been described as another expression of that colonial habit of mind the Mountie in part represents. His fate as an authentic literary image may be a small but significant indication of what becomes of the "primary cultural values" of a nation which imports its entertainment, especially in an age when mass media make its influence so pervasive. Some of the effects of this imported popular culture on the contemporary fiction of the prairies will be considered in Chapter VII.

The other stream of "popular" fiction in these middle decades of prairie writing, the sentimental comedies, are closely related to the earlier sentimental romances and in some instances probably owe a debt to writers like Connor and McClung. The heroes and heroines of these stories face obstacles to their desires which are not usually serious enough to be threats to their existence, and these obstacles are overcome in an ending which redeems most of the apparent evil in their world.[6] The action does not, however, take place in a garden world, though the comic resolution may restore one very like it. In Ralph Allen's *Peace River Country*, for example, Bea Sondern and her children live through the worst of depression conditions in Saskatchewan, but the Peace River Country is always before them as a possibility and an ideal to rely on. The comedies are also capable of irony toward their main characters and a generally more skeptical view of humanity, though they stop short of any tragic conception of man's fate. Where the prairie realists saw man as alienated from his environment in a fallen world which demanded sacrifice and atonement, the writers of comedy portray a sometimes wicked world which can be purified by the sentimental reformation of a villain or the driving out of a comic scapegoat. Man is not in any essential way alienated from his environment. His harmony with the land may be obscured by human error, but can be recovered if man is placed in touch with his basically good natural impulses.

The comic genre includes fewer excellent novels than the darker realist tradition, but like the adventure romance, it is of cultural interest beyond its literary achievements. It provides a light view to balance the dark, a recognition of the prairie as still potentially that glimpse of the first creation O'Hagan saw in unnamed country. Its literary significance lies mainly in the fact that it culminates in the work of W. O. Mitchell and can provide a suitable context in which to see his work, but it has also held out an alternative to contemporary writers who cannot accept the prairie experience as defined by the realists of the critically received tradition.

I would include in this genre such books as Wilfrid Eggleston's *The High Plains* (1938), Arthur Storey's *Prairie Harvest* (1959) and the novels of Barbara Cormack, which may include incidental folk humour but are otherwise sober in tone. They are comic in the broader sense because of the nature and resolution of their central action. Eggleston's novel lies very near that end of the scale where comedy blends imperceptibly into romance. His pioneers, the Barnes family, are gradually failing on a homestead in the dryest part of the Palliser Triangle while their gifted son Eric is similarly withering in the intellectual aridity of the isolated farm. Eric is a type of the culturally deprived prairie child, but he is not potentially tragic; unlike Grove's Len Sterner, he is never disfigured by his lack of opportunity. His problem remains external and even his circumstances never appear hopeless. In the end a kind of *deus ex machina* provides the money to send Eric away for an education and to shift the Barnes family to an irrigated farm in the Lethbridge area—a restored bit of Eden.[7]

As comedy moves further from the romantic pole of its axis it develops more of an interest 165

in man as a social animal. The elements of social comedy
had been present in earlier prairie fiction from the time
of Zero's *One Mistake* in 1888, particularly in the work
of British writers, and in this period the interest in
society and manners still appears frequently from an old-
country point of view. C. L. Cowan's *Sandy's Son*
(1931)[8] is a good example. The last half is set in
Winnipeg around the turn of the century and follows the
fortunes of a young Scotsman who comes over, enters
the ministry, wins the girl he loves by dint of devotion,
and thrives in his calling. The setting is a new world
where new beginnings are made—at least by the
right sort of young chaps from home—but otherwise
it could be anywhere. The tone and the assumptions
are all very British, and that could be said too of
John Dolliver Freeman's *Kennedy's Second Best*
(1926) despite the fact that Freeman was a Baptist
minister who came West from Ontario. His hero, a
young minister from a good neighbourhood in Toronto,
comes out to visit his ranching brother in Alberta and
falls in love on the train, in a sequence of narration and
dialogue Freeman sustains very capably. Kennedy, after
his new bride's family is disgraced, thinks of staying in the
West as a kind of "second best" field for his ministry,
but as a reward for his selflessness he is offered the
pulpit of a great church in Montreal regarded as "the
most influential Protestant pulpit in Canada," along with
a stone mansion in Westmount. He is tempted: "He
wondered how many western congregations he would
need to face before he could talk to as much money as
was represented in Metropolitan Church."[9] But Kennedy
decides to go West again because, as he says to his wife,
"Those neglected people of the prairies have captured my
heart. Day and night I think of their terrible spiritual
destitution" (p. 302). The gross materialism of this
author together with his patronizing, missionary
approach to the West is typical of what westerners have
long thought of as the spirit of central Canada, and set
beside Cowan's novel it is a fair indication of why internal

colonialism is so much more offensive than the foreign variety. Certain imperial assumptions which connected earlier with the garden view of the prairie never entirely disappear, especially from social comedy, though by the time of Denis Godfrey's *No Englishman Need Apply* in 1965, for example, the English immigrant is at least registering the fact that the Canadian West regards itself as a separate and distinctive place.

Among writers of a more authentically local comedy, John Beames is one who does not deserve to be as completely forgotten as he has been. His novels are not only structurally comic but humorous, and they are sentimental only in their outcomes, not in tone. His irony toward his characters and their society actually moves him toward that other pole of comedy where it blends into satire, but he does not cross the boundary as Paul Hiebert, for example, does in his *Sarah Binks* (1947). Hiebert's work is a highlight of prairie humour but not properly a part of the stream of fiction we are looking at here. Beames's *An Army Without Banners* (1930) is a novel of pioneering, unusually vivid and precise in its description of the hardships encountered by settlers in what is now northern Saskatchewan around the turn of the century. It includes the effects of hard winters, grass fires, crop failures, and falling markets, but unlike the romances of pioneering which were inclined to be introspective, it represents these effects largely in the visible externals of the pioneers, their speech, manners, and actions. Seen externally in this way the characters are distanced enough for comedy of a stringently ironic tone. Beames's main figures, Billy and Maggie Clovelly, are admirable for their hardihood and their basic goodness of heart, but they are not given any implausible graces of mind or manner as conventional signs of that goodness. Here is a typical incident in their domestic lives:

> Preachers of various denomina-
> tions made their appearance in the settlement.

The women welcomed them, but the general
attitude of the men was one of tolerant contempt. Services were held quite regularly in the
schoolhouses.

Men drove their wives over, but
stayed outside themselves to talk or pitch
horseshoes.

. . . .

Billy refused to attend church.
"When preachers commence to snoop around,
that means the country's all shot," he said. "I
knowed this district was goin' on the bum, but
this proves it. It's gettin' around time for me to
move on."

"Why, Billy, I didn't know you
was such a heathen," said Maggie. "You used to
come to church back in Wenderton with me."

"Uh-huh, I used to go with you,"
grinned Billy. "Back in them days I'd go any
place with you. But I seen a lot of you since then,
an' I ain't so anxious."

They had one of their differences
of opinion, an affair of hot words, shouts, tears,
a swift reconciliation and kisses. But Billy continued not to go to church.[10]

The relations between the Clovellys are never much better
than this; their love does not rise to poetry or ecstasy, but
it endures, which is a considerable testimony to it, given
their circumstances. When Billy finally decides to move
on, alone if necessary, he finds Maggie has already
decided to go with him. Beames creates something
unusual in prairie fiction, a rural social comedy, with
characters a reader can assent to because their
weaknesses and strengths are appropriate to their
situation.

In a later novel, *Gateway* (1932), Beames
turns to a northern Saskatchewan small town where the
people are more pretentious and therefore more

outwardly comic. The story is about a young man, Dick Black, who wastes his inheritance courting the belle of Gateway, an empty and slightly vicious coquette. He is temporarily ruined by a villainous rival, Conquest Gates, but recovers himself in the end. There are romantic shadows behind the ironic tone, but Beames's descriptions of the characters are unflinching and appropriate to the prairie setting. Here, for example, is the villain's father, owner of the flour mill: "Old Tom Gates was in the office too. Failing eyesight and a chronic state of intoxication made it impossible for him to take any active part in the business, but when he was not in the Imperial bar or in a drunken stupor at home, he liked to potter about the place, giving his son the benefit of maxims that had governed his own long and dishonourable career."[11] Of an eager young prairie girl who manages to capture the eligible Dick Black for a dance, Beames says, "her heart was light but her tread was heavy." The small town humanity Beames describes so sardonically is redeemed in the end when the hero, recovering from disgrace and from his own vanity, is accepted by his neighbours and marries the innocent sister of the villain. The outcome is sentimental, some of the dark complications in the plot have nothing to do with the setting, but Beames has a sharp eye for the prairie townspeople, as he has for the homesteaders.

A more complete pattern for sentimental comedy on the prairie can be found in Ross Annett's *Especially Babe* (1942) and Ralph Allen's *Peace River Country* (1958). Centred somewhere between romantic and satiric extremes, they are both inclined to be sentimental in tone as well as in resolution and humorous as well as structurally comic. Like Mitchell's *Who Has Seen the Wind* they are both set in Saskatchewan during the years of depression and drought, yet they radiate a faith in the hopeful endurance of the people and in the reluctance of the prairie to absolutely blight their hope. The kind of humour Annett and Allen find in the prairie people is probably

authentic, since it anticipates much of what Barry
Broadfoot would later catch with his tape recorder when
he interviewed the survivors of the depression for his
book *The Ten Lost Years 1929-1939*.[12] Something about
their ironic view of humanity seems distinctively western.
Annett, for example, shows a typically broad acceptance
of eccentric manners as something insignificant, scarcely
touching the moral nature of a character. In *Especially
Babe*, Big Joe needs credit from the one remaining store
in town:

> In court, an accused person is considered
> innocent until proved guilty. In Hindson's store a
> person is considered broke until he proves
> otherwise. You had to tell Ed what you wanted
> and show him the money to pay for it before he
> would get up out of his chair by the pot-bellied
> stove. That's what six years of drought had done
> to Ed Hindson. He was glad to see you, though;
> there were so few people to talk to.[13]

Hindson is a bit crotchety, but he's all right, and he
proves it by overlooking Joe's clumsy attempt to walk
off with a drum of tractor oil (which is also all right,
under the circumstances) and by eventually giving Joe
the oil he needs.

Big Joe is a widowed farmer trying to
bring his children through the drought and depression
decently, with the somewhat dubious help of "Uncle
Pete," who lives for the home brew he can distill from
potato peelings. Their adventures are episodic like
Mitchell's *Jake and the Kid* stories, so their structure is
clear from the first episode. A long-buried tractor and
granary of seed wheat are uncovered by the wind so that
the family at last have a chance to relieve their poverty.
The weather cooperates with unexpected rain, the
necessary fuel is found, nature and man seem to conspire
with them except for the implement company (the
villain) which has a lien on the crop as soon as it is

harvested. At the last moment, the document proves ineffective because the crop is on Uncle Pete's section, not Big Joe's, and the sheriff's deputy who serves the papers is driven out, fuming and impotent like a comic scapegoat, while the family enjoy the elation of a world freed from the shadow of unjust authority. The ridicule of unjust authority is a consistent feature of these comedies, as it is in so much of the popular comedy we see in film and on television. The weight of the encompassing social order which has grown so oppressive by the time of Ross's *As For Me and My House* is thrown off in these comedies, just as the terrors of the drought wind are disarmed in this episode by having it uncover the tractor it had once buried. As Mitchell has one of his characters say in "The Liar Hunter," "If a man can laugh . . . he's won half the battle."[14]

    Ralph Allen's *Peace River Country* is a darker comedy and humanly more complex. Bea Sondern and her children are seeking the Peace River Country while fleeing her alcoholic husband, Chris, who serves as a villain though without malice. Initially Allen exposes the meanness of human motives around him ruthlessly. His description of the longsuffering Mr. Chatsworth's quietly destructive marriage, for example, is painfully convincing. He also exposes some harmless pretenses and self-deceptions which are dear to everyone's memories of small towns. The passage in which young Harold Sondern talks with reverence to the town baseball hero Dutch Reiseling, while Dutch is totally absorbed in eyeing the shapely figure of Vanny Chatsworth across the street is a rich memory of childhood delusions and one of the funniest scenes in prairie fiction.[15]

    Allen's sentimental resolution of the obstacles to love and happiness is all-embracing and soft. Chris sacrifices his life rather than be a burden to his family; Mr. Chatsworth finally asserts himself so that Vanny can marry Dutch; Mrs. Chatsworth is made the 171

comic scapegoat, exposed and despised for her meddling
in the affairs of both families. The Sonderns do not
reach the Peace River Country; nor is there any
guarantee that they will, but they are seeking now
without fleeing from anything. Casting alcohol as the
ultimate villain may even be appropriate in a prairie
comedy, establishing as it does the tension between
understandable human weakness and the gods of
propriety which rule the small prairie town.

W. O. Mitchell might not be pleased to
find himself associated with these minor writers of
comedy. His work expresses the kind of subtle and
poetic awareness of man's precarious hold on the prairie
we associate with realists like Grove and Ross. His
sensibility enlivens fairly traditional comic forms to a
breadth and depth of human comedy never approached
by Allen or Annett. This is true of the popular *Jake and
the Kid* radio serials which were so much a part of
prairie life in the 1940's and of his second novel, *The
Kite* (1962), but especially of *Who Has Seen the Wind*,
where Mitchell's irresistible urge to affirm life finds its
best expression. More than the other writers of comedy
he faces seriously the questions of man's relationship to
the prairie which preoccupy the realists. And Mitchell is
the only major writer in the period of "prairie realism" to
present a reconciliation of the human spirit with the
prairie. Not that he is less sensitive than his contemporaries to the ambivalent power of the landscape. For
Mitchell too the stillness and vacancy of the prairie
landscape has an elusive beauty and power to excite the
imagination. It is "the least common denominator of nature,
the skeleton requirements simply, of land and sky."[16]
Its paucity of detail imposes few limits on either the
extent or the direction of the feelings it evokes; it holds
the same promise of freedom and the same threat of
chaos it holds in Ross, but by emphasizing the promise,
Mitchell presents in *Who Has Seen the Wind* the
converse of Ross's prairie. The prairie becomes less a
challenge to the imagination than a temptation young Brian

must resist. Though the novel is set in the years of depression and drought, the prairie is not desert or Waste Land. It is fertile with creation and with destruction, a delicate balance of contradictions:

> It lay wide around the town, stretching tan to the far line of the sky, shimmering under the June sun and waiting for the unfailing visitation of wind, gentle at first, barely stroking the long grasses and giving them life; later, a long hot gusting that would lift the black topsoil and pile it in the barrow pits along the roads, or in deep banks against the fences. (p. 3)

The wind is the active spirit, the will of the prairie which controls the balance, quite capriciously; yet there is nothing in the tone to suggest a wilderness indifferent to men either. Nature is simply indifferent to man's moral designs; natural order has nothing to do with moral order.

Brian O'Connal is an imaginative child. He begins his search for God at the age of four, for example, and the vividness of his imaginings gets him into some trouble when he holds too stubbornly to the reality of his little friend R. W. God, B.V.D. But Brian is not simply given an overactive fancy; he has moments of transcendental awareness, the most minutely described on a "very Sabbath" Sunday morning when he is about six:

> A twinkling of light caught his eye; and he turned his head to see that the new, flake leaves of the spirea were starred in the sunshine— on every leaf were drops that had gathered during the night. He got up. They lay limpid, cradled in the curve of the leaves, each with a dark lip of shadow under its curving side and a star's cold light in its pure heart. As he bent more closely over one, he saw the veins of the leaf magnified under the prefect crystal curve of the drop. The

173

barest breath of a wind stirred at his face, and its
caress was part of the strange enchantment too.
Within him something was
opening, releasing shyly as the petals of a flower
open, with such gradualness that he was hardly
aware of it. (p. 107)

This recurring experience which Brian
comes to think of as "the feeling" is his moment of
transcendence, of apocalyptic contact with the divine, his
"intimations of immortality" as the school principal Mr.
Digby would have it. In the perfection of the dewdrops,
the unity of the crystal sphere, Brian has intuited a
oneness which he goes on searching for through the rest
of the novel. Later the same day, in church, he equates
the feeling of his newfound natural religion with the
purpose of the formal worship he is attending. When the
congregation sings "Holy, holy, holy," he interprets it to
mean "unbelievably wonderful—like his raindrop—a
holy holy holy drop lying holy on a leaf" (p. 111). He
believes the presence of the Chinese children and the
Bens in the same congregation with Mrs. Abercrombie
and Rev. Powelly betokens the same holy oneness he has
felt. All, of course, is irony, and Brian has yet to learn
the dangers of his naive assumptions of the unity of man
and nature, of the harmony among men, and of the
benevolence of nature.
Brian at first experiences "the feeling"
only in nature and identifies it with the prairie, the wind,
and God. This is to be expected, since Brian has been
powerfully stirred by the prairie ever since his first
encounter with it. Mitchell's very vivid descriptions of
these encounters have several qualities usually found in
romance or in lyric verse—a freedom of metaphor
opening up expanses of feeling and generating a warm
identification with the young hero. Here is one of Brian's
first impressions: "The hum of telephone wires along the
road, the ring of hidden crickets, the stitching sound of
grasshoppers, the sudden relief of a meadowlark's song,

were deliciously strange to him" (p. 11). There is, through the wind especially, a romantic animism in Mitchell's prairie: "And all about him was the wind now, a pervasive sighing through great emptiness, unhampered by the buildings of the town, warm and living against his face and in his hair" (p. 11). Quite naturally the boy identifies his "feeling" with the prairie and not with the town.

Mitchell's town, like Ross's Horizon, is mean, petty and bigoted. Just as sharp little Mrs. Finley rules over Horizon, Mrs. Abercrombie the banker's wife rules this town, and with her servant the Reverend Mr. Powelly she imposes a regularized form of decency which stifles life and which is never without malice. It is strange that Mitchell should twice refer to Conrad's *Heart of Darkness* in connection with the iniquities of this town. The phrase in Conrad's novel signifies a giving way to a dark primitive nature within, while the Mrs. Abercrombies seek to drive out natural people like the Bens and to deny all natural impulse in themselves as though they feared it. Brian, because he is a child, is unaware of the deeper villainies of the town, such as their bigotry in turning out Mr. Hislop, their efforts to imprison the Young Ben, or their hounding the old Chinese to his death. We see them through older characters, and some critics have accused Mitchell of losing his focus by shifting away from his main character to develop the social comedy of the town, but they overlook the fact that there are two protagonists in the action, Brian and Digby the school principal.[17] Mitchell develops a second focus of this sort in most of his fiction; there is not only the Kid, but Jake, and in *The Kite* there are David Lang and Daddy Sherry. It is a method of pinpointing reality by triangulation, the younger and the older consciousness at work on an experience—possibly even the younger and the older Mitchell—so that in *The Vanishing Point* (1973) you do find the older Sinclair looking back at the younger. Brian is more important, but Digby is indispensable, not   175

only to reveal the character of the town but to provide
an access to Brian's character. The threads of their
separate actions touch at vital points and are finally
woven together at the end when Brian begins to grow up.

Brian himself encounters only the
outworks of the town consciousness in the regimentation
of the school and especially the discipline of the embit-
tered old spinster teacher who inspires in him presentiments
of a mean and spiteful God. The God in nature that
Brian himself visualizes requires a great deal of imaginative sweep, and the town is an enemy to imagination. Brian's
companions Arty and Fat are true children of the town,
as can be gathered from their version of the book's
title verse.

> "Who has seen the wind?" Fat chanted.
> "Neither you or I," returned Brian.
> "But when the trees bow down their heads—"
> "Nobody gives a damn," Art finished up.
> Fat laughed. (p. 191)

Brian, needless to say, cannot share his "feeling" with his
playmates.

Brian is at first tempted to follow his
"feeling" in the direction of the prairie, to become like
the young Ben whom he identifies with the prairie. After
seeing the strange boy who lives on the prairie Brian says
he does not want to live in a house, that he wants to
have "prairie hair" like the young Ben's. But Brian is
warned back by a number of things. He begins to see the
moral ambivalence of the prairie. The terror of the
young Ben's merciful killing of the tailless gopher and his
attack on Arty for mutilating the animal, Brian can ride
over with a kind of exultation in animal spirits; the later
sight of the gopher's putrescent and fly-blown body he
cannot. "Prairie's awful, thought Brian, and in his mind
there loomed vaguely fearful images of a still and
brooding spirit, a quiescent power unsmiling from
everlasting to everlasting to which the coming and

passing of the prairie's creatures was but incidental" (p. 128). Though he does not long retain any sense of cosmic indifference, Brian does gradually separate natural process from ethical process. There is another less tangible fear that assails him the night he runs away from his Uncle Sean's farm. It is the first time he has been quite alone, away from the town, surrounded by the prairie at night.

> He was filled now with a feeling of nakedness and vulnerability that terrified him. As the wind mounted in intensity, so too the feeling of defenselessness rose in him. It was as though he listened to the drearing wind and in the spread darkness of the prairie night was being drained of his very self. He was trying to hold together something within himself, that the wind demanded and was relentlessly leaching from him. (p. 236)

Because of Brian's sensitive imagination, the prairie has the power to excite him, but also a frightening power to annihilate him. Brian can quite happily return to the human security of the unimaginative town.

Brian returns, too, because he is proven too social an animal to belong entirely with the prairie. He feels the growing responsibility of belonging with his family, particularly when his father dies, and he also needs thinking, articulating human beings like Mr. Digby. Total rejection of the town is represented for Brian by Saint Sammy, "Jehovah's hired man," who lives in a piano box on the prairie raising a herd of Clydesdale horses as pets. There is something about the immediacy of Sammy's faith, the fervour of his Jeremiads on the town as "Sodom and Gomorrah" which excites Brian, but the boy always turns back to the sane, if corrupt town. "Listening to Saint Sammy, he had been carried away by the fervor of his words; He had felt for a while that he was closer, but it couldn't be right. Saint

Sammy was crazy, crazy as a cut calf, Uncle Sean had said. A thing couldn't come closer through a crazy man gone crazy from the prairie" (p. 198). The Saint Sammys and the Bens are no acceptable alternative to the Mrs. Abercrombies and the Rev. Powellys of the town. Brian, while drawn in both directions, finds his element among the people on the edge of the town, Milt Palmer, Mr. Digby, Miss Thompson, and with his Uncle Sean who is spiritually on the edge of the prairie. Brian's grandmother is another vitally important influence, with her years of pioneer experience of living with the land and with her stake in the human community.

Brian's most significant experiences in fact occur not in the town or on the prairie but at the point of contact between the two, nature's order and man's. Most of his transcendental moments occur on the edge of town and the edge of the prairie, and the action of the novel grows out of the tension between the claims they make upon Brian, with the imagination drawing Brian in the direction of the prairie, and common sense and social instinct drawing him back toward the town. His compromise of becoming a "dirt doctor," an intermediary between the two, resolves that tension. This resolution ought to be a victory for the imagination. It is certainly an affirmation of life. The last pages of the novel become a vivid romantic lyric on the prairie as a living cosmic organism. But in some respects the ending is a disappointment because the harmony is achieved only by a limitation of the claims of imagination. Brian does not, like his "cousin" Huck Finn, hold a place in his mind where he is always "lighting out for the Territories." The temptations of the imagination are put quite firmly behind Brian. There is a scene in which he tells Digby, "I don't get the feeling any more." Digby thinks of Wordsworth's "Intimations" ode and says, "Perhaps you've grown up" (p. 296). Growing up seems to mean not only accepting social responsibilities but also accepting spiritual compromise, mediation between conflicting forces in place of the imagination's search for a divine unity.

The ending provides a very convenient rounding out of the action, especially the action in town where some very unpleasant things have happened. It is not until we examine this ending that we recognize with a start that Mitchell belongs not in the grim tradition of prairie realism but in the popular tradition of sentimental comedy. His *Jake and the Kid* stories, *The Kite*, everything but his most recent *The Vanishing Point*, which will be discussed later, is characterized by this same final, total affirmation. *Who Has Seen the Wind* is the consummate example of the popular tradition, with the classic shape of comedy.[18] It begins with the good people, Digby, Miss Thompson, Hyslop, excluded from their proper community, and Brian in particular seeking a way into the community of both man and nature. The human community is at first too bigoted, petty, and hypocritical to join, but in the school-board meeting at the end, Mrs. Abercrombie is ritually driven out, a scapegoat with all the sins of the town loaded upon her. The community thus purged is a fit place to welcome the sympathetic characters. (Forgotten are the firing of Hyslop, the attempts to imprison the young Ben, the hounding to death of old Wong.) At the same time, the prairie is humanized in the comic scene of Saint Sammy calling down the wrath of God on miserly old Bent Candy. Evidently man was never seriously alienated from his natural environment, and in becoming a "dirt doctor" Brian is joining forces with Uncle Sean, who has fairly explicit plans for returning the prairie to the state of a garden.

Anyone reading the novel carefully, of course, would know that Mitchell has no delusions about the prairie blossoming as the rose or the townspeople putting away pettiness and bigotry. What his comic resolution offers is a new beginning in hope, sparked by a moment of ritual reaffirmation of the good in man and nature. The habit of beginnings, of starting again, is deeply ingrained in the western consciousness, and comedy is its necessary expression. As Mitchell himself

would say, it is illusion, like all art, but no nearer to
delusion than the tragic form of Grove's novels. In fact,
Mitchell's good-humoured irony at man's failings sets off
the eternal humourlessness of the realists which amounts
almost to narrowness, a lack of awareness of the broader
human comedy in their settings. Without intending to
diminish the value of the intensities they create, I would
say that the realists generate an unrelieved grimness of
outlook which no healthy human being could long
sustain. Even in Ole Rolvaag's *Giants in the Earth*, a
book which invites comparison especially with Grove's
work, there is a wealth of gently ironic humour.[19] The
non-fiction accounts of the Canadian prairie also testify
to the pioneers' capacity for mirth and joy, and in a
book such as James Gray's *The Winter Years* we can see
how human compassion and a sense of humour survived
even the darkest years of depression and drought.[20]

The methods of the realists may have been
well suited only to portraying the prairie of those who
were alienated from the land, and in that respect they
reflect the limitations of the ethnic group they represent.
It is easy to forget that the English-speaking were only
one of several ethnic groups settling the plains. Though a
dominant minority, they probably had a poorer record of
adaptation to the plains than other groups such as the
German, Slavic, or French. A look at the French-
Canadian fiction of the prairies reveals a different
fundamental attitude toward the progress which was
alienating man from the land. While Stead, Ostenso, and
Grove were chronicling the opening of the West, Georges
Bugnet, in his *Nipsya* and Constantin-Weyer in his *A
Man Scans his Past* were lamenting the end of the
West.[21] They clearly identify with a different West, one
which was not dominated by man and machine. In
Bugnet and later in Gabrielle Roy there is a great deal of
cyclic imagery suggesting that man is a part of the
elemental life of the plains. The English-language fiction
has less imagery of such cyclic involvement in eternal
processes. Man is there· caught in linear time, the kind of

time defined by progress.[22] When man identifies with nature as a beneficent order, man and nature are to be united in some moment of apocalyptic perfection, not in the slow round of the days.

Once we begin to look for what is missing from prairie realism we discover some surprising gaps. During the 1930's two national political parties were formed in Saskatchewan and Alberta, yet with the exception of McCourt's *Music at the Close,* these novels give us practically nothing of the very active political life of the time. And where are such staples of prairie life as the cooperatives, grain growers' associations, and other farm organizations? Where is the Prairie Farm Rehabilitation Administration? The radio? The *Winnipeg Free Press*? Where, in effect, is the outside world? Like most English-Canadian fiction, the prairie novel is inclined to be private and domestic rather than public. Compare *As For Me and My House*, for example, with Sinclair Lewis's *Main Street*. While Ross's novel is private, confessional, Lewis's is public, drawing in farm movements, making generalizations about the Midwest, slipping even into essays on moral and cultural issues. *As For Me and My House* is, in my opinion, the better novel because of the discipline induced by its very limitations of scope, but that is another matter. We must recognize the nature and limitations of its subject if we are to avoid being misled by the term "realism" into expecting a balanced or comprehensive view. The missing elements, from the United Farmers of Alberta to Eaton's catalogue, are only fragments which suggest whole areas of prairie life untouched by the realists.

The comedies and to a lesser extent the adventure romances help to expand the portrayal of prairie life, but up to the mid-1950's, they share some of the most basic limitations of the realist novels. They too tend to be private and domestic, and in their own way confined within the assumptions of the dominant ethnic minority on the plains. It is not until the 1960's and 1970's that we see, among the younger writers, a strong 181 consciousness of the limitations of the earlier fiction. They live, of course, in a different world, literary and factual, but they also have a new consciousness of the old experience and a desire to find a fictional form for it. When they draw upon the older fiction it is not only the realists but what I have described here as the popular tradition. Robert Kroetsch and Ken Mitchell, for example, write comedies; Rudy Wiebe is conscious of the adventure romances and the history they just fail to bring to life; Kroetsch's novels search out the spirit of the West and the mythology that has attached to it, particularly through the effects of popular fiction and the entertainment media. All the younger writers draw areas of experience silently excluded from the earlier critical tradition into their very deliberate re-examination of the prairie past.

Contemporary
Fiction

Prairie novelists in the 1960's and 1970's have begun to
look back, and their desire to re-examine the prairie past
is understandable. To begin with, the West of which they
write, the agrarian West, is past, absorbed into the new
urban-industrial environment as "Agribusiness." They
could have taken this as an occasion to view it
sentimentally, as a lost heroic age, in the way Wister
treats the frontier West in *The Virginian*, but instead
they see it as a completed cycle, the record of man's
faltering attempts to make himself at home on the land,
and as such it invites reflection and re-interpretation.
This circumstance has had a profound effect on the new
fiction, but does not in itself explain the urgency with
which the novelists are questioning the past. They may,
as Margaret Laurence says, feel a need to come to terms
with their roots or ancestors. The present generation of
writers, including Laurence, Robert Kroetsch, and Rudy
Wiebe are the first who can claim ancestors in the prairie
soil, but then Sinclair Ross and W. O. Mitchell have also
turned, in the 1970's, to a more retrospective approach.
Evidently the end of the older West has coincided with a
time of historical curiosity when Canadians at last
consider their local roots worth understanding.
        The current popularity of first person
narrators and the confessional form would also
encourage retrospective fiction, but this again would not
explain the prairie novelists' consistent skepticism about
the past as given. It is as though they regarded their past
as something that must be rediscovered because it has
been somehow misrepresented to them. Laurence
articulates this attitude in a sequence at the beginning of
her last novel, *The Diviners*. Her narrator, Morag Gunn,
is reviewing her memories of her parents who died when
she was very young. By reflecting upon a series of old
snapshots and the scenes they represent, she sketches an
early life for herself consistent with popular notions of
what childhood should be, then says, *"And that is the
end of the totally invented memories. I can't remember
myself actually being aware of inventing them, but it*   183

must have happened so." (Laurence's italics) Her
parents, the ancestors who might have helped to define
her, are "Two sepia shadows whose few remaining
words and acts I have invented."[1] As a novelist,
Morag knows that the memory creates, that there
is no accessible past which has not been creatively
shaped by human desires and convictions. In Morag,
Laurence presents the self-reflective image of the
contemporary novelist's dilemma. What to do with the
invented past, not the personal past only but the
collective past which surrounds it. As a girl, Morag has
been confronted with three versions of the history of the
West: school history, her uncle Christie's Scots legends of
Piper Gunn and the Selkirk Settlers, and old Lazarus's
tales of Rider Tonnerre, a legendary hero of the Metis
nation. Morag comes to realize that none of these is
"true" in the sense that her school history purports to be,
though each is true to the human spirit which created it.

A similar skepticism about the given past
can be seen in most of the recent novels. In *The
Temptations of Big Bear*, Rudy Wiebe is creating an
Indian consciousness of a phase of history we have
known only within a White, Victorian frame of mind. In
W. O. Mitchell's *The Vanishing Point*, Carlyle Sinclair is
slowly and painfully learning to see his White world of
Victorian assumptions in an entirely new perspective.
The novelists do not appear to be interested in
substituting a revised version of prairie history, only in
freeing their past from the constrictions of that British
imperial view which has dominated the development of
the prairie in fact and fiction. And like contemporary
novelists elsewhere, they seem to be exploring the
relationship between history and fiction, between the
fictions of the historian and the other fictions with which
man attempts to order the chaos of experience. In
Kroetsch's work especially, where there is a constant
tension between historical and legendary or mythic
realities, there is also an ironic awareness of the
184 storyteller's own creative tendency to shape the past to

his desires.

A sense of the prairie as past haunts contemporary fiction, not in a nostalgic or elegiac tone, but in persistent imagery of death and burial. Laurence's Hagar Shipley is compared with a stone angel in the Manawaka cemetery; her Rachel Cameron in *A Jest of God* lives over her father's mortuary. Wiebe's *Big Bear* chronicles the death of the independent Cree nation. George Ryga's narrator in *Ballad of a Stone Picker* ends by burying his own father. Kroetch's Johnny Backstrom, the undertaker in *The Words of My Roaring*, appears again in *Gone Indian*, a novel Kroetsch had first entitled "Funeral Games"; *The Studhorse Man* ends with Hazard Lepage's death which is also the death of a phase of western history; Anna Dawe in *Badlands* goes in search of her dead father who has spent his life searching for the bones of dinosaurs. There are coffins everywhere in Kroetsch. This imagery does not always carry the simplest implication of the death of the agrarian prairie. In Kroetsch, Laurence, and Ryga it can also imply the hard but necessary death of something else in the prairie milieu, often an aspect of the transplanted culture which has hampered westerners in coming to terms with the land. Johnny Backstrom, for example, contends with Old Doc Murdoch, the transplanted easterner, for dominance of the town. Backstrom is appropriately an undertaker because he must bury the paternal influence of the old eastern establishment and launch the West on a period of self-reliance, however crude it may be. The choice of imagery suggests not only the moribund state of the old culture but that failure to adapt which we have been examining: no metamorphosis is possible, nothing short of a death and rebirth into one of the West's endless beginnings.

An accompanying change can be seen in familiar archetypes of prairie fiction. Houses, for example, are inclined to be more incongruous and more ruinous than ever. They are still cultural expressions, and they continue to express dynastic ambitions, like the 185

homes of Laurence's exiled Scots. It is important that
Jason Currie's house in *The Stone Angel* is one of a
"half a dozen decent brick houses" in Manawaka. It is
equally important that the Connor house in *A Bird in
the House* is "sparsely windowed as some crusader's
embattled fortress in a heathen wilderness,"[2] because the
houses still embody a reaction of hostility and fear
toward the environment. That reaction in current fiction
becomes more conscious and explicit, just as Laurence's
heroine, Vanessa, becomes acutely conscious of the
attitudes the house embodies but remains powerless to
change them in herself. Laurence's houses are hardly a
celebration of the tradition Vanessa recognizes as her
own. The mortuary Rachel Cameron grows up in only
makes explicit the sense of something moribund in the
heavy propriety of all the brick houses on Laurence's
prairie. The absurd reduction of Laurence's imperial
houses is the mansion in which Kroetsch's studhorse man
keeps his horses. Its English builder, Derek Hardwick,
having completed it on the day Queen Victoria died,
"intended to keep everything intact as it was on the day of
its completion."[3] Taking the news that the Great War
was over as a German plot to make him surrender his
"fort," Hardwick had barricaded himself in and
apparently drowned in a well he was digging in the
cellar—a wild image of the garrison culture overcome by
its own repressed subconscious.

     Water imagery in the new fiction is also
inclined to be sophisticated, often ironic, like the water
beside which Rachel Cameron acts out her passion for
Nick Kaslik, or the rain Johnny Backstrom promises the
farmers in *The Words of My Roaring*. In the midst of
the drought of the 1930's the rain carries all the
suggestions of fertility it has in the medieval romances
which echo ironically through the pages of the novel.
Johnny has other mock-heroic trappings such as a
mysterious birth and he is running on the ticket of the
messianic William Aberhart. He takes on the traditional
quest of restoring fertility to a Waste Land when he

rashly asks a heckler at a rally, "Mister, how would you like some rain?"[4] His comic predicament is relieved by rain on the night before the election, but it is typical of the imagery in contemporary fiction that the rain has a sadly ambivalent value. It wins Johnny the election but confirms him in his fraud; it restores the people's hopes without giving them any substance. It is, like the water in the earlier fiction, identified with dreaming which escapes unpleasant realities, yet as a final twist, we recognize that what Backstrom's depression-weary constituents need most is hope, given on any basis whatever.

In contemporary fiction the typical balance between prairie man and prairie woman also shifts. Patriarchs still appear, like Deacon Block in Wiebe's *Peace Shall Destroy Many* and the hardened old Baptist father in *First and Vital Candle*. Laurence too has her stern Old Testament, Scots Presbyterian fathers like Jason Currie, who erects the stone angel over his wife's grave to "proclaim his dynasty," but in Laurence's novel the shift can be seen. In the generation after the pioneers, Hagar is cruelly strong while Bram Shipley gives in gradually to weakness and misfortune. Their sensitive son John is the victim of his father's failure as well as his mother's domination. What might be called the disappearing father emerges in current fiction as a consistent pattern. Rachel Cameron's father dies, leaving her tied to a domineering and dependent mother; in *A Bird in the House* Vanessa's father dies when she is a child, leaving her to the authority of her stubborn old pioneer grandfather; Morag's father is a "sepia shadow" in an old snapshot, and her foster-father Christie is a weak substitute, a man she can eventually love but never quite respect. In Kroetsch's novels the vanished fathers are emphasized by the way in which his characters search for substitutes. Johnny is in an uneasy filial relationship with Doc Murdoch; Demeter seems to be trying to make a father out of Hazard Lepage; Jeremy Sadness, whose father is said to have taken one look at him and disappeared, is dependent upon Professor Madham. In 187

Mitchell's *Vanishing Point,* Carlyle Sinclair's remembered childhood is dominated by his aunt Pearl rather
than by his father who seems to have ceased all vital
contact with the boy at an early age.

  The disappearing father is far more
universal than the prairie patriarch ever was, and his
range of significance is correspondingly broader, but
each novelist uses the figure in a roughly consistent way.
The waning male figures in Laurence give way to a
growth in the strength and independence of the women.
The same is true to a degree in Mitchell, but more
significantly the lost fathers in *Who Has Seen the Wind,*
The Kite, and *The Vanishing Point* leave their sons to
approach the mysteries of maturity and manhood alone
without the appropriate guide or initiator. In Kroetsch
the loss of the father does not seem as traumatic in itself
as the search that ensues. His characters' relationships
with surrogate fathers are shot through with an oedipal
bitterness and hostility. Demeter appears to make a
father of Hazard in order to bring about his death (as
the name Proudfoot suggests); Johnny is more reluctant
to destroy Doc Murdoch because he is still childishly
dependent upon him. The extreme example is Jeremy's
relationship in *Gone Indian* with the slightly sinister
Madham, who sends him on his perilous quest for the
spirit of western virility. If the true father, as Mitchell
suggests, is a figure of authority from whom the child
seeks approval and guidance into manhood, then
Kroetsch creates the false counterpart, a threatening
master who forces Jeremy through dangerous initiation
rites.

  In Sinclair Ross's latest novel, *Sawbones
Memorial,* Doc Hunter is also a surrogate father to both
the Ukrainian boy, Nick, and the town's leading citizen,
Duncan Gillespie. There is nothing demonic about Doc
Hunter, yet there is the suspicion of a manipulative hand
in his secret decision to favour the young outcast Nick,
and the pattern is more pronounced in Ross's earlier
novels. Philip Bentley, as the bastard son of an intellec-

tual small-town preacher, has spent his life trying
to live up to, yet live down, his heritage, and in the
orphan boy Steve he evidently sees an opportunity to set
another generation to work at the same fruitless task. In
The Well old Larson attempts to make a son of the
young drifter Chris in response to his own needs. For
Ross, in fact, the failure of any natural father-son
relationship is a major concern and one of his most
consistent themes long before the disappearing father
becomes a feature of contemporary fiction.

      Whatever particular themes disappearing
fathers may suggest in individual novels, the very
pervasiveness of this motif in post-pioneer fiction is
significant in itself. Nothing could more emphatically
declare the end of the patriarchal prairie of earlier
fiction. The missing or false fathers, like Morag's "sepia
shadows" also suggest dead, lost, or obscured
antecedents. The search for a father is, of course, a
classic form of search for one's own identity, but there is
a more specific implication here of lost continuity with
the past. The current generation, looking for the
ancestors who might help define their present identity,
are shown like Pip in *Great Expectations*, searching the
gravestones of lost parents.

      Time takes on a new importance when the
fiction is turned back upon the West as a completed
cycle. The prairie becomes less a thing "out there" which
must be shaped physically as well as imaginatively and
more a territory within the psyche which must be
explored and understood, and in this internal prairie that
contemporary novelists explore, time is the essential
dimension they must travel. Demeter Proudfoot makes
such a discovery while composing the biography of
Hazard Lepage; he says, "It is then *time* that I must
reconstruct, not space."[5] Kroetsch probably intended
Demeter's statement to comprehend more than the
realization that Hazard exists only in the past, in his
biographer's mind. Hazard as the last of the studhorse
men is significant in relation to the time rather

189

than the space he passes through, and like Demeter, contemporary novelists are discovering time as the missing dimension of prairie experience. In the earlier fiction, not only is space a dominant visual impression and a constant practical concern, but it also provides the metaphors for intangible qualities. In *As For Me and My House*, for example, the Bentleys' failure and frustration is imaged in a series of receding "horizons," while the promise of change is suggested by the spatial image of the railroad running beyond those horizons. The fiction may here reflect a quality of the "westering" mind, which seeks spiritual change in physical movement without much concern for time. As Kroetsch says of westerners in a conversation with Donald Cameron: "There's very little credence given to the notion that we exist in history, in time."[6] Kroetsch is talking about time in human dimensions, measured by the movement of human affairs, the reach of human memory, the descent of generations. The westerner tends to have rather an apocalyptic sense of time, to situate himself in relation to the gigantic movements of Christian history of the world—creation, the fall, redemption, the apocalypse. That is certainly true of fictional westerners, as we can gather from successive views of the land as Eden or the wilderness. In *As For Me and My House*, for example, the dust storms obviously belong to the drought of the 1930's but the year is deliberately vague. The days are marked but we are not conscious of a movement of history beyond them. Grove's heroes are confident that they set foot on the plains on the last day of creation, but they gradually discover they are taking part in the story of the Fall.

When we compare prairie fiction with, say, that of the Atlantic provinces the contrast is striking. The characters of Charles Bruce and Ernest Buckler are preoccupied with time as measured by the generations that inhabit their world, alive or in memory. In the stories of Bruce's *Township of Time* there is an intricate multiple awareness of time, as one generation is imposed upon another.[7] They have what the western fiction most often lacks, a sense of time as cyclic, eternal in its periodic repetition of day, season, generation, but they also show the encroachment of the linear time of the new industrial society. The most complete example is Buckler's *The Mountain and the Valley,* in which David is torn between his youthful, individualistic linear view of time as something he must catch before it passes him by, and the old tribal, cyclic view of time which governs the valley people who are so close to the land.[8] Closeness to the land may be essential to that organic sense of time. Until recently not enough generations had yet been buried on the prairie to give time its full human dimensions, so its emergence in contemporary fiction is a very natural result of the writers having a human past to reflect upon. The present generation of writers begin to search through past time and to explore the significance of time. In Laurence's Manawaka there is even a sense of generations living through each other, as when Vanessa recognizes her grandfather in herself: "I had feared and fought the old man, yet he proclaimed himself in my veins,"[9] or when Stacy in *The Fire Dwellers* or Morag in *The Diviners* feels a hereditary guilt for the injustices done the Tonnerre family.

The fact that the prairie has been absorbed by a new urban-industrial environment also encourages a more consciously artistic approach to it. The things of farm and small town life become less and less objects of use, more and more objects of contemplation. Urbanites collect churns, lanterns, singletrees, days in the country, land. As Marshall McLuhan says, "Each new technology creates an environment that is itself regarded as corrupt and degrading. Yet the new one turns its predecessor into an art form."[10] Perhaps because of this changed relationship to their subject, the novelists too have become more self-consciously "artistic," more concerned with technique, more varied and experimental in the forms they develop. Their searches into the past range from deliberate

191

historical fiction like Wiebe's *Big Bear* to the absurdist
fantasies of Kroetsch's Demeter Proudfoot, and in
varying degrees they exhibit a growing dissatisfaction
with the methods of earlier writers. Kroetsch is the most
explicit about this dissatisfaction, just as he is more
innovative in technique and form than his contemporaries. In "A conversation with Margaret Laurence,"
Kroetsch says, "As I explore that [Western] experience,
trying to make both inward and outward connections,
I see new possibilities for the story-teller. In the process I
have become somewhat impatient with certain traditional kinds of realism."[11] In part Kroetsch's impatience
may stem from the general distrust contemporary
novelists harbour for the structures of the traditional
realistic novel and the conclusions implicit in those structures. Alain Robbe-Grillet voices that distrust very clearly
in his *For a New Novel*.[12] But the dissatisfaction of
Kroetsch and the other prairie writers seems to have a
more particular object. Their frequent use of various
kinds of discontinuity, from the digressions of George Ryga's
stone picker, to the senile wanderings of Laurence's
Hagar, to the shifting points of view in *Big Bear*, to disrup-
tions of narration and logic in *The Studhorse Man*, all
suggest a desire to loosen those traditional structures
and make the symbols of prairie experience tell a
different story.

      Margaret Laurence is probably the nearest
of the younger writers to the prairie realists in spirit and
in method, which may help to explain why *The Stone
Angel* is the most thoroughly realized fiction of the
period so far. Laurence's techniques are familiar, and she
writes with the assurance of having a usable tradition of
prairie fiction behind her. She can confidently evoke the
prairie desert in a few words, for example, as though she
assumed that the chronicles of the drought, including the
work of Ross and Mitchell, had established a common
understanding of the time. Yet there is a difference in the
way a reader sees the familiar images of the prairie in
Laurence's fiction. They are held up for conscious

scrutiny, filled with an awareness of the types they represent because they are distillations of the shared imagery of the earlier fiction. The one main image of water in "Horses of the Night" from *A Bird in the House,* for instance, is powerful and comprehensive. Vanessa's cousin Chris, in from remote northern Manitoba to attend high school, is in many ways the culturally deprived child found in earlier fiction. He is imaginative and stirs Vanessa's own imagination, taking her beyond her family practicality. She comes to realize that his two racing horses, Duchess and Firefly "only ever existed in some other dimension,"[13] yet she goes on believing in Chris. In some way his imaginative world is for her identified with Lake Manitoba as he has described it to her, and when he takes her there to camp she recognizes in the lake the terrible loneliness of Chris's world.

> No human word could be applied. The lake was not lonely or untamed. These words relate to people, and there was nothing of people here. There was no feeling about the place. It existed in some world in which man was not yet born. I looked at the grey reaches of it and felt threatened. It was like the view of God which I had held since my father's death. Distant, indestructible, totally indifferent. (pp. 147-148)

As an image of what the unsheltered imagination must confront in the prairie wilderness, this is chilling. It is reminiscent of the darkest intimations gathered by early travellers such as Butler and Grant, as though the first generations of pioneers have had no effect, even as though the terrain defies man permanently with its solitude and desolation. The situation is reminiscent of the scenes of Len Sterner and Lydia beside this same lake just before their sacrificial death. Chris, whose name suggests sacrifice, is later driven mad by the barbarities of war. In Laurence's story it seems only a choice of   193 which horror the imagination will be sacrificed to. The familiar threat of the landscape to the imagination seems intensified, distilled from the earlier fiction.

The Stone Angel includes a synoptic view of archetypal town pioneers, alienated from the new land by pride and an arrogant will to dominate. Feeling themselves exiles in a barbaric wilderness, they are further isolated by their stern Calvinist self-repression. But for Laurence's narrator Hagar the problem is no longer to contend with the prairie but to deal with the residue of prairie experience which lies within, controlling the character. Hagar in a sense is still paying for the conquest of the land which demanded that the pioneers so ruthlessly conquer themselves,[14] but for Hagar the difficulty is that she cannot "un-conquer" herself. Even when she marries a common man of the soil, Bram Shipley, she finds she has done it out of pride, to defy her father. Ultimately her inability to give herself to life ruins the lives of Bram and her favourite son John. Laurence characteristically presents Hagar's dilemma in both imagery and statement, and as usual the imagery is wiser than the statement. Hagar traces her lack of love, life, and joy to inborn pride:

> Pride was my wilderness, and the demon that led me there was fear. I was alone, never anything else, and never free, for I carried my chains within me, and they spread out from me and shackled all I touched.[15]

It is hard not to take this eloquent explanation as authorial comment. Laurence can be bluntly explicit about her themes. Because the statement is explicit, it is limiting and it does no justice to the rich mixture of forces conflicting in Hagar's large personality. Hagar is trying to break out, but she is also trying to find her way in, toward those shadowy recesses of herself where love and joy and grace may just survive.

There are two images of water which seem

to display Hagar's agony and Laurence's art much better.
Throughout the novel Hagar moves painfully from the
hard dry sunlit prairie toward the deep shadowy sea. She
also moves from the sunlit logic of conscious will back
toward dark recesses of fluid unconscious desires and
presentiments. The sea both beckons and menaces her.
When she first escapes to the old fish cannery by the
shore, the ocean suggests surrender, release, freedom
from her chains. "Now I could fancy myself there among
[the drowned] tiaraed with starfish thorny and purple,
braceleted with shells linked on limp chains of weed,
waiting until my encumbrance of flesh floated clean away
and I was free and skeletal and could journey with
tides and fishes" (p. 162). The image is given point by
Hagar's declared humiliation at being imprisoned in her
massive flesh. The sea offers rebirth, a cleansing
baptismal plunge. Hagar does deck herself out in sea
shells a little later, and she does plunge into depths of
her memories, where Murray Lees, with his wine and his
own confessions, helps to free Hagar from some of the
weight of her guilt for the death of her son John. But
that much yielding up of herself is a painful and
frightening experience to Hagar. The stone angel cannot
easily bend that much, and after the confessional she
cannot bear the sight of Lees. She has another vision of
the sea as a black gulf to swallow her, suck her out of
herself, annihilate her:

> Outside, the sea nuzzles at the floorboards that
> edge the water. If I were alone, I wouldn't find
> the sound soothing in the slightest. I'd be drawn
> out and out, with each receding layer of water to
> its beginning, a depth as alien and chill as some
> far frozen planet, a night sea hoarding sly-eyed
> serpents, killer whales, swarming phosphorescent
> creatures dead to the daytime, a black sea
> sucking everything into itself, the spent gull, the
> trivial garbage from boats, and men protected
> from eternity only by their soft and fearful flesh   195

and their seeing eyes. (pp. 224-225)

The sea threatens too much exposure of the "soft and
fearful flesh"; Hagar regards it as her prairie people
regard the wilderness surrounding their "embattled
fortresses." Like the lake in "Horses of the Night" it
appalls the imagination. Also, Hagar knows in the
unvisited depths of herself the sly-eyed serpents wait,
created by her guilt, but equally by her stubborn will to
remain consciously in control. It must be through her
trip to the water that Hagar reaches whatever degree of
grace she may have attained at her death. Her final
gesture of grasping the cup could suggest that in her own
imperious way, Hagar admits the need for the baptismal
water or the sacramental cup.

The great technical achievement of *The
Stone Angel* is in Laurence's creation of her narrator.
Hagar is, in her own words, "rampant with memory,"
and her age and personality provide aesthetic distance as
well as the shifting time scales, the necessary
discontinuities which allow for new connections of events
and feelings in the prairie past. Yet Laurence creates this
effect with what are essentially two simple time sequences
laid one over the other. One sequence covers the weeks
from the opening until Hagar's death, the other the years
from her childhood to the present. The illusion of
random association in the old woman's mind is smoothly
maintained, but the connections between the time scales
actually preserve deeper parallels in the action. When
Hagar is planning to run away from Marvin's house to
the sea, for example, she recalls running away from
Bram's house to the coast. Both escape sequences, begun
together in this way, converge on the experience of
John's death, the thing Hagar would most like to escape,
but which she remembers in the earlier time sequence,
and imagines to be happening again in the present. This
point is a kind of nexus in the action. In Hagar's alcohol
haze the present seems to have touched the past in such
a way as to change it. They touch at the point where her

196

pride has caused the one event in her life she can never accept. Dazed by the wine, Hagar forces Murray Lees to play the part of John and to absolve her of guilt for his death. Whether by this absolution or by the act of seeking forgiveness, Hagar is eased of some of her burden.

All of Laurence's prairie heroines are in some way imprisoned by pride and guilt, and they are seeking the absolution that could free them. At the same time they are victims of the prairie's Manawaka culture —its bigotry, its Calvinist self-repression, its dedication to a few limited and life-denying truths which may have sustained the pioneers but which stifle the next generation and isolate them from the life which should be accessible to them. What Laurence finds most consistently in her search through the past is confirmation of a need to be freed from that past and the burden of guilt it has left.

A somewhat similar inference could be drawn from the latest novels of Sinclair Ross and W. O. Mitchell. Ross's *Sawbones Memorial* reveals the moral character of a small prairie town, especially through the privileged understanding of the doctor who has served it for forty-five years. Presented entirely through dialogue and personal reflections at a retirement party, the novel provides Ross with some of the structural discipline his writing has been lacking since *As For Me and My House*. There is some return of the intensity which the constricted focus of that first novel generated. Knowing the moral as well as the physical ailments of the town, Old Doc Hunter is prescribing one last bitter pill for the dominant Anglo-Canadian minority to swallow. He has arranged for the outcast Ukrainian boy, Nick, to return as their new doctor, hoping to force the town to accept its wider humanity. The old doctor is paradoxically attempting to free the town from its past.

The Vanishing Point is for Mitchell a more pronounced change of direction. Like his earlier novels it is a comedy, and it does convey the solid

197

affirmation of life we identify with Mitchell's work.
Carlyle Sinclair's impending marriage to the Indian girl,
Victoria, indicates that the teacher has accepted nature
within himself and in the Stony Indians. But to reach
this point of acceptance Sinclair must reject the world of
Victorian values he has been hired to impose upon the
Indians, and in the ending that White world is not
redeemed as we would expect it to be in Mitchell's earlier
novels. Nonetheless, Sinclair's rejection of it is in another
sense positive, since his White world has come to
represent a denial of life, as the title of the novel
suggests. The term "vanishing point" comes from the
perspective exercises forced upon Carlyle by his primary
school teacher, Old Kacky. It is the point in the drawing
at which the converging lines of roads, fences, and
telephone lines meet, the completion, so to speak, of the
ordering impulse in a perspective drawing. Into Old
Kacky's rigorously disciplined picture of the prairie,
young Carlyle had felt compelled to insert a tiger. The
image is a rich one, because perspective is not only a way
of drawing, but a way of seeing the world, and young
Carlyle has the natural impulse to go beyond the
imposed perspective, to sense the presence of the tiger in
that constrained world.[16] The older Carlyle must find his
way slowly and painfully back from the vanishing point
of his civilized perspective to that earlier state of natural
perception. When he believes, for example, that he is
simply trying to keep Victoria in the paths of virtue, he
does not realize that he is involuntarily responding to the
beauty of the young Indian girl—not until he recognizes
her as his "tiger." Paradoxically, Mitchell's image of the
vital energy which disturbs Sinclair's Victorian
perspective is drawn from elsewhere in the British
tradition. His "tiger," like his "lamb," is clearly taken
from William Blake. While Blake could hardly be
identified with Victorian values or sensibilities, it is
evident that Mitchell is not rejecting his British heritage,
merely criticizing certain life-denying aspects of it.

Mitchell's central image of the traditional

way of seeing the prairie recalls, ironically, Wallace Stegner's description of the landscape as "circles, radii, perspective exercises."[17] To Stegner, twenty years earlier, that seemed the appropriate way of perceiving the prairie, and though the physical landscape has not changed in the intervening time, Mitchell is insisting on a less abstract, more human perception as vital to the prairie-dweller's health and sanity.

Mitchell's choice of the Indian viewpoint as a possible alternative marks another major development in contemporary prairie fiction, and one that has been very slow to emerge. In American western fiction as early as 1941, Frank Waters was creating strong and sympathetic portrayals of the Pueblo Indians of New Mexico in his *The Man Who Killed the Deer*. As we have seen, the Canadian Indian virtually disappeared from prairie fiction around the turn of the century and has not reappeared in any substantial way until now. This could be one unfortunate effect of Canadians' smugness at not having dealt with the native peoples in as violent and genocidal a manner as their American neighbours. We have felt free to forget the Indian entirely, which may say something about the robustness of our consciences or merely about how thoroughly we have been confined to the perspective of Old Kacky. It has not been until contemporary novelists began breaking out of this perspective that they discovered the Indian culture—somewhere near the vanishing point. The appearance of Kroetsch's *Gone Indian* and Wiebe's *Big Bear* in the same year as Mitchell's novel might raise a suspicion that the writers are capitalizing on the current wave of romantic primitivism, but I think it is more a matter of seeing at last that the Indian culture can be useful in understanding their own prairie past. They identify the Indian as the one potential "ancestor" who is close to the soil, organically and elementally connected with it, and whose culture may reveal what the land has been trying to tell us from the beginning. In this view the land tends to emerge not only sympathetically but as an 199 embodiment of darker subconscious states of the human mind and spirit with which we must re-establish contact. W. F. Butler, of course, saw these suggestions in the prairie as early as 1869. In Kroetsch's *Gone Indian* both the natives and the land exist mainly in these psychological and archetypal terms. "Indian" is something within the overcivilized white man which Jeremy Sadness is drawn to search for; the land is a darkness into which he must disappear with his earth goddess Bea Sunderman.

The impression that contemporary novelists are attracted to the Indian as a link with the land they have been alienated from is reinforced by the fact that the most thorough exploration of Indian culture is carried out by Rudy Wiebe. His previous novels have been largely devoted to his own Mennonite past, and the shift is not as abrupt as it may seem. The Mennonites who, as J. B. McLaren put it in 1882, "at once accommodated themselves to the climate and all the material conditions"[18] of the prairie, share with the Indians this experience of accommodating themselves to the land as well as the experience of facing the dominant Anglo-Canadian society from without. To both peoples, alienation from the land was something imposed upon them by others.

Big Bear belongs roughly to the genre of the historical novel, yet it shows that Wiebe has come further from the realist tradition than Margaret Laurence. His first novel, *Peace Shall Destroy Many* (1964), is a fairly traditional realistic novel with an omniscient narrator, a continuous time scheme, and the expected continuity of action. By the time he writes *Big Bear* Wiebe has moved gradually into a mixture of techniques specially adapted to the prairie realities as he sees them. The narration is discontinuous as Wiebe works with an interplay of a number of voices, a method he also uses to good effect in *The Blue Mountains of China* (1970). A third person narrator is joined by

several first-person narrators—Lieutenant Governors

Morris and Dewdney, missionary John McDougall,
trader's daughter Kitty MacLean, and others. The effect
is more than distancing or verisimilitude. It resembles the
way the lenses of a stereoscope draw the separate two-
dimensional aerial photographs into a single three
dimensional illusion. The different viewpoints uncover
depth and contour invisible to one, and the "reality" of
the vision is not a compromise between views but a new
perception entirely.

The several narrators have also been
introduced to allow their own characters to become part
of the story. Wiebe in some of the narration has tried to
capture the sound of their world and the style of the
characters as these appear in documents. Inspector
Francis Dickens, for example, the son of Charles
Dickens, was chased out of Fort Pitt with his small
garrison of NWMP on Tuesday, 14 April 1885. His diary
entry for 15 April reads simply, "Very cold weather,
snow. Travelled."[19] Here Wiebe has quoted directly from
a copy of the diary,[20] evidently because its silences are
eloquent, but also for the "voice" of Dickens and for the
general air of authenticity that the style of such
documents lends. On the other hand, documentary
fidelity is not in itself a main achievement of the novel.
In the section by John McDougall, for example, there
are occasional echoes of McDougall's own writing in
phrases such as "our dear wives," but no sustained
attempt to copy his style. We are given not McDougall
writing but McDougall thinking, his journal style
modulated into a stream of consciousness so that it can
encompass much broader subjects in shorter spaces. We
are reminded of the delicacy of that task when
McDougall says after some digressing, "Believe me I am
not one to let my mind wander" (p. 40).

Much of the narration, aside from the
very sharp action sequences, has the appearance of being
suspended in reflection. Big Bear's own reflections
provide the richest medium of suspension whenever the
omniscient narrator chooses his as the shaping

consciousness of the narration. In Big Bear's mind a judgment of political strategy may be interrupted by a reflection on the taste of buffalo liver or the softness of his second wife. It is partly because of this logic of reflection that the narration, despite its vividness of sensory description and frankness of revelation, remains somehow slightly opaque. It is unlike Laurence's transparent self-explanatory narration, or Kroetsch's narration with its occasional obscurities which demand interpretation. More than most fiction or even most lyric, Wiebe's narration is overheard; it does not demand interpretation but rather patience, a suspension of judgments to wait for delayed significance. What we are first conscious of is the sensory reality of these neglected nineteenth-century prairie experiences. Lieutenant Governor Morris, for example, while waiting for the signing of Treaty Number Six at Fort Pitt can look out of history at "the huge river turning past the tiny peaks of the buildings, coils of it spinning in circles like suns, its grey water so thick, so heavy with silt it seemed to bulge up out of its bed, lean against hills" (p. 11). Gradually the larger significance of these experiences also appears, as when McDougall connects for us a routine government delay, the absence of the savage Plains Cree from this treaty signing, and the Cree part in the Northwest Rebellion (p. 42). We see gradually that these incidents are as interconnected and as significant to our lives as the chronicled events of civilized Europe.

We see still more slowly that Wiebe is bringing the sensory experience and the larger significance together, though at first they seem to draw the mind in separate directions. At their meeting is the reality of Big Bear's world, which is both more immediate and more eternal than the intensely time-bound world of mechanical values he faces—the world of progress, empire, commerce, and material possession. Big Bear's world is presented, first of all, with greater sensory richness than the White world. Here is a scene of
202 hospitality when his women tend a buffalo carcass that

hangs over the fire in the chief's lodge:

> Into the coned warmth of the lodge, a thick
> weighed darkness of roasting meat and women
> and firelight and fur; soft darkness of leather and
> people sweat; darkness moving like raw yearling
> buffalo hung headless, turning in the complete
> circle of living and solid sweet immovable and
> ever changing Earth; darkness of fat's slip and
> dripping, of birch bark curling light, a darkness
> soft in flares of burning blood like the raw heat
> of woman tunneled and spent for love. (p. 51)

Anyone looking for McLuhan's tactile world of pre-
literate tribal man should recognize here not only the
richness but the different balance of the senses before the
tyranny of the eye that we find in the White world, even
the world of Governor Morris glimpsed a moment ago.
Big Bear is a man who likes "to smell his friends about
him" (p. 57).

Big Bear is also credited with more
enduring values than his Victorian adversaries who are
so closely identified with the mechanical horror of the
steam locomotive. He sees the basic absurdity of the
abstractions they and their surveyors would lay over the
land to serve their unnatural greed. He questions how
anyone can choose for himself a piece of the mother
earth or how, in accordance with the treaty, he can
receive one square mile of land: "'who can receive the
land? From whom would he receive it?' " (p. 29). In his
last buffalo running especially we are shown that for Big
Bear the ultimate significance must visit the immediate
experience. The buffalo are, for his band, "hardly more
than one belly-stretching meal yet everything for life and
this moment that could ever be asked" (p. 127). They
provide, for Big Bear, not so much meat as, in the act of
hunting and eating them, access to all that is essential
and permanent in his world. When he has "run" the
fattest cow his condition is one of reaching all eternal

human experience in the moment: "In the circle of sun and sky and earth and death he stood complete" (p. 129). With this image we seem to have moved, in Wiebe's fiction, from a linear historical view of time to a natural cyclical view which again gives man his place in eternity—and reunites him with the earth. While *The Temptations of Big Bear* chronicles the coming of the time-bound mechanical society which in *Peace* destroys the Mennonite's closeness to the soil, the novel is like a return to that state, because we are drawn gradually into the world-view of Big Bear himself. That is also the tragedy felt in the novel, of course, since at the trial we understand his logic as well as that of the Whites who convict him.

The fiction of Robert Kroetsch introduces a third way of reinterpreting the past. Laurence and the older novelists examine the past critically, but largely in its own terms; they generate a new awareness of traditional values rather than a radical rearrangement of them. In a way this is a logical development because unlike the literature of the American West which has always tended to look westward toward the frontier, Canadian prairie fiction has always tended to look East toward the centres of civilized order and refinement. It is only fitting that it should now demonstrate its independence by looking East with a scathingly critical eye. The same tendency could, for that matter, be encouraging the motif of the disappearing father, the delinquent figure of authority who has betrayed a naive trust. Wiebe, whose fathers do not disappear and who was not a child of the British-Ontario tradition in the first place, creates instead a separate consciousness through which to see the dominant culture, and the tension between the two kinds of awareness is revealing. Kroetsch attempts to clarify and sharpen our vision of the past with irony, especially the sometimes bitter sometimes comic ironies generated by juxtaposing the mythical and historical realities of prairie experience.

Kroetsch designs his prairie trilogy to

span the history of the West. *The Words of My Roaring* (1966) is set in 1935, and each successive novel moves further forward as well as further back in time. *The Studhorse Man* (1969), set immediately after the Second World War, is equally concerned with the pre-depression life which is passing away. *Gone Indian* (1973) is set in the 1960's but preoccupied with the pre-settlement prairie of Indian and Buffalo. Though *Badlands* (1975) was apparently not part of the original design, it advances the narrative present to the 1970's and extends the past back into the pre-history of the prairie. Kroetsch is not mainly retrieving historical facts or, like Wiebe, vividly realizing moments in history; he is laying out the timespan over which both historical and mythical shapes of the prairie past were formed.

His point of beginning, the 1935 Alberta election, is crucial. Kroetsch, as we have seen, is interested in the western people's unusual sense of time, of not existing in history, and their alternately apocalyptic and millennial conception of their own position in cosmic time is probably the most basic element of their mythic awareness of themselves. The initial source of this mythic pattern was obviously a literal reading of the Bible. Many fundamentalists did settle the prairies, but for others as well the exposure to, and utter dependence upon, so extreme and capricious a climate must have encouraged a sense of being directly in the hands of an Old Testament God. That sense of being caught up in cosmic beginnings and endings might also be encouraged by the topography as well as the climate. The prairie resembles the desert of the Old Testament, where the sky is obtrusive, where God is not manifest in things about, which companion man, but in things above, which dominate him.[21] The Alberta people were well prepared for the appeal of "Bible Bill" Aberhart, when he rose with his Social Credit Party to proclaim the coming of the apocalypse in which the "whore of Babylon," the Eastern banking interests, would be driven out.[22] This coincidence of mythic consciousness and 205 specific event in the election of 1935 may have been what attracted Kroetsch to the Aberhart campaign as a starting point for his time scheme of the West. Johnny Backstrom is forced involuntarily into that cosmic calendar by the demands of the people, who want a Messiah. His opponent, Doc Murdoch, may be almost a father to Johnny, but he is also identified with the eastern, Babylonian oppressors. Like the Babylonians he keeps a lush garden, and his daughter is like a goddess of love in that garden. Johnny himself approaches the election as though it were the end of the world and he himself were uncertain of "election." The first of Kroetsch's novels, then, centres upon that moment in which the West distinguishes itself publicly and historically by its peculiar sense of its place in time. From that point Kroetsch's time scheme and world view expand like ripples from a dropped stone.

The coincidence of mythic awareness and historical event is, of course, ironic. Even as the rain falls at the end of *The Words of My Roaring* we know that the moment of renewal is illusory and that what Kroetsch chronicles is actually the fall of the West. *The Studhorse Man* is the central narrative of that fall; with Hazard's years in the West it spans roughly the time described in Chapter IV as the transition from rural agrarian to urban industrial West. The horse becomes the appropriate image for the vanishing agrarian prairie not only because of its literal part in pre-industrial farming but because it carries all the associations of freedom and power and pride we attach to the open spaces of the plains. Hazard's Poseidon, being a Mustang and one whose ancestor was passed on by an Indian, appears to represent the spirit of an earlier more untrammelled West. At the end of the war, when the novel opens, mechanization is in the final stages of replacing the free spirit of the Mustang, and Kroetsch gives this loss of the West in terms of fertility. The unpromising state of the prairie is signalled at once by the corn goddess Demeter appearing as a man, an unfruitful man. The fertilizing spirit, represented by the studhorse, is equally frustrated. Hazard can find servicing work only for himself. Because the spirits of virility and fertility are disoriented, the studhorse is finally put in the anomalous position of serving infertility and the sterile commercial world of Eugene Utter, who has been pictured as Hazard's pale shadow.

Just as Kroetsch ironically deflates the messianic and millennial myths of the prairie with Johnny Backstrom, he deflates later heroic myths with the character of Hazard Lepage. Hazard, the questing hero, the champion of the Old West, the agent of virility, might be expected to resemble a Hollywood Western hero, but he is neither strong nor handsome; he fights neither fairly nor well, and his most heroic wound is a charge of buckshot in the arse. He is never in control of his destiny; he is continually seduced by women, and he is finally killed by his own horse. Hazard is a comic travesty of the Western hero and his exploits, and this type of anti-hero must inevitably call to mind recent developments in the fiction of the American West— movies like *Cat Ballou* and novels like Thomas Berger's *Little Big Man*. Kroetsch's ironic treatment of popular myths does place him nearer than any other Canadian novelist to the "New Western" in America described by Leslie Fiedler in his *The Return of the Vanishing American*.[23] Kroetsch probably is more conscious of what happens in American fiction, since he has been living and writing in the United States for several years, but it should be remembered that for Kroetsch as for any western Canadian the dynamic between myth and history is entirely different from the one being worked out in the American West. The Canadian's problem of settling the relative claims of history and myth upon his consciousness is complicated by the fact that most of the myths carelessly attached to the Canadian West are foreign and have little connection with its actual past.

Most western Canadians think of themselves as living in a northern extension of the great   207 frontier West they know so well from American popular culture. Even Al Purdy, who should know better, can write of the cowboys in the Chilcotin having a ready-made mythology with which to identify. He says, "They love the movies of John Wayne and Gary Cooper; they listen to country and western music, practically standing to attention when Wilf Carter sings *Oh, That Strawberry Roan*."[24] A poet like Purdy should sense the anomaly of their condition. Beneath it and the fanfare that attends the Calgary Stampede and Edmonton's Klondike Days there lies a careless assumption of a tradition of frontier values, a past which may have been quieter, more respectable than the American frontier, but which had vaguely the same significance in the development of the nation. This, apparently, is what becomes of the "primary cultural values" we discussed earlier when a nation imports its popular entertainment. Western Canadians are, in effect, assuming a new colonial state of mind before they have outgrown the older one dominated by British-Ontario culture.

As we can see from *The Words of My Roaring* and *The Studhorse Man*, Kroetsch is very conscious of the need to dispel both of these forms of false or misleading order which have been imposed upon the West. Before he can hope to find the appropriate mythical patterns which will make the experience of the prairie past intelligible, he must first de-mythologize the West. I would be inclined to add that someone must begin teaching western Canadians their own history. But for Kroetsch the problem is deeper and more pervasive than the anomalous presence of a few Wild West myths. It is incorporated into the language itself, as Kroetsch says in a recent article:

> The Canadian writer's particular predicament is that he works with a language, within a literature, that appears to be authentically his own, and not a borrowing. But just as there was in the Latin word a concealed Greek experience, so there is in

the Canadian word a concealed other experience, sometimes British, sometimes American. In recent years the tension between this appearance of being just like someone else and the demands of authenticity has become intolerable—both to individuals and to the society. In recent Canadian fiction the major writers resolve the paradox—the painful tension between appearance and authenticity—by the radical process of demythologizing the systems that threaten to define them.[25]

For Kroetsch at least the task of renaming the prairie experience entails this radical process. His revolt against the techniques of the prairie realists is part of a larger effort to jar the language out of familiar contexts which reinforce that hidden, other experience. His irony, often so comprehensive as to leave readers feeling lost, bewildered, hostile, is a deliberate attempt to unsettle all settled expectations about the experience he is recreating. The process of de-mythologizing has, at least initially, a tendency to shred the world back to its original chaos, and Kroetsch has a considerable tolerance for chaos, for the formless and fecund darkness of the mind. His resort to absurdity, madness, and hallucination in his fiction again aligns him with the writers of the "New Western" in America. Berger's narrator finds his hero Jack Crabb in a psychiatric ward; Ken Kesey's *One Flew Over the Cuckoo's Nest* is set in a mental hospital; Demeter writes from a mental asylum, and Professor Madham, as the name suggests, has a strangely obsessive interest in shaping Jeremy Sadness's story. The madness in the New Western, according to Fiedler, signifies the ultimate West, the final escape from the White reason and intellect which has tyrannized over America from the beginning.[26] In Kroetsch's novels it would be more accurate to say that the madness *is* that White reason and intellect. Demeter in particular is the historical consciousness attempting to 209 impose reason and significance on the wanderings of Hazard, which are legitimately mythic when seen as the decline of the West but which become absurdly pompous when Demeter casts Hazard as a new Odysseus. Demeter and Hazard are like the paired characters which appear again and again in recent Canadian fiction. In Hugh MacLennan's *The Watch That Ends the Night,* George Stewart is the historian, Jerome Martell the mythic hero; in Leonard Cohen's *Beautiful Losers,* "I" is the historian, "F" the man of myths; in Robertson Davies' *Fifth Business,* Dunstan Ramsay is the historian, Boy Staunton the liver of myths. In every case these paired or split characters are engaged in a very complex action involving shared identity and love of the same woman which cannot be examined here, but the frequency of their appearance suggests that Canadians' particular kind of national schizophrenia stems from a disparity between the historical and the mythic shapes given to their experience. Through Demeter and later through Professor Madham, Kroetsch treats the historian's shaping impulse as ironically as he does the false myths.

There are indications in *The Studhorse Man* that Demeter's is specifically the madness of the creative writer. From the beginning Demeter's relationship with his subject is uneasy, slightly hostile. He draws attention to his own editing of Hazard's story, and the reader can see his tendency to manipulate his subject, to make Hazard tell Demeter's own story. Hazard is obliged to serve as hero of Demeter's id, acting out sexual fantasies Demeter is too timid to realize. The whole theme of the virility of the Old West in fact acquires a strange, introverted, onanistic quality. Whenever Hazard or Poseidon gets involved in a sexual adventure there is some mention of Demeter's own slow sexual awakening, and his eventual identification with Hazard, assuming his role as studhorse man, confirms his exploitive use of Hazard as a figure in his own fantasies.

210   The contention between Demeter and

Hazard, is, on one plane, an opposition between art and life. When his subject stubbornly refuses to fulfill the patterns Demeter has established, when Hazard appears to be willing to give up his quest and accept Martha, the biographer lays down his pen and steps into the action, becoming "D. Proudfoot, Studhorse Man" and indirectly destroying Hazard. It is the violence, not of man to man but of artist to subject which is important here. It completes a long sequence in which Demeter has questioned whether Hazard's reality or his own has priority, whether Hazard's crude remarks or his polished account is the more authentic. Demeter shows that he is troubled by the question as he sets out to describe the horse:

> I hardly know where to suggest you begin. Those old Chinese artists, they drew their horses true to life, true to the rhythm of life. They dreamed their horses and made the horse too. They had their living dreams of horses. . . Ah, where to begin? Why is the truth never where it should be? Is the truth of the man in the man or in his biography? Is the truth of the beast in the flesh and confusion or in the few skillfully arranged lines. . . . [Kroetsch's ellipses][27]

The dilemma remains. As Kroetsch says, the artist's imagination must impose order if we are to live with the flesh and confusion. At the same time, Demeter's obvious manipulations, his willingness to do the ultimate violence to his subject for the sake of his art, can be taken as a sardonic comment upon the patterns imposed by novelists, especially prairie novelists. In one direction it is self-irony, in the other it is the absurdist image of the traditional prairie novelist. Demeter in his madhouse of fiction, seeking refuge within the insane culture which is destroying his subject, seeing the prairie only through a mirror and a window like the Lady of Shalott, Demeter is the madness just visible beneath the brittle

211

orderliness of Mrs. Bentley's mind in *As For Me and My House*. On Kroetsch's ironic prairie the final irony is turned back upon the artist himself, the one who presumes to impose order on the chaos.

Contemporary prairie novelists going back to re-name the past are in a sense facing the same obstacles encountered by their pioneer ancestors who confronted an unnamed country: the new land and the old culture. But there is this difference; the novelists are acutely aware of the difficulties imposed by the old culture and of the need to create a fictional idiom which is indigenous, a language in which the buried experience is their own. Wiebe, for example, has a scene in his *Big Bear* in which the impossibility of real understanding between Cree Indian and White Victorian is represented vividly in their failure to find words in each language for the essential experiences of the other culture. For the English concept of treason interpreter Peter Houri can find no nearer Cree equivalent than "throwing sticks at the queen's hat."[28] Between Cree and English, of course, the difficulty of naming is clear; the otherness of the experience is not buried under a similarity of words.

Robert Kroetsch, as we have seen, acknowledges the difficulty of re-naming more explicitly. He has decided, in fact, that the first duty of the Canadian writer is to *unname* his experience, to uninvent his world.[29] Despite the danger of a kind of creative nihilism which lurks in these phrases, Kroetsch has done much to create the prairie past by drawing its legendary or mythic forms closer to immediate, local experience. He passes essentially romantic figures like Backstrom and Hazard through small town churches, cafes, fairgrounds, community halls, and beer parlours, and through weddings, rodeos, auctions, and election rallies which were the social staples of rural life in the West and which have not yet quite disappeared. For Albertans especially Kroetsch is making their experiences more real by turning them into fiction, adding the necessary imaginative dimension. At the same time that he is de-

212

mythologizing the West, he is offering the prairie imagination its local past in usable terms by mythologizing the commonplaces of prairie life.

Margaret Laurence expresses a slightly different sense of the re-naming process. In *The Diviners,* Morag Gunn says, "*A popular misconception is that we can't change the past—everyone is constantly changing their own past, recalling it, revising it. What really happened? A meaningless question. But one I keep trying to answer, knowing there is no answer.*"[30] (Laurence's italics.) Like Kroetsch's irony toward the creative act, this expresses a healthy skepticism about the absoluteness, the finality of the naming process. Re-naming is not just a thing to be done now but something which must be begun now. Howard O'Hagan has an apt description of how inconclusive the storyteller's art is in his *Tay John,* if I may return to the point at which we began:

> Indeed, to tell a story is to leave most of it untold. You mine it, as you take ore from the mountain. You carry the compass around it. You dig down—and when you have finished, the story remains, something beyond your touch, resistant to your siege; unfathomable, like the heart of the mountain. You have the feeling that you have not reached the story itself, but have merely assaulted the surrounding solitude.[31]

The image for the inviolate mystery could as easily have been a prairie as a mountain, and I think the current generation of prairie novelists would share O'Hagan's humility. The re-naming of that early, generative prairie will undoubtedly go on, not merely as repetition or as the urge of each generation to re-write its history, but as a continuing effort to approach the central mystery of life that is in it. The mining, the digging down, that Laurence and Kroetsch and Wiebe are doing now is the first necessary step.

Notes

Notes to Preface

1. *Tay John* [1960; Reprint (rpt.), Toronto: McClelland and Stewart, 1974], p. 80.
2. While the pioneers could well have read various pre-settlement accounts of the prairies such as those of William F. Butler and George Monro Grant, these works, like the plethora of immigration pamphlets issued by government, railroads, and land companies, tended to be superficially informative but profoundly misleading. Grant's assurance, for example, that sixty acres would be sufficient for a grain farm would tend to confirm the prospective settler in his assumption that the ways of his previous environment were appropriate to this new one. *Ocean to Ocean* (1873; rpt. Edmonton; Hurtig, 1967), p. 73.
3. *As For Me and My House* (1941; rpt. Toronto: McClelland and Stewart, 1957), p. 100.
4. *Who Has Seen the Wind* (1947; rpt. Toronto: Macmillan, 1969), p. 199.
5. "The Prairie: A State of Mind," *Transactions of the Royal Society of Canada*, vol. 6: series 4, June 1968, p. 173.
6. I am working from descriptions given in W. A. Mackintosh, *Prairie Settlement, The Geographical Setting* (Toronto: Macmillan, 1934).
7. *The Canadian West in Fiction*, rev. ed. (Toronto: Ryerson, 1970, first published, 1949), p. 6.

Notes to Chapter I

1. *Homesteader* (Toronto: Macmillan, 1973), p. 29.
2. *Clearing in the West* (1935; rpt. Toronto: Thomas Allen, 1964), p. 58.
3. *Gully Farm* (Toronto: McClelland and Stewart, 1955), p. 186.
4. Russell M. Brown, "An Interview with Robert Kroetsch," *University of Windsor Review*, VIII (Spring 1972), p. 2.
5. James W. Whillans, *First in the West, The Story of Henry Kelsey* (Edmonton: Applied Arts Products, 1955), p. 106.
6. For a more extensive treatment of the responses of early explorers, see John Warkentin, ed., *The Western Interior of Canada* (Toronto: McClelland and Stewart, 1964).
7. *York Factory to the Blackfeet Country, The Journal of Anthony Hendry, 1754-55*, ed. Lawrence J. Burpee, *Transactions of the Royal Society of Canada*, 3rd series, 1907-08, vol I, section II.
8. *Voyages* (1801; rpt. Toronto: Courier, 1911), p. cii.
9. *Voyages*, p. cxxxi.
10. *The Great Lone Land* (1872; rpt. Edmonton: M. G. Hurtig, 1968), pp. 199-200.
11. *Butterfly on Rock* (Toronto: University of Toronto Press, 1970), p. 34.

214

12. *Picturesque Canada* (Toronto: Belden Bros., 1882) p. 340.
13. *Wolf Willow* (New York: Viking, 1955), p. 7.
14. *The Long Journey* (Toronto: University of Toronto Press, 1968).
15. *Virgin Land: The American West as Symbol and Myth* (Cambridge: Harvard University Press, 1950).
16. Stegner, pp. 6-7.
17. *The North-West Passage by Land* (1865; rpt. Toronto: Coles Canadiana Collection, 1970), p. 178.
18. *As For Me and My House* (1941; rpt. Toronto: McClelland and Stewart, 1957), p. 59—subsequent page references are to this edition.
19. *Who Has Seen the Wind* (Toronto: Macmillan, 1947), p. 3— subsequent page references are to this edition.
20. *My Antonia* (Boston: Houghton Mifflin, 1918), p. 7.
21. *Voyages*, p. xxv.
22. "Seeing an Unliterary Landscape," *Mosaic*, III (Spring 1970), 3.
23. *Stories from Indian Wigwams and Northern Campfires* (1893; rpt. Toronto: Coles Canadiana Collection, 1970), p. 118.
24. "The House on the Prairies," *Canadian Literature,* 42 (Autumn 1969), 46-55. See also Warren Tallman's "Wolf in the Snow," *Canadian Literature*, 5 (Summer 1960), 7-20.
25. Grant, p. 292.
26. Joseph Kinsey Howard, *Strange Empire* (New York: William Morrow, 1952), p. 98.
27. See Margaret Arnett MacLeod and W. L. Morton, *Cuthbert Grant of Grantown* (Toronto: McClelland and Stewart, 1963).
28. *The Opening of the Canadian West* (London: Heineman, 1968), p. 33.
29. Hill, p. 162.
30. "Seeing an Unliterary Landscape," p. 2.
31. Grant, p. 321.
32. "A Prairie Sampler," *Mosaic*, III (Spring 1970), 92.
33. *Wanderings of an Artist* (1859; rpt. Toronto: Radisson Society, 1925), p. xxxiii.
34. *Painting in Canada* (Toronto: University of Toronto Press, 1966), p. 150.
35. Kane, *Wanderings*, p. 49.
36. *The Story of Louis Riel* (1885; rpt. Toronto: Coles Canadiana Collection, 1970), p. 12.
37. *Clearing in the West,* p. 56.
38. For a study of these immigration pamphlets, see Bruce Peel's "The Lure of the Wheat," *Papers of the Bibliographical Society of Canada*, vol. V (Toronto, 1966).
39. *The Prairie Wife* (New York: A. L. Burt, 1915), pp. 59-60.
40. C. A. Dawson and Eva R. Younge, *Pioneering in the Prairie Provinces: The Social Side of the Settlement Process* (Toronto: Macmillan, 1940), p. 30.
41. Jones, p. 73.

42. Harper, p. 267.
43. *150 Years of Art in Manitoba: Struggle for a Visual Civilization* (Winnipeg: Art Gallery, 1970), pp. 16-17.
44. Dawson and Younge, pp. 120-121.
45. Gray, *Men Against the Desert* (Saskatoon: Western Producer, 1967), pp. 13, 15, 3, 190.
46. Gray, p. 9.
47. Arthur Storey's *Prairie Harvest* (Toronto: Ryerson, 1959), though undistinguished as fiction, is an informative guide to agricultural ideals and attitudes in Saskatchewan from the first days of settlement through the boom years to the drought. Storey's hero (transparently named "Torey") has an ideal: 1000 acres of wheat. When his single-minded pursuit of his ideal impoverishes his land, the curious reaction of the entire Torey Family is a violent hatred of the land, as though *it* had betrayed *them.*
48. Harper, p. 351.
49. Harper, p. 391.
50. William Kurelek himself has provided the following explanation of the painting:
   "We Make All Kinds of Excuses"
   The setting for this painting is on my father's farm near Winnipeg back in the 40's. It is a winter scene looking in the direction of Stoney Mountain. Our cows and horses, the ones who were unproductive and which we had no room for in the barn, had to spend the winter under the straw pile. They ate it around for food and shelter till it resembled a toad stool. I carry my empathy for them backward symbolically to the situation of the Holy Family on the first Christmas. There is a big difference though, in that on that occasion they at least found shelter in the moist warmth of a stable. Today people reject Christ even more totally so that there is not even room in the barn for Him and His Mother. Then the poor at least accepted him—the shepherds, the farmers. Today even the workers and peasants feel they are above child-like faith in Him. A common excuse of North Americans for neglecting their obligation to worship Him is that they are too busy. This I represented by my father ignoring the plight of the Holy Couple by turning his back on them as he spreads the manure. Besides WORK I've included symbolically the other 2 main activities of mankind in general, namely PLAY (represented by the fox and geese game and skis in the background) and WAR (represented by the snow fight). I've depicted the Holy Couple in rags because they represent also the Third World which we comfortable North Americans by and large turn a blind eye to in pursuit of material-istic pleasures.
   Letter to the author, 3 Jan 1977.
51. "A Conversation with Margaret Laurence," in Robert Kroetsch and James Bacque, *Creation* (Toronto: New Press, 1970), p. 55.
52. Kroetsch, *Creation*, p. 53.

53. *The Studhorse Man* (Toronto: Macmillan, 1969).

Notes to Chapter II

1. Robert Kroetsch also discusses prairie man as exile in
   Conversations With Canadian Novelists—1, by Donald Cameron
   (Toronto: Macmillan, 1973), p. 94.
2. *On the Indian Trail* (London: The Religious Tract Society), p. 89.
3. *Red Cloud, the Solitary Sioux* (London: Burns and Oates, n.d.).
4. *Oowikapun or How the Gospel Reached the Nelson River Indians*
   (Chicago: Student Missionary Campaign Library, 1896).
5. John McDougall, *Pathfinding on Plain and Prairie* (Toronto:
   William Briggs, 1898), p. 181.
6. *From Cliché to Archetype* (New York: Viking, 1970), p. 82.
7. *The Story of Louis Riel, The Rebel Chief* (Toronto: Rose, 1885)
   and *Annette the Metis Spy* (Toronto: Rose, 1886).
8. *Annette*, p. 143.
9. *Strange Empire* (New York: William Morrow, 1952).
10. Norah Story, *The Oxford Companion to Canadian History and
    Literature* (Toronto: Oxford, 1967).
11. *Lords of the North* (Toronto: Ryerson, 1900).
12. *Mine Inheritance* (Toronto: Collins, 1940).
13. Margaret Arnett McLeod and W. L. Morton, *Cuthbert Grant of
    Grantown* (Toronto: McClelland and Stewart, 1963).
14. *Red Man's Revenge* (Toronto: Musson, 1886).
15. Joan Selby, "Ballantyne and the Fur Traders," *Canadian
    Literature*, 18 (Autumn 1963), 40-46.
16. *In the Land of the Moose the Bear and the Beaver* (London: T.
    Nelson, 1885).
17. *The Devil's Playground* (New York: Frederick A. Stokes, 1894),
    Sinners Twain, A Romance of the Great Lone Land (London: T.
    Fisher Unwin, 1895), *The Prodigal's Brother* (London: Jarrold &
    Sons, 1899), *The Heart of the Prairie* (London: Nisbet, n.d.
    [1899]), *The Rising of the Red Man, a Romance of the Louis Riel
    Rebellion* (London: Jarrold, n.d. [1904]).
18. Story.
19. *The Prodigal's Brother*, p. 127.
20. "Departure from the Bush," *The Journals of Susanna Moodie*
    (Toronto: Oxford University Press, 1970), p. 26.
21. *Polson's Probation* (Toronto: Wm. Briggs, 1899).
22. "My Four Years of Experience in the North-West of America:
    Roughing it in the Far West," unpublished, Public Archives of
    Canada.
23. *A Home in the Northwest* (London: Society for Promoting
    Christian Knowledge, n.d. [1894]), and *Red House by the Rockies*
    (Toronto: Musson, 1896).
24. *A Home*, p. 67.

25. *A Home*, p. 64.
26. A. E. M. Hewlett, *A Saskatchewan Historic Site, Cannington Manor Historic Park* (Saskatchewan Diamond Jubilee and Canada Centennial Corporation, 1967), p. 2. Subsequent information and quotations about Cannington Manor are from this source.
27. *Cannington Manor*, p. 20.
28. *The Land of Napioa* (Moosomin, NWT: Spectator Printing and Publishing Company, 1896).
29. *Dot it Down* (Toronto: Hunter Rose, 1871).
30. *Warden of the Plains* (Toronto: Wm. Briggs, 1896).
31. Story.
32. *Warden*, p. 240.
33. Story.
34. *Tales of Western Life* (Ottawa: C. W. Mitchell, 1888).
35. *Prairie Pot-Pourri* (Winnipeg: The Stoval Company, Printers, 1895).
36. Diary of Lizzie McFadden, 1879, unpublished, Public Archives of Canada.
37. See, for example, Ronald Atkin, *Maintain the Right* (London: Macmillan, 1973).

Notes to Chapter III

1. *Virgin Land* (Cambridge: Harvard University Press, 1950), p. 193.
2. "Clio in Canada: The Interpretation of Canadian History," *University of Toronto Quarterly*, XV (3), April, 1946.
3. Quoted in Edwin Fussell, *American Literature and the American West* (New Jersey: Princeton University Press, 1965), p. 11.
4. *The Homesteaders* (Toronto: Musson, 1916), pp. 58 and 60-61.
5. *The Virginian* (London: Macmillan, 1902), p. 13.
6. *Corporal Cameron* (Toronto: Westminster, 1912), pp. 307-308.
7. *Purple Springs* (Toronto: Thomas Allen, 1921), pp. 37-38.
8. C. A. Dawson and Eva R. Younge, *Pioneering in the Prairie Provinces: The Social Side of the Settlement Process* (Toronto: Macmillan, 1940), pp. 31-32.
9. *The Canadian West in Fiction*, rev. ed. (Toronto: Ryerson, 1970), p. 74.
10. *The Foreigner* (Toronto: Westminster, 1909), p. 157.
11. Dawson and Younge, p. 34.
12. *Love in Manitoba* (Toronto: Musson, n.d.), p. 287.
13. *Lorimer of the Northwest* (New York: A. L. Burt, 1909), p. 28.
14. *The Way of the Strong* (Toronto: Copp Clark, 1914).
15. *The Sky Pilot* (Toronto: Westminster, 1899), p. 46.
16. *Sowing Seeds in Danny* (Toronto: William Briggs, 1908).
17. See, for example, *The Next of Kin* (Toronto: Thomas Allen, 1917).

18. Nellie McClung, *The Stream Runs Fast* (1945; rpt. Toronto: Thomas Allen, 1965), p. 75.
19. Hopkins Moorhouse, *Deep Furrows* (Toronto and Winnipeg: George J. McLeod, 1918), p. 90.
20. Norah Story, *The Oxford Companion to Canadian History and Literature* (Toronto: Oxford, 1967), p. 320.
21. Moorhouse, p. 261.
22. *The Homesteaders*, p. 88.
23. *The Bail Jumper* (London: T. Fisher Unwin, 1914), p. 161.
24. See A. T. Elder, "Western Panorama: Settings and Themes in Robert J. C. Stead," *Canadian Literature,* 17 (Summer 1963), 44-56.
25. *The Prairie Wife* (New York: A. L. Burt, 1915); *The Prairie Mother* (Toronto: McClelland and Stewart, 1920); *The Prairie Child* (Toronto: McClelland and Stewart, 1922).
26. *Prairie Wife*, p. 80.
27. *Prairie Mother*, p. 344.
28. *As For Me and My House* (1941; rpt. Toronto: McClelland and Stewart, 1957), p. 4.
29. *The Prairie Child*, p. 42.
30. *Painted Fires* (Toronto: Thomas Allen, 1925), p. 119.
31. *Gwen, An Idyll of the Canyon* (Toronto: Fleming H. Revell, 1899).
32. Charles W. Gordon, *Postscript to Adventure* (New York: Farrar and Rinehart, 1938), p. 151.
33. *Sky Pilot*, pp. 163-164.
34. *The Mud Lark* (Indianapolis: Bobbs-Merrill, 1931), pp. 299-300.
35. *Wolf Willow* (1955; rpt. New York: Viking, 1971), pp. 28-29 and 291.
36. *Bail Jumper*, p. 8.
37. *Alberta* (Toronto: Macmillan, 1968), p. 7.

Notes to Chapter IV

1. "The 1920s," in *The Canadians 1867-1967,* ed. J. M. S. Careless and R. Craig Brown (Toronto: Macmillan, 1967), p. 210.
2. *Fruits of the Earth* (1933; rpt. Toronto: McClelland and Stewart, 1965), p. 138.
3. Norah Story's criticism of "Stead's romantic attitudes and his use of the stock villain and somewhat naive hero" has very little application to *The Smoking Flax* or *Grain. The Oxford Companion to Canadian History and Literature* (Toronto: Oxford, 1967), p. 776.
4. *Grain* (1926; rpt. Toronto: McClelland and Stewart, 1963), p. 15.
5. "The Prairie: A State of Mind," in *Contexts of Canadian Criticism,* ed. Eli Mandel (Chicago: University Press, 1971), p. 264.

6. Carlyle King, Introduction to *Wild Geese* (1925; rpt. Toronto: McClelland and Stewart, 1961).
7. *Wild Geese*, p. 11.
8. *Butterfly on Rock* (Toronto: University of Toronto Press, 1970), p. 57.
9. "Snow," in Robert Weaver, ed., *Canadian Short Stories* (Toronto: Oxford, 1967), p. 63.
10. "Realism in Literature," in his *It Needs to be Said* (Toronto: Macmillan, 1929), p. 58.
11. *Settlers of the Marsh* (1925; rpt. Toronto: McClelland and Stewart, 1966), p. 15.
12. Hopkins Moorhouse, *Deep Furrows* (Toronto and Winnipeg: George J. McLeod, 1918), p. 230.
13. *It Needs to be Said*, p. 73.
14. *It Needs to be Said*, pp. 70-71.
15. *Dream Out of Dust* (London: Ward Lock, 1956), p. 11.
16. *The Curlew Cried* (Seattle: Frank McCaffrey, 1947), p. 13.
17. *On A Darkling Plain* (New York: Harcourt Brace, 1939).
18. *As For Me and My House* (1941; rpt. Toronto: McClelland and Stewart, 1957), p. 35.
19. *Music at the Close* (1947; rpt. Toronto: McClelland and Stewart, 1966), p. 132.

Notes to Chapter V

1. "The Aim of Art," in his *It Needs to be Said* (Toronto: Macmillan, 1929), p. 96.
2. *Grain* (1926; rpt. Toronto: McClelland and Stewart, 1969), p. 19.
3. *Wild Geese* (1925; rpt. Toronto: McClelland and Stewart, 1961), p. 33.
4. *Settlers of the Marsh* (1925; rpt. Toronto: McClelland and Stewart, 1965), p. 122.
5. Susan Jackel, "The House on the Prairies," *Canadian Literature,* 42 (Autumn 1969), 50.
6. In *In Search of Myself* (Toronto: Macmillan, 1946), p. 385, Grove describes the house as appearing to him a fit habitation for the character of Abe Spalding which had been growing in his mind for several years. In the introduction to *Fruits of the Earth* (1933; rpt. Toronto: McClelland and Stewart, 1965), p. xiv, it is cited as *the* germinal idea.
7. *Fruits of the Earth* (1933; rpt. Toronto: McClelland and Stewart, 1965), p. 150.
8. *As For Me and My House* (1941; rpt. Toronto: McClelland and Stewart, 1957), pp. 44 and 58.
9. *It Needs to Be Said,* p. 95.
10. *In Search of Myself,* p. 227.
11. Laurence Ricou also defends the ending very ably, though he does

not carry the argument quite as far as I do. *Vertical Man/Horizontal World* (Vancouver: University of British Columbia Press, 1973), p. 50.

12. *It Needs to Be Said,* p. 88.
13. Mitchell's children are conspicuous exceptions, but they belong in a slightly different tradition and will be discussed separately.
14. "Pattern in the Novels of Edward McCourt," *Queens Quarterly, LXVIII* (Winter 1962), 557-578.
15. *Fasting Friar* (Toronto: McClelland and Stewart, 1963), p. 11.
16. *Music at the Close* (1947; rpt. Toronto: McClelland and Stewart, 1966), p. 57.
17. *Fasting Friar,* p. 133.
18. Laura Goodman Salverson, *The Viking Heart* (Toronto: McClelland and Stewart, 1925) and Vera Lysenko, *Yellow Boots* (Toronto: Ryerson, 1954).
19. "Sinclair Ross's Ambivalent World" in *Writers of the Prairies,* ed. D. G. Stephens (Vancouver: University of British Columbia Press, 1973), p. 187.
20. *As For Me and My House,* p. 29.

Notes to Chapter VI

1. *The Six-Gun Mystique* (Bowling Green: Bowling Green University Popular Press, 1975), pp. 31-33 and passim.
2. Ronald Atkin, *Maintain the Right* (London: Macmillan, 1973), pp. 331-332.
3. "Natuk. Experiences in the Life of Dr. H. G. Esmonde. Told by Major George Bruce," *Blackwoods* (Feb., 1944), pp. 105-110.
4. *Steele of the Royal Mounted* (1911; rpt. Montreal: Pocketbooks of Canada, 1947).
5. *Canadian Magazine,* 22 Sept. 1973, p. 10.
6. My definition of comedy is adapted from Northrop Frye, "The Mythos of Spring: Comedy," *Anatomy of Criticism* (Princeton: Princeton University Press, 1957), pp. 163-186.
7. *The High Plains* (Toronto: Macmillan, 1938).
8. *Sandy's Son* (Toronto: John M. Poole, 1931).
9. *Kennedy's Second Best* (Toronto: McClelland and Stewart, 1926), p. 292.
10. *An Army Without Banners* (Boston: Little Brown, 1930), pp. 181-182.
11. *Gateway* (London: Ernest Benn, 1932), p. 85.
12. *The Ten Lost Years 1929-1939* (Don Mills: General Publishing, 1973).
13. *Especially Babe* (Toronto: Ryerson, 1942), p. 8.
14. "The Liar Hunter" in his *Jake and the Kid* (Toronto: Macmillan, 1961), p. 101.
15. *Peace River Country* (Garden City: Doubleday, 1958), pp. 57-69.   221

16. *Who Has Seen the Wind* (Toronto: Macmillan, 1947), p. 3.
17. Irene Hanson, "W. O. Mitchell and Robert Kroetsch; Two Prairie Humorists," Master's Thesis, Idaho State University, 1976, p. 35.
18. Frye, pp. 163-186.
19. *Giants in the Earth* (New York: Harper and Row, 1927).
20. *The Winter Years* (Toronto: Macmillan, 1966).
21. George Bugnet, *Nipsya,* trans. Constance Davies Woodrow (Montreal: Louis Carrier, 1929); M. Constantin-Weyer, *A Man Scans His Past,* trans. Slater Brown (Toronto: Macmillan, 1929).
22. For a fuller discussion of this distinction, see E. D. Blodgett, "The Concept of 'prairie' in Western Canada Fiction," *Proceedings of the VIIth Congress of the International Comparative Literature Association, Montreal-Ottawa 1973,* 2 vols., ed. M. V. Dimić (Stuttgart and Budapest, 1977), in press.

Notes to Chapter VII

1. *The Diviners* (Toronto: McClelland and Stewart, 1974), pp. 9 and 15.
2. *A Bird in the House* (Toronto: McClelland and Stewart, 1970), p. 3.
3. *The Studhorse Man* (1969; rpt. Richmond Hill, Ontario: Pocket Books, 1971), p. 52.
4. *The Words of My Roaring* (Toronto: Macmillan, 1966), p. 8.
5. *Studhorse,* p. 85.
6. Donald Cameron, *Conversations with Canadian Novelists—1* (Toronto: Macmillan, 1973), p. 84.
7. *The Township of Time* (Toronto: Macmillan, 1959).
8. *The Mountain and the Valley* (1952; rpt. Toronto: McClelland and Stewart, 1961).
9. *Bird in the House,* p. 207.
10. *Understanding Media* (New York: Signet, 1964), p. ix.
11. "A Conversation with Margaret Laurence," in Robert Kroetsch and James Bacque, *Creation* (Toronto: New Press, 1970), p. 53.
12. *For a New Novel,* trans. Richard Howard (New York: Grove Press, 1966).
13. *Bird in the House,* p. 145.
14. "The Prairie: A State of Mind," in Eli Mandel, ed. *Contexts of Canadian Criticism* (Chicago: University of Chicago Press, 1971), p. 263.
15. *The Stone Angel* (1964; rpt. Toronto: McClelland and Stewart, 1968), p. 292.
16. *The Vanishing Point* (Toronto: Macmillan, 1973), p. 319.
17. *Wolf Willow* (New York: Viking, 1955), p. 6.
18. *Picturesque Canada* (Toronto: Belden Bros., 1882), p. 321.
19. *The Temptations of Big Bear* (Toronto: McClelland and Stewart, 1973), p. 271.

20. Vernon LaChance, "The Diary of Francis Dickens," *Queens Quarterly*, XXXVII (Spring 1930), 312-334.
21. All or some of these factors may have contributed to the prominence of Old Testament imagery in prairie fiction which Sandra Djwa discusses in her article, "False Gods and the True Covenant: Thematic Continuity Between Margaret Laurence and Sinclair Ross," *Journal of Canadian Fiction*, I, no. 4 (1972), 43-50.
22. In Saskatchewan the protest against Eastern domination took the form of the CCF, and while that party had no explicitly messianic leader, its ideals of collectivism had equally millennial overtones.
23. *Return of the Vanishing American* (New York: Stein and Day, 1969), pp. 159-168.
24. "Boozy Saddles," *MacLeans* (May 1975), p. 82.
25. "Unhiding the Hidden: Recent Canadian Fiction," *Journal of Canadian Fiction*, III, 3 (1974), p. 43.
26. Fiedler, p. 185.
27. *Studhorse*, p. 134.
28. *Big Bear*, p. 387.
29. "Unhiding the Hidden," p. 43.
30. *Diviners*, p. 49.
31. *Tay John* (1939; rpt. Toronto: McClelland and Stewart, 1974), p. 167.

Primary Sources

Allen, Ralph. *Peace River Country.* New York: Doubleday, 1958.
Amy, Wm. Lacey. *Blue Pete at Bay* by Luke Allan, pseud. London: Herbert Jenkins, 1951.
    Blue Pete, Indian Scout by Luke Allan, pseud. London: Herbert Jenkins, 1950.
    Blue Pete and the Kid by Luke Allan, pseud. London: Herbert Jenkins, 1953.
    Blue Pete and the Pinto by Luke Allan, pseud. London: Herbert Jenkins, 1954.
    Blue Pete Rides the Foothills by Luke Allan, pseud. London: Herbert Jenkins, 1953.
    Blue Pete, Unofficially by Luke Allan, pseud. London: Herbert Jenkins, n.d.
    Blue Pete Works Alone by Luke Allan, pseud. London: Herbert Jenkins, n.d.
    The Return of Blue Pete by Luke Allan, pseud. New York: George Doran, 1922.
Annett, Ross. *Especially Babe.* Toronto: Ryerson, 1942.
Ballantyne, R. M. *Red Man's Revenge.* Toronto: Musson, 1886.
Bashford, H. H. *The Manitoban.* New York: John Lane, 1905.
Beames, John. *An Army Without Banners.* Boston: Little Brown, 1930.
    Gateway. London: Ernest Benn, 1932.
Begg, Alexander. *Dot It Down.* Toronto: Hunter Rose, 1871.
Beynon, Francis. *Aleta Dey.* London: C. W. Daniel, 1919.
Bindloss, Harold. *The Broken Net.* London: Ward Lock, 1928.
    Carson of Red River. New York: Grosset and Dunlap, 1924.
    The Frontiersman. New York: Stokes, 1929.
    The Girl From Kellars. Toronto: George J. McLeod, 1917.
    Harding of Allenwood. Toronto: McLeod and Allen, 1915.
    Lorimer of the Northwest. New York: A. L. Burt, 1909.
    The Mistress of Bonaventure. Toronto: McLeod and Allen, n.d. [1908?].
    Prescott of Saskatchewan. Toronto: McLeod and Allen, 1913.
    Ranching for Sylvia. New York: Stokes, 1912.
    Sweetwater Ranch. New York: Stokes, 1935.
    Winston of the Prairie. New York: Stokes, 1907.
Blondal, Patricia. *A Candle to Light the Sun.* Toronto: McClelland and Stewart, 1960.
Bridle, A. *Hansen; A Novel of Canadianization.* Toronto: Macmillan, 1924.
Brooker, Bertram. *Think of the Earth.* Toronto: Nelson, 1936.
Butler, William F. *Red Cloud the Solitary Sioux.* London: Burns and Oates, 1882.

Bruce, Major George (pseud?). "Natuk. Experiences in the Life of Dr. H. G. Esmonde. Told by Major George Bruce." *Blackwoods* (Feb., 1944), pp. 105-110.

Campbell, R. W. *A Policeman from Eton.* London: J. Murray, 1923.

Collins, J. E. *Annette, the Metis Spy.* Toronto: Rose-Belford, 1886.

The Story of Louis Riel. 1885; rpt. Toronto: Coles Canadiana Collection, 1970.

Cormack, Barbara. *The House.* Toronto: Ryerson, 1955.

Local Rag. Toronto: Ryerson, 1951.

Cowan, C. L. *Sandy's Son.* Toronto: John M. Poole, 1931.

Cullum, Ridgwell. *Child of the North.* New York: George Doran, 1926.

The Hound from the North. Toronto: Copp Clark, 1904.

The Night-Raiders. London: Chapman and Hall, 1906.

The Riddle of Three-Way Creek. Toronto: McClelland and Stewart, 1925.

The Story of Foss River Ranch. Toronto: Copp Clark, 1903.

The Trail of the Axe. New York: A. L. Burt, 1910.

The Way of the Strong. Toronto: Copp Clark, 1914.

The Wolf Pack. Toronto: Copp Clark, 1927.

Curwood, James Oliver. *The River's End.* Philadelphia: Blakiston, 1919.

Steele of the Royal Mounted. 1911; rpt. Montreal: Pocketbooks, 1946.

Daunt, Achilles. *In the Land of the Moose, the Bear and the Beaver.* London: Thomas Nelson, 1890.

Dickson, Lovat. *Out of the West Land.* London: Collins, 1944.

Durkin, Douglas. *The Lobstick Trail.* Toronto: Musson, 1921.

Dyker, Bob. *Get Your Man.* London: Sampson, Low, Marston, n.d. [*1934*]

Eggleston, Wilfrid. *The High Plains.* Toronto: Macmillan, 1938.

Evans, Allen Roy. *All in a Twilight.* Garden City: Doubleday, 1944.

Dream Out of Dust. London: Ward Lock, 1956.

Footner, Hulbert. *The Fur Bringers.* London: Hodder and Stoughton, 1920.

Jack Chanty. Toronto: Musson, n.d.

Two on the Trail. Toronto: Musson, 1911.

Fraser, W. A. *Mooswa and Others of the Boundaries.* Toronto: William Briggs, 1900.

Freedman, Benedict and Nancy. *Mrs. Mike.* New York: Coward-McCann, 1947.

Freeman, John Dolliver. *Kennedy's Second Best.* Toronto: McClelland and Stewart, 1926.

Garrioch, A. C. *A Hatchet Mark in Duplicate.* Toronto: Ryerson, 1929.

Gill, E. A. W. *Love in Manitoba.* Toronto: Musson, n.d.

Godfrey, Denis. *No Englishman Need Apply.* Toronto: Macmillan, 1965.

Goodchild, George. *Saskatoon Patrol* by Wallace Q. Reid, pseud. London: Collins, 1934.

Trooper O'Neill. New York: A. L. Burt, 1923.

Gordon, Charles. *Corporal Cameron.* Toronto: Westminster, 1910.

The Foreigner. Toronto: Westminster, 1909.

Gwen, An Idyll of the Canyon. Toronto: Fleming H. Revell, 1899.

The Major. Toronto: McClelland and Stewart, 1917.

Patrol of the Sundance Trail. New York: Hodder and Stoughton, 1914.

The Sky Pilot. Toronto: Westminster, 1899.

To Him That Hath. New York: Doran, 1921.

Grove, F. P. *Fruits of the Earth.* 1933; rpt. Toronto: McClelland and Stewart, 1965.

Our Daily Bread. Toronto: Macmillan, 1928.

Settlers of the Marsh. 1925; rpt. Toronto: McClelland and Stewart, 1966.

"Snow" in Robert Weaver, ed. *Canadian Short Stories.* Toronto: Oxford, 1967.

Tales from the Margin: The Selected Stories of Frederick Philip Grove. Edited by Desmond Pacey. Toronto: McGraw-Hill Ryerson, 1971.

The Yoke of Life. Toronto: Macmillan, 1930.

Harker, Herbert. *Golden Rod.* New York: Random House, 1972.

Harrison, Frank. *Step Softly on the Beaver.* London: Carsell, 1971.

Hayes, K. *Prairie Pot-Pourri.* Winnipeg: The Stovel Co., Printers, 1895.

Aweena. Winnipeg: John Hart, 1906.

Hendryx, James Beardsley. *Gold and the Mounted.* Garden City: Doubleday Doran, 1928.

Henham, Ernest G. *Menotah, A Tale of The Riel Rebellion.* London: Hutchinson, 1897.

Hiebert, Paul. *Sarah Binks.* 1947; rpt. Toronto: McClelland and Stewart, 1964.

Willows Revisited. Toronto: McClelland and Stewart, 1967.

Hunter, Francis J. *Colonel Gascoigne, V.C. A Story of Travel, Adventure and Love.* Montreal: Author, n.d.

Hunter, Robert. *Erebus.* Toronto: McClelland and Stewart, 1968.

Ingersoll, Will E. *Daisy Herself.* Toronto: Musson, 1920.

The Road That Led Home. New York: Harper, 1918.

Jarvis, W. H. P. *Letters of a Remittance Man to His Mother.* London: John Murray, 1908.

Kendall, Ralph S. *Benton of the Royal Mounted.* Toronto: Gundy, 1918.

The Luck of the Mounted. Toronto: Gundy, 1920.

Kingston, W. H. G. *Rob Nixon, The Old White Trapper.* London: Society for the Propagation of Christian Knowledge, n.d.

Kreisel, Henry. *The Betrayal.* Toronto: McClelland and Stewart, 1964.

Kroetsch, Robert. *Badlands.* Toronto: New Press, 1975.

    But We Are Exiles. Toronto: Macmillan, 1965.

    Gone Indian. Toronto: New Press, 1973.

    The Studhorse Man. Toronto: Macmillan, 1969.

    The Words of My Roaring. Toronto: Macmillan, 1966.

Kroetsch, Robert and James Bacque. *Creation.* Toronto: New Press, 1970.

Laurence, Margaret. *A Bird in the House.* Toronto: McClelland and Stewart, 1970.

    The Diviners. Toronto: McClelland and Stewart, 1974.

    A Jest of God. Toronto: McClelland and Stewart, 1966.

    The Stone Angel. 1964; rpt. Toronto: McClelland and Stewart, 1968.

Laut, Agnes C. *Lords of the North.* Toronto: Ryerson, 1900.

Livesay, Dorothy. "A Prairie Sampler," *Mosaic,* III (Spring 1970), 85-92.

Loeb, Harold. *Tumbling Mustard.* New York: Horace Liveright, 1929.

Lysenko, Vera. *Westerly Wild.* Toronto: Ryerson, 1956.

    Yellow Boots. Toronto: Ryerson, 1954.

Lyttleton, E. J. *The Lawbringers.* New York: Hodder and Stoughton, 1913.

McClung, Nellie. *Black Creek Stoppinghouse.* Toronto: William Briggs, 1912.

    Flowers for the Living. Toronto: Thomas Allen, 1931.

    Painted Fires. Toronto: Thomas Allen, 1925.

    Purple Springs. Toronto: Thomas Allen, 1921.

    The Second Chance. New York: Doubleday Page, 1910.

    Sowing Seeds in Danny. New York: Grosset and Dunlap, 1908.

    When Christmas Crossed "The Peace." Toronto: Thomas Allen, 1923.

McCourt, Edward. *Fasting Friar.* Toronto: McClelland and Stewart, 1963.

    The Flaming Hour. Toronto: Ryerson, 1947.

    Home is the Stranger. Toronto: Macmillan, 1950.

    Music at the Close. 1947; rpt. Toronto: McClelland and Stewart, 1966.

    Walk Through the Valley. Toronto: McClelland and Stewart, 1958.

McDougall, John. *Wapee Moostoch; or White Buffalo.* Calgary: The Author, 1908.

Mackie, John. *Canadian Jack. Toronto: Bell and Cockburn, 1913.*

    The Devil's Playground, A Story of the Wild Northwest. New York: Frederick A. Stokes, 1894.

    The Heart of the Prairie. London: Nisbet, n.d.

    The Prodigal's Brother, a Story of Western Life. London: Jarrold and Sons, 1899.

The Rising of the Red Man, a Romance of the Louis Riel Rebellion. London: Jarrold, n.d. [1904].

Sinners Twain, a Romance of the Great Lone Land. London: T. Fisher Unwin, 1895.

MacLean, John. *The Warden of the Plains and Other Stories of Life in the Canadian North-west.* Toronto: William Briggs, 1896.

Macmillan, Don. *Rink Rat.* Toronto: Dent, 1949.

McNamee, James. *Them Damn Canadians Hanged Louis Riel!* Toronto: Macmillan, 1971.

Marlyn, John. *Under the Ribs of Death.* 1957; rpt. Toronto: McClelland and Stewart, 1964.

Mercier, Anne and Violet Watt. *A Home in the North-West.* London: Society for Promoting Christian Knowledge, n.d. [1894].

The Red House by the Rockies. Toronto: Musson, 1896.

Mitchell, Ken, *The Meadowlark Connection.* Regina: Pile of Bones Publishing, 1975.

Wandering Rafferty. Toronto: Macmillan, 1972.

Mitchell, W. O. *Jake and the Kid.* Toronto: Macmillan, 1961.

The Kite. Toronto: Macmillan, 1962.

The Vanishing Point. Toronto: Macmillan, 1973.

Who Has Seen the Wind. Toronto: Macmillan, 1947.

Moore, Amos. *Royce of the Royal Mounted.* Winnipeg: Harlequin, 1950.

Morton, James. *Polson's Probation, A Story of Manitoba.* Toronto: William Briggs, 1897.

Mowrey, William Byron. *Tales of the Mounted Police.* New York: Airmont Books, 1953.

The Black Automatic. Boston: Little Brown, 1937.

Niven, F. J. *The Flying Years.* London: Collins, 1935.

Mine Inheritance. London: Collins, 1940.

Oakes, Christopher. *The Canadian Senator.* Toronto: National Publishing, 1890.

Olson, Oscar. *Mountie on Trial.* Toronto: Ryerson, 1953.

Ostenso, Martha. *Wild Geese.* 1925; rpt. Toronto: McClelland and Stewart, 1961.

Parker, Gilbert. *An Adventurer of the North.* London: Methuen, 1895.

Neighbours, Toronto: Hodder and Stoughton, 1922.

The Smoking Flax. Toronto: McClelland and Stewart, 1924.

Wild Youth and Another. Toronto: Copp Clark, [1919].

World for Sale. Toronto: Gundy, 1916.

Parsons, Nell W. *The Curlew Cried.* Seattle: Frank McCaffrey, 1947.

Pocock, H. R. A. *The Cheerful Blackguard.* Indianapolis: Bobbs-Merrill, 1915.

Tales of Western Life. Ottawa: C. W. Mitchell, 1888.

Reville, F. D. *A Rebellion.* Brantford: Hurley Printing, 1912.

Robinson, Frank. *Trail Tales of Western Canada.* London: Marshall Bros., [1914].

Ross, Sinclair. *As For Me and My House.* 1941; rpt. Toronto: McClelland and Stewart, 1957.

    The Lamp at Noon and Other Stories. Toronto: McClelland and Stewart, 1968.

    Sawbones Memorial. Toronto: McClelland and Stewart, 1974.

    The Well. Toronto: Macmillan, 1958.

    Whir of Gold. Toronto: McClelland and Stewart, 1970.

Russell, Sheila Mackay. *The Living Earth.* Toronto: Longmans, 1954.

Ryga, George. *Ballad of a Stone Picker.* Toronto: Macmillan, 1966.

    Hungry Hills. Toronto: Longman's, 1963.

Sallans, G. H. *Little Man.* Toronto: Ryerson, 1942.

Salverson, L. G. *The Dark Weaver.* Toronto: Ryerson, 1937.

    The Viking Heart. Toronto: McClelland and Stewart, 1925.

Saxby, Argyll. *The Taming of the Rancher.* London: Partridge, n.d.

Sinclair, Bertrand. *Raw Gold.* New York: Dillingham, 1907.

Sluman, Norma Pauline. *Blackfoot Crossing.* Toronto: Ryerson, 1959.

Snell, LeRoy. *The Spirit of the North.* New York: Cupples and Leon, 1935.

Stead, R. J. C. *The Bail Jumper.* London: T. Fisher Unwin, 1914.

    The Cow Puncher. Toronto: Musson, 1918.

    Dennison Grant. Toronto: Musson, 1920.

    Grain. 1926; rpt. Toronto: McClelland and Stewart, 1963.

    The Homesteaders. Toronto: Musson, 1916.

    Neighbours. Toronto: Hodder ans Stoughton, 1922.

    The Smoking Flax. Toronto: McClelland and Stewart, 1924.

Steele, H. E. R. *Ghosts Returning.* Toronto: Ryerson, 1950.

    Spirit-of-Iron. New York: A. L. Burt, 1923.

Stegner, Wallace. *Big Rock Candy Mountain.* New York: Hill and Wang, 1938.

    On A Darkling Plain. New York: Harcourt Brace, 1939.

Storey, Arthur. *Prairie Harvest.* Toronto: Ryerson, 1959.

Stringer, Arthur. *The Mudlark.* Indianapolis: Bobbs-Merrill, 1931.

    The Prairie Child. Toronto: McClelland and Stewart, 1922.

    The Prairie Mother. Toronto: McClelland and Stewart, 1920.

    The Prairie Wife. New York: A. L. Burt, 1915.

Taylor, Gladys Tall. *Pine Roots.* Toronto: Ryerson, 1956.

Tennyson, Bertram. *The Land of Napioa and Other Essays in Prose and Verse.* Moosomin, NWT: Spectator Printing and Publishing Co., 1896.

Van der Mark, Christine. *Honey in the Rock.* Toronto: McClelland and Stewart, 1966.

    In Due Season. Toronto: Oxford, 1947.

White, S. A. *North of the Border.* New York: Phoenix, 1940.

    Northwest Crossing. New York: Phoenix, 1944.

    Northwest Law. New York: Phoenix, 1942.

Northwest Raiders. London: Wright and Brown, n.d.

Wiebe, Rudy. *The Blue Mountains of China.* Toronto: McClelland and Stewart, 1970.

First and Vital Candle. Grand Rapids: Eerdmans, 1966.

Peace Shall Destroy Many. Toronto: McClelland and Stewart, 1962.

ed. *Stories from Western Canada.* Toronto: Macmillan, 1972.

The Temptations of Big Bear. Toronto: McClelland and Stewart, 1973.

Williams, Flos. *Fold Home.* Toronto: Ryerson, 1950.

New Furrows. Ottawa: Graphic, 1926.

Wiseman, Adele. *Crackpot.* Toronto: McClelland and Stewart, 1974.

The Sacrifice. Toronto: Macmillan, 1956.

Young, Egerton Ryerson. *Oowikapun or How the Gospel Reached the Nelson River Indians.* Chicago: Student Missionary Campaign Library, 1896.

Zero [pseud.]. *One Mistake.* Montreal: Canadian Banknote Company, 1888.

Bibliographies

Bell, Inglis F., ed. *"Canadian Literature—1959: A Checklist,"* Canadian Literature, no. 3 (Winter 1960), 91-108 [a Continuing Annual Compilation through 1971 under changing compilers].

Bell, Inglis F. and Susan W. Port. *Canadian Literature/ Litterature Canadienne, 1959-1963.* A checklist of creative and critical writings, Vancouver: University of British Columbia Press, 1966.

Canadian Index to Periodicals and Documentary Films 1948-1959; 1960-. Ottawa, Canadian Library Association and National Library of Canada, 1960-. Monthly.

Canadian Periodical Index. Windsor: Public Library, 1932. Cumulation of quarterly issues 1929-31, continued issues, 1932.

Canadian Periodical Index. 1938-1947. Toronto: Public Libraries Branch, Ontario Department of Education, 1939-1949.

Canadiana: A List of Publications of Canadian Interest. Ottawa: Bibliographic Center, National Library, 1950—.

Klinck, Carl F., comp. "Canada" in "Annual Bibliography of Commonwealth *Literature* 1965," *Journal of Commonwealth Literature,* no. 2 (December 1966), 39-55 [a continuing annual series with changing compilers].

ed. "Canadian Literature—1959, a Checklist: Theses,"

Canadian Literature, no. 3 (Winter 1960), 108 [Annual to 1971].
comp. "Post-Graduate Theses in Canadian Literature: English and English-French Comparative," *Journal of Canadian Fiction*, I (Summer 1972), 68-73 [an annual compilation under changing compilers].

Naaman, Antoine Youssef. *Guide bibliographique des theses litteraires canadiennes de 1921 a 1969*. Montreal: Cosmos, 1970.

Nesbitt, Bruce, ed. "Canadian Literature 1972; An Annotated Bibliography," *Journal of Canadian Fiction*, II (Spring 1973), 99-150, annual [?].

Peel, Bruce Braden, comp. *Bibliography of the Prairie Provinces to 1953*. 2nd ed., Toronto: University of Toronto Press, 1973.

Watters, R. E., comp. *A Checklist of Canadian Literature and Background Materials, 1628-1960*. Toronto: University of Toronto Press, 1972.

Watters, R. E. and Inglis F. Bell, comps. *On Canadian Literature 1806-1960*. Toronto: University of Toronto Press, 1966.

History and Background

Atkin, Ronald. *Maintain the Right*. London: Macmillan, 1973.

Atwood, Margaret. *Journals of Susanna Moodie*. Toronto: Oxford, 1970.

Barr, John J. and Owen Anderson, eds. *The Unfinished Revolt; Some Views on Western Independence*. Toronto: McClelland and Stewart, 1971.

Braithwaite, Max. *The Night We Stole the Mountie's Car*. Toronto: McClelland and Stewart, 1971.

Broadfoot, Barry. *The Ten Lost Years 1929-1939*. Don Mills: General Publishing, 1973.

Butler, William F. *The Great Lone Land*. 1872; rpt. Edmonton: M. G. Hurtig, 1968.

Careless, J. M. S. and R. Craig Brown, eds. *The Canadians 1867-1967*. Toronto: Macmillan, 1967.

Cheadle, W. B. and Viscount Milton. *The North-West Passage by Land*. 1865; rpt. Toronto: Coles Canadiana Collection, 1970.

Coues, Elliott, ed. *The Manuscript Journals of Alexander Henry and David Thompson 1799-1814*. 2 vols. Minneapolis: Ross and Haines, 1897.

Dawson, C. A. and Eva R. Younge. *Pioneering in the Prairie Provinces: The Social Side of the Settlement Process*. Toronto: Macmillan, 1940.

Gard, Robert E. *Johnny Chinook*. 1945; rpt. Edmonton: Hurtig, 1967.

Grant, George Monro. *Picturesque Canada.* 2 vols. Toronto: Belden
　　Bros., 1882.
　　Ocean to Ocean. 1873; rpt. Edmonton: Hurtig, 1967.
Gray, James H. *The Boy from Winnipeg.* Toronto: Macmillan, 1970.
　　Men Against the Desert. Saskatoon: Western Producer, 1967.
　　The Winter Years. Toronto: Macmillan, 1966.
Grove, F. P. *Over Prairie Trails.* 1922; rpt. Toronto: McClelland and
　　Stewart, 1960.
　　The Turn of the Year. Toronto: Macmillan, 1929.
Harper, J. Russell. *Painting in Canada.* Toronto: University of
　　Toronto Press, 1966.
Henday, Anthony. *York Factory to the Blackfeet Country, The
　　Journal of Anthony Hendry, 1754-55.* Edited by Lawrence
　　Burpee. *Transactions of the Royal Society of Canada,* 3rd
　　ser., I (1907-08), Section II.
Hewlett, A. E. M. *A Saskatchewan Historic Site, Cannington Manor
　　Historic Park.* Saskatchewan Diamond Jubilee and Canada
　　Centennial Corporation, 1967.
Hiemstra, Mary. *Gully Farm.* Toronto: McClelland and Stewart,
　　1955.
Hill, Douglas. *The Opening of the Canadian West.* London:
　　Heineman, 1967.
Horn, Michiel, ed. *The Dirty Thirties.* Toronto: Copp Clark, 1972.
Howard, Joseph Kinsey. *Strange Empire.* New York: William
　　Morrow, 1952.
Kane, Paul. *Wanderings of an Artist. 1858;* rpt. Toronto: Radisson
　　Society, 1925.
Kirby, George W. *The Broken Trail.* Toronto: William Briggs, 1909.
Kroetsch, Robert. *Alberta.* Toronto: Macmillan, 1968.
Lachance, Vernon. "The Diary of Francis Dickens," *Queens
　　Quarterly,* XXXVII (Spring 1930), 312-334.
Livesay, Dorothy. "A Prairie Sampler," *Mosaic,* III (Spring 1970), 85-
　　92.
McClung, Nellie. *The Next of Kin.* Toronto: Thomas Allen, 1917.
McDougall, John. *Pathfinding on Plain and Prairie.* Toronto:
　　William Briggs, 1898.
MacGregor, James G. *A History of Alberta.* Edmonton: Hurtig, 1972.
　　North-West of 16. Toronto: McClelland and Stewart, 1958.
Mackenzie, Alexander. *Voyages.* 1801; rpt. Toronto: Radisson
　　Society, 1927.
Mackintosh, W. A. *Prairie Settlement, The Geographical Setting.*
　　Toronto: Macmillan, 1934.
MacLeod, Margaret Arnett and W. L. Morton. *Cuthbert Grant of
　　Grantown.* Toronto: McClelland and Stewart, 1963.
McLuhan, Marshall. *Understanding Media.* New York: Signet, 1964.
McLuhan, Marshall and Wilfred Watson. *From Cliché to Archtype.*
　　New York: Viking, 1970.
Milton, Viscount and W. B. Cheadle. *The North-West Passage by*

Land. 1865; rpt. Toronto: Coles Canadiana Collection, 1970.

Minifie, James M. *Homesteader.* Toronto: Macmillan, 1973.

Moorhouse, Hopkins. *Deep Furrows.* Toronto and Winnipeg: George J. McLeod, 1918.

Morton, Arthur S. *History of the Canadian West to 1870-71.* London: Thomas Nelson, n.d.

Morton, W. L. "Clio in Canada: The Interpretation of Canadian History," in Carl Berger, ed., *Approaches to Canadian History,* Canadian Historical Readings I, Toronto: University of Toronto Press, 1967, pp. 42-49.
Manitoba, a History. 2nd ed. Toronto: University of Toronto Press, 1967.
"Seeing an Unliterary Landscape," *Mosaic,* III (Spring 1970), 1-10.

150 Years of Art in Manitoba: Struggle for a Visual Civilization. Winnipeg Art Gallery, 1970.

Palliser, John. *Exploration—British North America.* London: Her Majesty's Stationery Office, 1863.

Peel, Bruce. "The Lure of the Wheat," *Papers of the Bibliographical Society of Canada,* vol. V, Toronto, 1966.

Public Archives of Canada. *The Diary of Lizzie McFadden,* ca. 1879. 39p.
"Extracts from a Diary of the March with Colonel Otter to Relieve Battleford." 24p.
"Jottings on the March from fort Garry to Rocky Mountains, 1874," by James Finlayson. 21 p.
"My Four years of Experience in the North-West of America." 20 p.
Notes from George Murdoch's Diary, first Mayor of Calgary, 1883-1886.
"Old Fort Garry in the Seventies," by William Morris, 1900-1912. 15 p.

Public Archives of Saskatchewan. "The Battleford Trail," by E. Pauline Johnson, 1902. 7 p.
Extracts of a memoir of life in Manitoba and British Columbia, 1872-1928, by Henry Halpen. 18 p.
"Iteskawin," the story of the Sioux wife of NWMP Inspector Jervis, by John O'Kute-sica. 15 p.
"Life of an English Emigrant," by P. D. Wotton, 10 p.
Reminiscences of pioneering in Estevan area from 1905, by August Dahlman. 25 p.
"Thirty Years Ago on the Whitemud River or the Last of the Open Range," by Harry Otterson, ca. 1937. 22 p.

Rasky, Frank. *The Taming of the Canadian West.* Toronto: McClelland and Stewart, 1967.

Reaney, James. "Manitoba as a Writer's Environment," *Mosaic,* III (Spring 1970), 95-97.

Stanley, G. F. G. *Louis Riel.* Toronto: Ryerson, 1963.

Stegner, Wallace. *Wolf Willow.* New York: Viking, 1955.
Story, Norah. *The Oxford Companion to Canadian History and Literature.* Toronto: Oxford, 1967.
Turner, Frederick Jackson. *The Frontier in American History.* New York: Henry Holt, 1920.
Warkentin, John, ed. *The Western Interior of Canada.* Toronto: McClelland and Stewart, 1964.
Whillans, James W. *First in the West; The Story of Henry Kelsey, Discoverer of Canadian Prairies.* Edmonton: Applied Art Products, 1955.
Wright, James F. C. *Saskatchewan: the History of a Province.* Toronto: McClelland and Stewart, 1955.
Young, Egerton Ryerson. *On the Indian Trail and Other Stories of Missionary Work among the Cree and Salteaux Indians.* London: The Religious Tract Society, n.d.
Stories from Indian Wigwams and Northern Campfires. 1893; rpt. Toronto: Coles Canadiana Collection, 1970.

General Criticism and Scholarship

Anderson, Allan. "Aspects of the Canadian Novel," Canadian Broadcasting Corporation, Program no. 5, 2 Dec. 1972.
Atwood, Margaret. *Survival: A Thematic Guide to Canadian Literature.* Toronto: Anansi, 1972.
Blodgett, E. D. "The Concept of the 'Prairie' in Western Canadian Fiction," *Proceedings of the VIIth Congress of the International Comparative Literature Association, Montreal-Ottawa 1973,* 2 vols., ed. M. V. Dimić, Stuttgart and Budapest, 1977.
Cameron, Donald. *Conversations with Canadian Novelists.* 2 vols. Toronto: Macmillan, 1973.
Cawelti, John G. *The Six-Gun Mystique.* Bowling Green: Bowling Green University Popular Press, 1975.
Davey, Frank. *From There to Here, A Guide to English-Canadian Literature Since 1960, Our Nature—Our Voices,* vol. II. Erin, Ontario: Press Porcepic, 1974.
Eggleston, Wilfrid. *The Frontier and Canadian Letters.* Toronto: Ryerson, 1957.
Folsom, James K. *The American Western Novel.* New Haven: College and University Press, 1966.
Frye, Northrop. *Anatomy of Criticism.* Princeton: Princeton University Press, 1957.
Fussell, Edwin. *American Literature and the American West.* New Jersey: Princeton University Press, 1965.
Gross, K. "'Looking Back in Anger' Frederick Niven, W. O. Mitchell,

234

and Robert Kroetsch on the History of the Canadian West,"
Journal of Canadian Fiction, III, 2 (1974), 49-54.

Grove, F. P. *It Needs to Be Said*. Toronto: Macmillan, 1929.

Harrison, Dick. "The Beginnings of Prairie Fiction," *Journal of
Canadian Fiction*, vol. IV, no. 1 (1975), 159-177.

"Cultural Insanity and Prairie Fiction," in D. E. Bessai and
D. Jackel, ed. *Figures in a Ground*, Saskatoon: Prairie
Books, in press.

"The Mounted Police in Fiction," in Hugh Dempsey, ed.
Men in Scarlet, Calgary: McClelland and Stewart West,
1974, pp. 163-174.

Hornyansky, Michael. "Countries of the Mind," *Tamarack Review*,
no. 26 (Winter 1963), 58-68.

"Countries of the Mind, II," *Tamarack Review*, no. 27
(Spring 1963), 80-89.

Jackel, Susan. "The House on the Prairies," *Canadian Literature*, no.
42 (Autumn 1969).

Jones, D. G. *Butterfly on Rock*. Toronto: University of Toronto
Press, 1970.

Klinck, Carl F., gen. ed. *Literary History of Canada*. Toronto:
University of Toronto Press.

Kreisel, Henry. "The Prairie; a State of Mind," *Transactions of the
Royal Society of Canada*, 4th ser., VI (June 1968), 171-180.

McCourt, Edward. *The Canadian West in Fiction*. Revised Edition.
Toronto: Ryerson Press, 1970.

MacLulich, T. D. "Last Year's Indians," *Essays on Canadian Writing*,
I, pp. 47-50.

Mandel, Eli, ed. *Contexts of Canadian Criticism*. Chicago: University
of Chicago Press, 1971.

"Romance and Realism in Western Canadian Fiction," in A.
W. Rasporich and H. C. Klassen, ed., *Prairie Perspectives 2*,
Toronto and Montreal: Holt, Rinehart and Winston, 1973.

Meyer, Roy W. *The Middle-Western Farm Novel in the Twentieth
Century*. Lincoln: University of Nebraska Press, 1965.

Moss, John. *Patterns of Isolation in English-Canadian Fiction*.
Toronto: McClelland and Stewart, 1974.

New, W. H. *Articulating West: Essays on Purpose and Form in
Modern Canadian Literature*. Toronto: New Press, 1972.

Pacey, Desmond. *Creative Writing in Canada*. Toronto: Ryerson,
1961.

Ricou, Laurence. *Vertical Man/Horizontal World*. Vancouver:
University of British Columbia Press, 1973.

Robbe-Grillet, Alain. *For a New Novel*. Translated by Richard
Howard. New York: Grove Press, 1966.

Smith, Henry Nash. *Virgin Land: The American West as Symbol and
Myth*. Cambridge: Harvard University Press, 1950.

Stephens, D. G., ed. *Writers of the Prairies*. Vancouver: University of

British Columbia Press, 1973.

Stevenson, Lionel. "Land of Open Spaces," in his *Appraisals of Canadian Literature*. Toronto: Macmillan, 1926, 236-244.

Story, Norah. *Oxford Companion to Canadian History and Literature*. Toronto: Oxford, 1967.

Sylvestre, Guy, Brandon Conron and Carl F. Klinck. *Canadian Writers/Ecrivains Canadiens*. Toronto: University of Toronto Press, 1964.

Tallman, Warren. "Wolf in the Snow: Part One, Four Windows on Two Landscapes," *Canadian Literature*, no. 5 (Summer 1960), 7-20.

"Wolf in the Snow: Part Two, The House Repossessed," *Canadian Literature*, no. 6 (Autumn 1960), 41-48.

Thomas, Clara. *Canadian Novelists 1920-1945*. Toronto: Longmans, 1946.

Warwick, Jack. *The Long Journey*. Toronto: University of Toronto Press, 1968.

Individual Authors

BALLANTYNE, R. M.

Quayle, Eric. "R. M. Ballantyne in Rupert's Land," *Queens Quarterly*, LXXV (Spring 1968), 63-71.

Selby, Joan. "Ballantyne and the Fur Traders," *Canadian Literature*, 18 (Autumn 1963), 40-46.

Beharriell, Ross. Introduction to *The Man From Glengarry* by Ralph Connor. 1901; rpt. Toronto: McClelland and Stewart, 1960, pp. vii-xii.

GORDON, CHARLES

Gordon, Charles. *Postscript to Adventure*. New York: Farrar and Rinehart, 1938.

Gordon, Charles, Jr. "Ralph Connor and the New Generation," *Mosaic* III (Spring 1970), 11-18.

Thompson, J. Lee and John H. Thompson. "Ralph Connor and the Canadian Identity," *Queens Quarterly*, LXXIX (Summer 1972), 159-170.

Watt, Frank W. "Western Myth, the World of Ralph Connor," *Canadian Literature* (Summer 1959), 26-36.

GROVE, F. P.

Ayre, Robert. "Canadian Writers of Today—Frederick Philip Grove," *Canadian Forum*, XII (April 1932), 255-257.

Birbalsingh, Frank. "Grove and Existentialism," *Canadian Literature*, 43 (Winter 1970), 67-76.

Clarke, G. H. "A Canadian Novelist and His Critics," *Queens Quarterly*, LIII (August 1946), 362-368.

Dudek, Louis. "The Literary Significance of Grove's Search," *Inscape*,

XI (Spring 1974), 89-99.

Eggleston, Wilfrid. "F.P.G.: The Ottawa Interlude," *Inscape,* XI (Spring 1974), 101-110.

"Frederick Philip Grove," in *Our Living Tradition.* First Series, edited by Claude Bissell, Toronto: University of Toronto Press, 1957, pp. 105-127.

Grove, F. P. "Apologia pro Vita et Opere Sua," *Canadian Forum,* XI (August 1931), 420-422.

"Grove's Letters from the Mennonite Reserve," introduced by Margaret Stobie, *Canadian Literature,* 59 (Winter 1974), 57-66.

"In Search of Myself," *University of Toronto Quarterly,* X (October 1940), 60-67.

In Search of Myself. Toronto: Macmillan, 1946.

"A Postscript to A Search for America," *Queens Quarterly,* XLIX (Autumn 1942), 197-213.

Hin-Smith, Joan. *Three Voices; the Lives of Margaret Laurence, Gabrielle Roy, Frederick Philip Grove.* Toronto and Vancouver: Clarke Irwin, 1975.

Holliday, W. B. "Frederick Philip Grove: An Impression," *Canadian Literature,* no. 3 (Winter 1960), 17-22.

Keith, W. J. "The Art of Frederick Philip Grove: *Settlers of the Marsh* as an Example," *Journal of Canadian Studies,* vol. IX, no. 3, 26-36.

"Grove's Over Prairie Trails: A Re-Examination," *Literary Half-Yearly,* XIII, no. 2, 76-85.

"Grove's Search for America," *Canadian Literature,* no. 59 (Winter 1974), 57-66.

McMullen, Lorraine. "Women in Grove's Novels," *Inscape,* XI (Spring 1974), 67-76.

McMullin, Stanley. "Evolution Versus Revolution: Grove's Perception of History," *Inscape,* XI (Spring 1974), 77-88.

"Grove and the Promised Land," *Canadian Literature,* no. 49 (Summer 1971), 10-19.

Morley, Patricia. "*Over Prairie Trails:* 'a poem woven of impressions,'" *Humanities Association Review,* vol. XXV, no. 3, 225-31.

Nesbitt, Bruce H. "*The Seasons:* Grove's Unfinished Novel," *Canadian Literature,* no. 18 (Autumn 1963), 47-51.

Noel-Bentley, Peter. "The Position of the Unpublished *Jane Atkinson* and *The Weatherhead Fortunes," Inscape,* XI (Spring 1974), 13-33.

Pacey, Desmond. *Frederick Philip Grove.* Toronto: Ryerson, 1945.

ed. *Frederick Philip Grove.* Toronto: Ryerson, 1970.

"Frederick Philip Grove: A Group of Letters," *Canadian Literature,* no. 11 (Winter 1962), 28-38.

"Frederick Philip Grove," *Manitoba Arts Review,* III (Spring 1943), 28-41.

"In Search of Grove in Sweden: A Progress Report," *Journal of Canadian Fiction,* I (Winter 1972), 69-73.

Parker, M. G. Introduction to *Fruits of the Earth* by F. P. Grove. 1933; rpt. Toronto: McClelland and Stewart, 1965, pp. vii-xiii.

Phelps, Arthur L. "Frederick Philip Grove," in his *Canadian Writers.* Toronto: McClelland and Stewart, 1951, pp. 36-42.

Pierce, Lorne. "Frederick Philip Grove (1871-1948)," *Transactions of the Royal Society of Canada,* 3rd ser., XLIII (1949), sec. II, 113-119.

Riley, Anthony. "The German Novels of Frederick Philip Grove," *Inscape,* XI (Spring 1974), 55-66.

Ross, Malcolm. Introduction to *Over Prairie Trails* by Frederick Philip Grove. Toronto: McClelland and Stewart, 1957, pp. v-x.

Sandwell, B. K. "Frederick Philip Grove and the Culture of Canada," *Saturday Night,* LXI (November 24, 1945), 18.

Saunders, Thomas. "The Grove Papers," *Queens Quarterly,* LXX (Spring 1963), 22-29.
Introduction to *Settlers of the Marsh* by F. P. Grove. 1925; rpt. Toronto: McClelland and Stewart, 1965, pp. vii-xiii.
"The Novelist as Poet: Frederick Philip Grove," *Dalhousie Review,* XLIII (Summer 1963), 235-241.

Skelton, Isobel. "Frederick Philip Grove," *Dalhousie Review,* XIX (July 1939), 147-163.

Spettigue, Douglas. *F.P.G. The European Years.* Ottawa: Oberon, 1973.
Frederick Philip Grove. Toronto: Copp Clark, 1969.
"Frederick Philip Grove in Manitoba," *Mosaic,* III (Spring 1970), 19-33.
"The Grove Enigma Resolved," *Queens Quarterly,* LXXIX (Spring 1972), 1-2.

Stanley, C. "Frederick Philip Grove," *Dalhousie Review,* XXV (January 1946), 433-441.
"Voices in the Wilderness," *Dalhousie Review,* XXV (July 1945), 173-181.

Stobie, Margaret. *Frederick Philip Grove.* New York: Twayne, 1973.

Sutherland, Ronald. *Frederick Philip Grove.* Toronto: McClelland and Stewart, 1969.
"What was Frederick Philip Grove," *Inscape,* XI (Spring 1974), 1-11.

Thompson, J. Lee. "In Search of Order: The Structure of Grove's *Settlers of the Marsh," Journal of Canadian Fiction,* vol. III no. 3 (1974), 65-73.

HIEBERT, PAUL

Hiebert, Paul. "The Comic Spirit at Forty Below Zero," *Mosaic,* III (Spring 1970), 58-68.

Wheeler, A. "Up from Magma and Back Again with Paul Hiebert," *Manitoba Arts Review,* VI (Spring 1948), 3-14.

Wheeler, Lloyd. Introduction to *Sarah Binks* by Paul Hiebert. 1947; rpt. Toronto: McClelland and Stewart, 1964, pp. vii-xiii.

KREISEL, HENRY

Warhaft, S. Introduction to *The Betrayal* by Henry Kreisel. 1964; rpt. Toronto: McClelland and Stewart, 1971, pp. v-x.

KROETSCH, ROBERT

Brown, Russell M. "An Interview with Robert Kroetsch," *University of Windsor Review,* VII (Spring 1972), 1-18.

Cameron, Donald. "Robert Kroetsch: The American Experience and the Canadian Voice," *Journal of Canadian Fiction,* I (Summer 1972), 48-52.

Hanson, Irene. "W. O. Mitchell and Robert Kroetsch; Two Prairie Humorists," M.A. Thesis, Idaho State University, 1976.

Moss, John. "Canadian Frontiers: Sexuality and Violence from Richardson to Kroetsch," *Journal of Canadian Fiction,* II (Summer 1973), 36-42.

New, W. H. "The Studhorse Quests," in his *Articulating West.* Toronto: New Press, 1972, pp. 179-186.

Ross, Morton. "Robert Kroetsch and his Novels," in Donald Stephens, ed., *Writers of the Prairies.* Vancouver: University of British Columbia Press, 1973, pp. 101-114.

Thomas, Peter. "Keeping Mum: Kroetsch's Alberta," *Journal of Canadian Fiction,* II (Spring 1973), 54-56.

LAURENCE, MARGARET

Bowering, George. "That Fool of a Fear; Notes on *A Jest of God,*" *Canadian Literature,* no. 50 (Autumn 1971), 41-56.

Cameron, Donald. "Margaret Laurence: The Black Celt Speaks of Freedom," in his *Conversations with Canadian Novelists—1.* Toronto: Macmillan, 1973.

Djwa, Sandra. "False Gods and the True Covenant: Thematic Continuity Between Margaret Laurence and Sinclair Ross," *Journal of Canadian Fiction,* I (Fall 1972), 43-50.

Gibbs, R. Introduction to *A Bird in the House* by Margaret Laurence, 1970; rpt. Toronto: McClelland and Stewart, 1974.

Gotlieb, Phyllis. "On Margaret Laurence," *Tamarac Review,* XLIX (Third Quarter 1969), 76-80.

Hin-Smith, Joan. *Three Voices; The Lives of Margaret Laurence, Gabrielle Roy, Frederick Philip Grove.* Toronto and Vancouver: Clarke Irwin, 1975.

Killam, G. D. Introduction to *A Jest of God* by Margaret Laurence. 1964; rpt. Toronto: McClelland and Stewart, 1974, v-ix.

Laurence, Margaret. *Heart of a Stranger.* Toronto: McClelland and Stewart, 1976.

"Sources," *Mosaic,* III (Spring 1970), 80-84.

"Ten Years Sentences," *Canadian Literature,* no. 41 (Summer 1969), 10-16.

New, W. H. Introduction to *The Stone Angel* by Margaret Laurence. 1964; rpt. Toronto: McClelland and Stewart, 1968, iii-x.

Pesando, Frank. "In a Nameless Land—the Use of Apocalyptic Mythology in the Writings of Margaret Laurence," *Journal of Canadian Fiction,* II (Winter 1973), 53-57.

Read, S. E. "The Maze of Life: The Work of Margaret Laurence," *Canadian Literature,* no. 27 (Winter 1966), 5-17.

Thomas, Clara. "A Conversation with Margaret Laurence and Irving Layton," *Journal of Canadian Fiction,* I (Winter 1972), 65-68.

The Manawaka World of Margaret Laurence. Toronto: McClelland and Stewart, 1975.

Margaret Laurence. Toronto: McClelland and Stewart, 1969.

"The Novels of Margaret Laurence," *Studies in the Novel,* University of Texas, 4 (Summer 1972), 154-164.

"Proud Lineage: Willa Cather and Margaret Laurence," *Canadian Review of American Studies,* II (Spring 1971), 3-12.

"The Short Stories of Margaret Laurence," *World Literature Written in English,* vol. II, no. 1 (1963), 25-33.

Thompson, Anne. "The Wilderness of Pride: Form and Image in *The Stone Angel,*" *Journal of Canadian Fiction,* vol. IV, no. 3 (1975), 95-110.

McCLUNG, NELLIE

McClung, Nellie. *Clearing in the West.* 1935; rpt. Toronto: Thomas Allen, 1964.

The Stream Runs Fast. 1945; rpt. Toronto: Thomas Allen, 1965.

McCOURT, EDWARD

Baldwin, R. G. "Pattern in the Novels of Edward McCourt," *Queens Quarterly,* LXVIII (Winter 1962), 574-587.

Bevan, Allan. Introduction to *Music at the Close* by Edward McCourt. 1947; rpt. Toronto: McClelland and Stewart, 1966, pp. 7-11.

MARLYN, JOHN

Mandel, Eli. Introduction to *Under the Ribs of Death* by John Marlyn. 1957; rpt. Toronto: McClelland and Stewart, 1964, pp. 7-14.

MITCHELL, W. O.

Barclay, Patricia. "Regionalism and the Writer: A Talk with W. O. Mitchell," *Canadian Literature,* no. 14 (Autumn 1962), 53-56.

Cameron, Donald. "W. O. Mitchell: Sea Caves and Creative Partners," in his *Conversations with Canadian Novelists—2.* Toronto: Macmillan, 1973.

Hanson, Irene. "W. O. Mitchell and Robert Kroetsch; Two Prairie Humorists," M.A. Thesis, Idaho State University, 1976.

McLay, C. M. "*The Kite:* A Study in Immortality," *Journal of*

Canadian Fiction, II (Spring 1973), 43-48.

New, W. H. "A Feeling of Completion: Aspects of W. O. Mitchell," *Canadian Literature,* no. 17 (Summer 1963), 22-33.

Phelps, Arthur L. "W. O. Mitchell," in his *Canadian Writers.* Toronto: McClelland and Stewart, 1951, pp. 94-102.

Sutherland, Ronald. "Children of the Changing Wind," *Journal of Canadian Studies,* V (November 1970), 3-11.

NIVEN, F. J.

Burpee, L. J. "Frederick Niven," *Dalhousie Review,* XXIV (April 1944), 74-76.

New, W. H. "Individual and Group Isolation in the Fiction of Frederick John Niven," M.A. Thesis, U.B.C., 1963. "A Life and Four Landscapes: Frederick John Niven," *Canadian Literature,* no. 32 (Spring 1967), 15-28.

Niven, F. J. *Coloured Spectacles.* London: Collins, 1938.

OSTENSO, MARTHA

King, Carlyle. Introduction to *Wild Geese* by Martha Ostenso. 1925; rpt. Toronto: McClelland and Stewart, 1961, pp. v-x.

MacLellan, W. E. "Real 'Canadian Literature,'" *Dalhousie Review,* VI (October 1926), 18-23.

Mullins, S. G. "Some Remarks on Theme in Martha Ostenso's *Wild Geese,*" *Culture,* XXIII (December 1962), 359-362.

Thomas, Clara. "Martha Ostenso's Trial of Strength," in Donald Stephens, ed., *Writers of the Prairies.* Vancouver: University of British Columbia Press, 1973, pp. 39-50.

ROSS, SINCLAIR

Chambers, Robert. *Sinclair Ross and Ernest Buckler.* Toronto: Copp Clark, 1975.

Daniells, Roy. Introduction to *As For Me and My House* by Sinclair Ross. 1941; rpt. Toronto: McClelland and Stewart, 1957, pp. v-x.

Djwa, Sandra. "False Gods and the True Covenant: Thematic Continuity Between Margaret Laurence and Sinclair Ross," *Journal of Canadian Fiction,* I (Fall 1972), 43-50. "No Other Way; Sinclair Ross's Stories and Novels," *Canadian Literature,* no. 47 (Winter 1971), 49-66.

Fraser, Keath. "Futility at the Pump: the Short Stories of Sinclair Ross," *Queens Quarterly,* LXXVII (Spring 1970), 72-80.

Kostash, Myrna. "Discovering Sinclair Ross: It's Rather Late," *Saturday Night,* LXXXVII, no. 7, 33-37.

Laurence, Margaret. Introduction to *The Lamp at Noon and Other Stories* by Sinclair Ross. Toronto: McClelland and Stewart, 1968, pp. 7-12.

New, W. H. "Sinclair Ross's Ambivalent World," *Canadian Literature,* no. 40 (Spring 1969), 26-32.

Ross, Sinclair. "On Looking Back," *Mosaic,* III (Spring 1970), 93-94.

Stephens, Donald. "Wind, Sun and Dust," *Canadian Literature,* no. 23 (Winter 1965), 17-24.

RYGA, GEORGE

Carson, Neil. "George Ryga and the Lost Country," *Canadian Literature*, 45 (Summer 1970), 33-40.

STEAD, R. J. C.

Elder, A. T. "Western Panorama: Settings and Themes in Robert J. C. Stead," *Canadian Literature*, no. 17 (Summer 1963), 44-56.

Saunders, Thomas. Introduction to *Grain* by R. J. Stead. 1926; rpt. Toronto: McClelland and Stewart, 1969, pp. v-xiii.

STRINGER, ARTHUR

Lauriston, Victor. *Arthur Stringer, Son of the North*. Toronto: Ryerson, 1941.

WIEBE, RUDY

Cameron, Donald. "Rudy Wiebe: The Moving Stream is Perfectly at Rest," in his *Conversations with Canadian Novelists—2*. Toronto: Macmillan, 1973.

Mandel, Eli. "Where the Voice Comes From," *Quill and Quire*, vol. XL, no. 12, 4, 20.

Melnyk, G. "An Interview with Rudy Wiebe," *Canadian Fiction Magazine*, no. 12, 29-34.

Robinson, J. M. Introduction to *Peace Shall Destroy Many* by Rudy Wiebe. 1962; rpt. Toronto: McClelland and Stewart, 1972, pp. 1-6.

Tiessen, Hildegard. "A Mighty Inner River: 'Peace' in the Fiction of Rudy Wiebe," *Journal of Canadian Fiction*, II (Fall 1973), 71-76.

Wiebe, Rudy. "Passage by Land," *Canadian Literature*, no. 48 (Spring 1971), 25-27.

WISEMAN, ADELE

Rosenthal, Helene. "Spiritual Ecology: Adele Wiseman's *The Sacrifice"* in Donald Stephens, ed., *Writers of the Prairies*. Vancouver: University of British Columbia Press, 1973, pp. 77-88.

Wiseman, Adele. "A Brief Anatomy of an Honest Attempt at a Pithy Statement about the Impact of the Manitoba Environment on my Development as an Artist," *Mosaic*, III (Spring 1970), 98-106.

243

244